FRIENDS
of
JUG BAY

Presented to the students of
Meade Middle School by the
Friends of Jug Bay
January 2004

SAVING THE BAY ∾

Saving the Bay

THE JOHNS HOPKINS UNIVERSITY PRESS

PEOPLE WORKING FOR THE FUTURE
∾ ∾ ∾ OF THE CHESAPEAKE

ANN E. DORBIN

Photographs by

RICHARD A. K. DORBIN

Baltimore & London

For more information on people working for the future of the Chesapeake, visit <www.press.jhu.edu/press/books/dorbin.htm>.

Printed in the United States of America on acid-free paper
9 8 7 6 5 4 3 2 1

The Johns Hopkins University Press
2715 North Charles Street
Baltimore, Maryland 21218-4363
www.press.jhu.edu

Library of Congress Cataloging-in-Publication Data
Dorbin, Ann E., 1960–
  Saving the Bay : people working for the future of the
Chesapeake / Ann E. Dorbin ; photographs by Richard A. K. Dorbin.
       p.   cm.
Includes bibliographical references and index.
  ISBN 0-8018-6628-6
  1. Environmental protection—Chesapeake Bay Region (Md. and Va.)—Citizen participation. 2. Water quality management—Chesapeake Bay Watershed (Md. and Va.) 3. Chesapeake Bay (Md. and Va.)—Environmental conditions. I. Dorbin, Richard A. K. II. Title.
  TD225.C43 D67   2001   333.91
  333.91′6416′0916347—dc21   DOR   00-011964

A catalog record for this book is available from the British Library.

Introduction photograph: Billy Moore, maintenance supervisor, William Preston Lane, Jr., Memorial Bridge, Maryland, May 1999.

To Joseph R. and Joline P. Frock,

who, like the Chesapeake's great blue heron,

stood steadfastly in the creeks of this project,

and without whom it would not have been possible

Old woman of the water

Trailing your torn hem—

   Fishbones, cups

  Rusted cans—

I hear you calling in the cool of the

  morning

  "Still I am beautiful"

—From "Early Spring, Sligo Creek"
by Cheryl Hellner, Sligo Creek, Maryland
(poet and volunteer stream monitor for the Audubon Naturalist Society)

CONTENTS

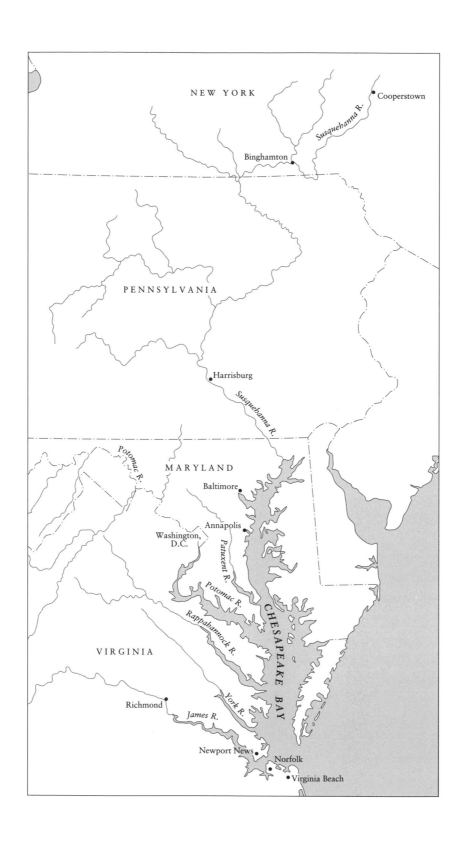

FOREWORD

Fifteen million of us live within the Chesapeake's watershed, and each of us has an impact on the Bay's well-being. That's so many people, the news surely has to be bad.

But almost miraculously, *Saving the Bay* turns that number into fifteen million reasons for hope. With their words and pictures, Ann and Richard Dorbin introduce us to dozens of individuals who are working in various, often surprising ways for the good of the Chesapeake. From New York's Otsego Lake at the headwaters of the Susquehanna, to the Cacapon River in the mountains of West Virginia, and along countless streams and rivers that flow toward the Cheapeake through Pennsylvania, Delaware, Maryland, and Virginia, the Dorbins found lives and efforts to celebrate. The result is inspiring.

Liz Hartwell fights to save the bald eagles of Mason Neck in northern Virginia. Alan Gregory works to undo the damage of acid mine drainage. Louisa Thompson advocates the use of native plants. Innovations in map making and advances in wastewater treatment share credit for helping the Bay. We hear the thoughts of a Chesapeake waterman, a marathon swimmer, and an F.B.I. agent who fights environmental crime. We meet longtime recyclers Joline and Joe Frock and the "Stream Team" at Westbrook Elementary School in Bethesda, Maryland.

To their wonderful stories of imagination, dedication, and effort on behalf of the Bay, I invite you to add your own. Let their stories inspire each of us to find our own ways of making a difference. Where the future of Chesapeake is concerned, we all matter. *Saving the Bay* reminds us how, in myriad ways, our daily activities have distant impacts far downstream and long into the future. Let this book also serve as a reminder that each of us, in ways unique to our experience and abilities, can make an enormous difference in the future of the Chesapeake.

WILLIAM C. BAKER
President and CEO
The Chesapeake Bay Foundation

ACKNOWLEDGMENTS

Before we embarked on this project, rambling lists of glorifying acknowledgments usually put us off. However, producing this book has enlightened us. What you hold in your hands is the result of a truly cooperative effort. If this book is the Chesapeake Bay, then the dedicated people who helped and encouraged us—from CEOs to "gofers"—over the past three years are its tributaries. Like the intricate branches of the Bay's vast watershed, hundreds of individuals have helped and supported us. As with any journey, even though at times we felt alone, we never were; there was always someone—a river or a creek or a spring of a person—along the way to keep our journey flowing on course. It would be impossible to acknowledge everyone who contributed to this project, but we would like to pay tribute to a few of them.

For generously sharing their expertise and opening doors in places where we otherwise might not have gained access: Kent Mountford and Kate Naughten of the Chesapeake Bay Program Office; Fran Flanigan, Ryan Davis, and Diane Dunaway of the Alliance for the Chesapeake Bay; Rick Leader and his staff at Pickering Creek Environmental Center; Carolyn Watson, Lauren Wentzel, and Darlene Walker of the Maryland Department of Natural Resources; Elizabeth Buckman, Roy Hoagland, Jeff Painter, and Michael Heller (Clagett Farm) of the Chesapeake Bay Foundation; Dave Mingus of the Chesapeake Bay Trust; Curtis Dalpra and Jim Cummins of the Interstate Commission of the Potomac River Basin; Albert McCullough and Cheryl May of Environment Concern Inc.; Tom Horton; John Tippett of Friends of the Rappahannock; Lisa Jo Fresch of Friends of the Nanticoke; Teresa Byler of the West Virginia Watershed Resource Center; Russ Brinsfield and Barbara Smith of the Wye Research and Education Center; Jacquelyn Bonomo of the Western Pennsylvania Conservancy; Cari Brandt and Billy Moore of the

Maryland Transportation Authority, Rebecca Barber of the Maryland Port Administration; Tom Simpson of Future Harvest; Gary Allen of the Center for Chesapeake Communities; Susan Stranahan for her insight on the people of the Susquehanna River; John Hostetler and Don Kraybill for their guidance in the Amish community; Will and Dorothy Howard; Jan Kirsh; Jeff Maynard; Peggy and John Ford; Chief Sewell Winterhawk Fitzhugh; Mark Christopher; Hunter Harris of Aloft, Inc.; Norm Brady; the Star Democrat circulation room; and our A-number-one mentor, Barbara Callahan.

The following people contributed moral support and exceptional artistic expertise: Bob Brugger, Melody Herr, Celestia Ward, and Wilma Rosenberger at the Johns Hopkins University Press; our friend and consulting editor, Dianne Lorang; Susan Bouse; Marion E. Warren; David Harp; Edwin Remsburg; Kim Weller of the Weller Agency; Tom McCall; Chris Smither; David Morrell; Carl Judd; and the University of Maryland University College (UMUC) Cooperative Education and EXCEL programs.

Our greatest thanks goes to our family and friends, who tirelessly kept the hectic "watershed" of our home alive and well: Joseph, Joline, and Kristin Frock, Lisa and Alan Willoughby, Walter, John, and Kathy Byrnes, Bruce Lee, Tom Tawney, Joe Davis, Rose Palombo, Amy and Eric Steward, and especially our children, April, Andrew, Conner, and Noah.

We extend special acknowledgment to the following people who generously and unhesitatingly gave their time and expertise to be a part of this project. Their profiles are available online at <www.press.jhu.edu/press/books/dorbin.htm>: E. Steuart Chaney, marina owner, Friendship, Maryland, and Tracey's Landing, Maryland; Thomas E. Harris, county administrator, King George, Virginia, and Cape Charles, Virginia; James H. Howdyshell, Bay Bridge Project engineer, William Preston Lane Memorial Bridge, Maryland; Eric Wakesa Kipruto, MESA agricultural intern from Kimilili, Kenya; Stephen P. Leatherman, shoreline applied scientist, Miami, Florida; Vincent O. Leggett, Blacks of the Chesapeake, Annapolis, Maryland; David L. Maase, Chesapeake College, Wye Mills, Maryland; Anne Pearson, Alliance for Sustainable Communities, Annapolis, Maryland; Russell L. Pettyjohn, Lititz Run Watershed Alliance, Lititz, Pennsylvania; Clyde Edward Watson (1905–1994), farmer, waterman, and hunter, Westwood, Maryland; and Stephen E. Haller, Clyde D. Kestner, C. Thomas Allen, Susan Zarecky, and Walter Jones, the Colonial Williamsburg Environmental Action Council, Williamsburg, Virginia.

INTRODUCTION

WHETHER BY THE TUG OF A "NUMBER ONE JIMMY" BLUE crab, the heady smell of salt marsh, the sight of ships pressing toward port, the tasty tang of a fresh-caught oyster, the splash of rough water on flesh, or the honking *Vs* of migrating geese moving across an autumn sky, when the Chesapeake Bay gets your attention, there's no shaking it. Those of us who know and love the Bay and its innumerable tributaries—from the breadth of its main stem to its breathtaking rivers and meandering upland streams—understand what author Norman Maclean meant when he wrote, "Eventually, all things merge into one, and a river runs through it. . . . I am haunted by waters."

It is an intimate haunting—a beckoning as rudimentary as basic biology, as profound as the human soul. The Chesapeake conveys a sense of place that creates a singular bond between the Bay and its people. It is *our Bay,* but it is also *my Bay.* At the 1983 Bay conference, William Ruckelshaus, director of the U.S. Environmental Protection Agency (EPA), called it a "people's bay." "Therein," states Bay writer Tom Horton, "lies both its infinite charm and the seeds of its destruction."

It is an irony with which ordinary people often grapple like a slippery eel in bare hands. On a cold winter day in 1998, in the living room of our small house near the Tuckahoe River, the idea for this book hatched, and, like the Bay and its people, persisted. Richard and I were innocently admiring a fancy color calendar of Bay landscapes, when, without warning, a notion—pure yet more than a little far-fetched—jumped out like a fish breaking water. Pointing to the glossy, picture-perfect pages, speaking the words almost before the thought had finished forming, I said, "What about all the *people* out there working to make this happen? How come we never read about them or see their pictures on the wall? They should be celebrated, too."

While the restoration efforts of professionals are vital, we wanted to bring home the fact that making a difference doesn't always mean being a biologist or an activist. We wanted to focus not on professional environmentalists or "green" gurus or (in the words of a scholarly colleague) "pointy-headed intellectuals" but on ordinary people (like us) using their everyday skills and talents to turn around the Bay's future.

One of my favorite authors, Barry Lopez, wrote, "Remember only this one thing, the stories people tell have a way of taking care of them. If stories come to you, care for them. And learn to give them away where they are needed." When this project took hold of us we barely knew the difference between SAV (submerged aquatic vegetation), a primary indicator of Bay health, and SUVs, major contributors to the region's air pollution. But we had cherished the Bay for most of our lives and knew that we could learn what it had to teach us and use our talents, Richard's photography and my writing, to pass on the wisdom of these stories.

By bringing these stories to the forefront we hope to educate readers, show that individual actions are critical, and accentuate positive rather than negative human impacts on the environment. Just as the wonder of the Bay is not reserved for experts or old-timers, neither is the work that lies ahead. Therein lies the premise of this project—that behind the reports and controversy over the human-induced decline of the Bay's health and the path of its future are many people doing their part, in different and necessary ways, for the future of the watershed.

Many refer to the Chesapeake Bay, our country's largest estuary, as the most-studied, least-understood body of water in the world. It has a rich maritime history and tradition that rivals those of larger waterways. A sea of marshes and an immense fishery, it exists in a region of wide-open vistas, stifling heat, sudden storms, and complex problems of the sort that occur when increasing numbers of people overtax a resource.

It is said that no one in the Chesapeake watershed lives more than a few minutes from one of its 100,000 streams and rivers. Yet the words *tributary* (a stream that flows into another stream and eventually into a larger body of water) and *watershed* (the land area that contributes to a specific body of water) have only recently become a part of our vocabulary. Ten major rivers and innumerable smaller rivers, creeks, streams, and springs flow out of Maryland, Virginia, Pennsylvania, the District of Columbia, Delaware, New York, and West Virginia to feed the Chesapeake Bay. The rivers bring the necessary elements and fresh water that, when mixed with the Atlantic Ocean's salt water, form the brackish conditions that are the lifeblood of the most productive estuary in the United States.

Every river, creek, and stream has a watershed, or subwatershed, which contains or receives (via atmospheric deposition) most of the potential sources of water pollution. With about 11,684 miles of shoreline (more than the entire U.S. West Coast), there is about nine times as much land surface in the Chesapeake watershed than there is water surface on the Bay. In other words, for every acre of water surface, there are nine acres of land from which water and everything in it—chemicals, manure, sediment, litter—drains into the Bay. While industry certainly contributes to pollution in the Bay, a bigger threat looms in the collective impact of the 15 million people living in the watershed. People produce sewage, use energy, drive cars, fertilize fields and lawns, and cut down trees to build homes and roads. All of these activities (and many others) contribute nutrients that negatively affect the Bay. Improving the health of the Chesapeake Bay and its tributaries can only be accomplished by reducing or eliminating active and potential sources of pollution throughout the watershed.

Only in the past several decades has the modern human populous, due in large part to our sheer numbers, taken a hard look at our place in the environment. At one time in its history, the Chesapeake Bay was self-sustaining. Native Americans of the past named it *chesepiook,* meaning "great shellfish bay." Fish were said to jump into boats right out of the water. Geese and ducks were so plentiful that early European settlers hunted them with cannons and punt guns. Perhaps the contrasts between then and now says it all.

In the 1960s, many people thought the Chesapeake was locked in an irreversible cycle of decline. Not only waterfowl but also aquatic life and habitat were disappearing. Early in that decade, Rachel Carson, credited with founding the modern environmental movement (a shift that science writer Laurence Pringle calls one of the most powerful social revolutions of the twentieth century), published her groundbreaking and controversial book, *Silent Spring.* About twenty years later, the Bay hit bottom. Parts of that bottom, once thriving with life, had turned into a foul, lifeless muck, referred to as "black mayonnaise," and some waterfowl populations had fallen nearly 80 percent from their mid-1950s levels. The Chesapeake, overstressed by human activity, shortsightedness, and apathy, was succumbing to exhaustion. At the same time, a new view of the Bay and its tributaries—as a single ecosystem, inextricably linked, for better or for worse—began to slowly evolve.

As a result, the Chesapeake Bay was America's first estuary targeted for restoration and protection. In 1967, a handful of people founded the Chesapeake Bay Foundation (CBF) and took up the battle cry of *Save the Bay.* Today CBF is the largest of many nonprofit Bay conservation organizations. Governmental efforts to halt the Bay's degradation started as early as 1973, when then-Maryland Senator Charles Mathias conducted a tour of water quality problems. This investigation eventually led to a five-year, $25 million study by the U.S. Environmental Protection Agency (EPA) to report on nutrient enrichment, toxic pollution, and the disappearance of SAV. The report, presented to congress in 1983, concluded that a chief factor in the decline of the Bay was excessive nutrient enrichment, also known as *eutrophication* or *cultural eutrophication*, the overnourishment (mostly from nitrates and phosphates) of aquatic ecosystems because of human activities such as agriculture, urbanization, and discharges from industrial plants and sewage treatment plants. Responding to the serious implications of the study's findings, officials signed the first Chesapeake Bay Agreement in December 1983 and soon established the Chesapeake Bay Program to begin reducing the input of nutrients and institute Baywide monitoring and modeling.

A second Bay Agreement, signed in 1987 by the governors of Maryland, Virginia, and Pennsylvania, the Mayor of the District of Columbia, and the heads of the Chesapeake Bay Commission and the EPA, expanded upon the first agreement and delineated state and federal participation through complementary goals and objectives. The agreement outlined specific commitments in such areas as water quality, public education, living resources, population growth, and land development. A direct outgrowth was the concerted, cooperative campaign in the Bay community to meet these commitments and manage the Bay's resources wisely.

In 1992, the Chesapeake Bay Program partners agreed to address nutrients at their sources: upstream in the Bay's tributaries. As a result, Pennsylvania, Maryland, Virginia, and the District of Columbia (often referred to as the signatory states) assembled Tributary Teams comprised of individuals from all walks of life, working within local communities to develop "tributary strategies," such as promoting watershed education and reducing nutrient pollution, for the ten major tributary basins. On the federal level, in 1998, Congress approved the Clean Water Action Plan (CWAP), which provides federal funding to address the nation's water quality problems and to fulfill the original goal of the Clean Water Act of 1973: safe waters for all Americans to enjoy. The CWAP stresses collaboration as a means to solve water pollution problems and brings together federal, state, and local governments, private and public sectors, and individual citizens to support restoring and maintaining watersheds nationwide.

Today, the Chesapeake's decline has slowed; important progress has been made, but the Chesapeake Bay Foundation's 1999 *State of the Bay* report pegged its health at less than one-third of its current potential. However, the Chesapeake Bay Executive Council has signed the new Chesapeake 2000 Agreement, which includes commitments that signal a new emphasis to not only clean up the Bay but also protect the land draining into it. This latest pact promises to slow the rate of sprawl within the watershed, preserve more open space rather than develop land, restore wetlands, voluntarily phase out "mixing zones" (discharge areas where pollutants are allowed to exceed water quality standards until they are diluted by river water), and increase the oyster population tenfold. The 64,000-square-mile watershed of the "Land of Pleasant Living" is in the midst of a profound transition. A fundamental change in viewpoint is occurring, as we move from an anthropocentric, human-centered view to one that is "biocentric," or life-centered. Residents are discovering a new direction that reaches out to everyone and educates them about the Bay's ecosystem and their place in it. We are learning that the water and land are inextricably connected in an environment of marvelous complexity.

The Chesapeake Bay has an awesome natural propensity to bounce back from negative impacts. Change and volatility are the Bay's self-defensive shield and sword. In her book about the Magothy River, Marianne Taylor writes, "Hope lies in the Bay's potential for change." She also asks, "What can we give back to this river?" and answers that "for Bay transformation to occur . . . river people must look to themselves to find their level of participation, whether it be joining conservation organizations, participating in citizen studies, leading youth to more awareness, or simply by observing boating regulations, speed limits, and . . . anti-pollution warnings. The bottom line for . . . Bay people in creating an environmental ethic lies in the care, the love and the participation we have of the watershed." Wise scientists realize that we do not perform our bay-saving in a laboratory where all parameters are under our precise control. Winning the battle to "save the Bay" will require awareness and effort, from the classroom to the boardroom to the restroom. With dozens of rivers and thousands of creeks, and a rapidly growing population disbursed across six states and the District of Columbia, this fight can seem like an overwhelming prospect. It is tempting to think of individual actions as little more than futile paddle-swipes across the surface of an imposing expanse of water. Yet anyone who has seen the Naval Academy rowing crew rhythmically pulling oars with confident strength across the Severn River knows that, working together, humans can make great, gliding strides.

This book celebrates a new era in the history of the Bay, an era in which the balance is shifting from negative human impact to people working hand-in-hand to reach mutual sustainability, from conquering nature to sustaining it. From Capitol Hill to Baltimore's Inner Harbor to Smith Island to the mountains of Virginia and Pennsylvania's Amish farm country, the Chesapeake's workforce is as diverse and dynamic as the resource itself. Tom Horton describes this unprecedented effort by scientists, government, and citizens as a "new and huge and devilishly interconnected concept of 'seeing the Bay whole.'"

A great deal of careful consideration went into selecting the subjects of this book. Decisions were primarily based on presenting a diverse, *representative* sample of a wide range of viewpoints and issues across a broad geographic region. Admittedly, Richard and I employed an instinctual and random method of deliberateness mixed with serendipity, characterized by blind faith, dumb luck, and wild goose chases. We often had to eliminate excellent candidates owing to duplication of location or profession. It was a difficult culling process, and we regretfully omitted many, many individuals who are deserving of inclusion. For every person featured there could be dozens more, and, likewise, every person profiled could fill his or her own book.

We already knew a few of the people featured here, but many we did not. Most we tracked down (some might say hounded) after hearing or reading about their work. Like still water swelling into whitecaps, our Rolodex grew from notes scrawled on napkins and scrap paper to a tabulated spiral notebook to a cabinet filled with file folders. Some profiles required months, even years, of persistence to complete. We invested countless hours, traveled thousands of miles, and engaged in endless phone calls. In all kinds of weather, we talked to people in offices, vehicles, forests, boats, homes, workshops, wetlands, and "greasy spoons" offering Muzak and burgers served by waitresses with bottle-blonde hair.

I worked from a home office at a desk always cluttered not only with books, papers, phone messages, photographs, and cassette tapes but also with baby bottles, business reports, calendars, report cards, grocery receipts, and toy trucks. We worked out countless details by squeezing in snippets of conversations separated by the closed darkroom door or the drawn shower curtain, during staff meetings, intermissions, desserts, and ninety-second breaks taken during day-shoots while waiting for Polaroid film to develop. Richard unhesitatingly lugged his camera equipment through rough neighborhoods, across gangways, over mud- and snow-covered trails, and to the top of the Bay Bridge. Our van was often called upon to double as a Land Rover. (Once a group of elderly locals at a two-bit filling station in Virginia—where we had stopped, desperate to use the only pay phone on that side of the mountain—collectively eyed our dirt-laden running boards. Finally, one of them dryly inquired, "What happened?!"). It was not unusual for us to visit a corporate conference room, a chemistry lab, a homey kitchen, and the backwoods all in a single day. Regardless of the stature or social position of our subjects, we were welcomed, our curiosities were satisfied, and our spirits were enriched.

Prior to the final draft, each subject had the opportunity to review his or her profile. In this information age of shifting technology, communication was a mixed bag—fax machines, cell phones, pagers, "snail mail," voice mail, email, websites, sound bytes, handheld "palm" computers, and even rotary telephones and handwritten letters. Often we had one foot in the past and the other in the future, yet we truly experienced a universality of commonplace genius and human spirit. Arriving in Blacksburg, Virginia, after months of planning and a six-hour drive, we were chided by a cohort of an inventive graduate student, "You mean you came all this way to talk to *him?*"

While most of the people we approached were pleased and excited to be included in the project, we were not always successful in our cajoling. Several outstanding candidates declined to be included because, finding enough reward working quietly behind the scenes, they humbly (and incorrectly) felt they were not worthy. Perhaps a poignant entry for these individuals would be a blank page, reflecting the dedicated and "invisible" efforts of many of the Chesapeake Bay's silent partners.

The people in this book shared with us their insights, their knowledge, and their time (several hours or more). They laughed with us and fed us. When we wavered—discouraged, "spinning our wheels," homesick and exhausted from traveling—and when our business suffered because of the time and expense of independently producing this project, the subjects of this book kept us going. They tolerated annoying traffic delays, exasperating computer glitches, and our younger children clamoring into their laps during interviews. Many of them have faced incredible obstacles. They didn't always win, but they stood their ground just the same. "It is not a slam dunk," an environmental specialist with the Maryland Department of Natural Resources (DNR) once said. "We're still working out the kinks." That resilient tenacity characterizes the Bay's people; that determination, against the odds and despite the naysayers, fueled this project.

Whatever their roles, the people we met are knowledgeable and realistically optimistic about the Bay. Their insights and convictions have educated, enlightened, and enriched us. Important, often-overlooked individual strides are being made. For centuries, humans' well-being has depended on the Bay's abundance; today, the Bay's well-being depends on human decisions and actions. No better classroom exists than the Bay itself. And there are no better teachers than those included here. We have shared their wisdom, intelligence, wit, frustration, and joy. In many cases, though I left it unwritten, they also related some of the suffering that is part of humanity: death, illness, abuse, divorce. We have been privileged to learn from the people in this book. We have listened and learned from them so that you can, too.

We can no longer rely on "them" to take care of problems in the Bay watershed; instead we must acknowledge that *we* must do the work ahead. It is "we" who will "save the Bay." As Harry Womack, professor of biological sciences at Salisbury State University, commented, "The story is not over—the battle is not won. The biggest battle is the battle to win the hearts and minds of the people. But the cost of a decent environment is eternal vigilance." Wherever we live in the watershed, we can be stewards of our own half-acre—at home, at work, at a town hall, where we ride a bike, paddle a boat, read a book, or just hang out. Taking care of the Bay means much more than planting trees and underwater grasses. The choices and actions of everyone who lives in the Chesapeake watershed—even if far away from the actual Bay—affect the Bay's health. In our extensive travels, perhaps the most concise statement of this concept comes from a sticker on a sinktop in rural Virginia that simply reads, "The River Starts Here."

SAVING THE BAY ❧

WILLARD N. HARMAN ⟆

Cooperstown, New York

Limnologist

BILL HARMAN IS A MAN AS COMFORTABLE IN HIS TERRITORY—the shores of Otsego Lake—as he is in his own skin. Harman's office, where he has worked for thirty years, is located at the Biological Field Station (BFS) near the northern margin of the Chesapeake Bay watershed, at the headwaters of the Bay's source river, the Susquehanna. A man whose true workplace is the great outdoors of upstate New York, Harman considers the office a necessary evil. The building bursts with the paraphernalia and accouterments of hands-on science. There are wildlife specimens: a turtle collection, brilliantly colored butterflies, mounted birds, sealed vials of insects, cabinets of meticulously cataloged shells and "voucher specimens," and meter-long fish floating in formaldehyde, tails folded over, put up in enormous glass carboys. The walls are covered with maps, some old and faded from decades of use, others glowing brightly with modern satellite images. There are buckets of rocks, dusty computers, and cluttered laboratory rooms. Shelves hold thousands of cockeyed books and periodicals. There are scuba diving suits, hip waders, Eskimo mittens, and footwear of every persuasion. It is an appropriate spot for the vast and complex interconnections of the Chesapeake Bay watershed to begin; and Harman, fascinating, learned, and muddy-booted, is a befitting keeper.

A professor of aquatic ecology and director of the BFS, a natural laboratory for aquatic and terrestrial biology and ecology, which serves the community as well as the State University of New York College at Oneonta, Harman explains that a limnologist is analogous to an oceanographer who studies fresh waters. In addition to directing research opportunities, Harman offers advanced training for science teachers, programs for school children, and seminars, workshops, field trips, and data for the general public. He oversees one full-time biologist, various faculty members, graduate students, and "a cadre of volunteers who do a heck of a lot of work for us because they think what we're doing is worthwhile." Public concern over the protection of Otsego Lake and the upper Susquehanna River has resulted in strong support for the lakeside facility.

Few lakes in the United States have been home to more romance, legend, and history than Otsego. Described in James Fenimore Cooper's Leatherstocking Tales as "the Glimmerglass," the narrow, north-south–oriented lake is eight miles long and has a maximum depth of 166 feet. Bounded to the east and west by slopes rising up to 482 feet above

the lake surface, its depth and temperatures provide ideal conditions for populations of game fish, such as Otsego bass (whitefish), greenbacks (cisco and lake herring), lake trout, and Atlantic salmon (found nowhere else in this region). The seventy-three-square-mile Otsego Lake watershed is home to about five thousand year-round residents, and agriculture and forestry are important resource-based local industries. The lake's access and proximity to the Susquehanna River, diverse fishery, and good water quality make it a hub for vacationing, tourism, and recreation.

While Otsego Lake is largely associated with fair-weather vacationers and tourists, who visit the Baseball Hall of Fame, Glimmerglass Opera, and other attractions, Harman conducts his work year-round. "We have projects we work on intermittently to document problems and evaluate mitigation," he explains, "but lake monitoring is the one thing we do in perpetuity." In all kinds of harsh weather (the area receives an average snowfall of seventy-eight inches), using divers, who swim under the ice, and high-tech equipment, Harman and his assistant, Matthew Albright, profile various water quality parameters, including temperature, oxygen, nutrient levels, conductivity, and water clarity. "All I'm doing is lowering this little doohickey down into the drink," Harman explains. "In the old days, it would take a good part of a week to do what we can do now in about a day. Automated sampling stations at various locations also allow us to compile an intensive watershed database."

He goes on to explain that because Otsego Lake teeters between a eutrophic system (rich in dissolved nutrients and seasonally deficient in oxygen in the depths) and an oligotrophic system (having abundant oxygen year round in deep water), it quickly responds to change. "It's really two lakes in summer," he elaborates. "A warm layer on top of a cold layer beneath, with silt on the lake bottom. So we have warm water fish—perch, pickerel, black bass, rock bass, sunfish—in the top layer, and populations of cold water fish like Atlantic salmon, lake trout, whitefish, brown trout, and cisco in the lower layer. In late summer, because of warmer water in the upper layer and oxygen loss in the lower portion of the deepest areas, the cold water dwellers end up with an increasingly restricted environment. It's easy to write a scenario," he cautions, "where that cold, oxygenated layer disappears and the lake loses its cold water fishery. However," he adds, "these species are the 'canaries in our mine.' The width of the cold layer by late summer is indicative of what's happened in the past year. We can really tell what's going on in the ecosystem."

Harman explains that the lake's problems are mostly biological rather than chemical. "As in other parts of the Bay watershed, we have problems with eutrophication," he begins. "But it's been exacerbated here because of introduced exotics, which are especially responsive to nutrients. For example, Eurasian milfoil, a nuisance aquatic plant that looks like stringy seaweed, flourishes, hindering both swimming and boating. If allowed to continue to proliferate," Harman warns, "it will upset the ecological balance and reduce the recreational value of the lake." Other imbalances can be found in the lake's fishery. "We've exchanged long-lived forage fish, like whitefish and cisco, with alewives, a smaller, short-lived species that recycles the nutrients they're fixing in their bodies much more rapidly. The result, aside from the ecological problems of making a food web less stable, is an increased rate of nutrient cycling favorable for algal growth."

With regard to introduced species, the BFS is taking somewhat of a "fight fire with fire" approach to restoring balance to the food chain. Harman is coordinating the reintroduction of eighty thousand walleye, a predator species, to reduce the lake's population of alewives, which are overconsuming plant-eating crustaceans and outcompeting larger game fish, such as Otsego bass. A few local individuals funded the project, with cooperation from the New York State Department of Environmental Conservation, Cornell University's Warm Water Fisheries Unit, BFS graduate students, and commercial growers statewide who are raising walleye fingerlings in ponds. "All that comes together here," Harman states. "We'll be returning the lake to the condition it was about seventy-five years ago."

Harman reports that today, erosion, agriculture, and increased development result in a runoff rate three times what it was in the 1930s, especially for phosphorous, which has significant impacts. Improvements in local water treatment processes and public education encouraging healthy choices and actions by citizens in everyday life are addressing residential issues. On the agricultural front, the BFS is involved in the Lake Friendly Farmer Program, which recognizes farmers who have identified and employed "best management practices" by voluntarily improving soil, managing nutrient waste, and controlling wastewater. "A few years ago, manure storage facilities were almost unheard of," Harman recounts.

"Farmers had no option but year-round, daily manure spreading—

not a good practice when snowmelt and precipitation wash it into the streams. In the early 1990s, we began working on nutrient budgets. We were in all the streams all the time. Because of our work and resultant funding, we're beginning to see manure lagoons and automated applicators. Next, we'll start monitoring the effectiveness of these practices. By compiling a comprehensive database, we can begin to put a price tag on how much phosphorus is being kept out of the lake and empirically predict a payback on investment in these applications."

It is essential, Harman summarizes, to develop a comprehensive land-use plan for the watershed based upon the lake's capacity to withstand the demands of increased residential, agricultural, and commercial uses. Full understanding of water quality, he advises, requires analysis of social and economic characteristics, soil attributes, land cover, elevations, and other considerations. "What it boils down to," he concludes, "is that tough choices have to be made if we want to develop land and maintain the lake with quality fisheries and scenic beauty. We need to take a systematic approach to getting things back into balance. The thrust of our research has been to gather and synthesize information necessary to determine the physical capabilities of Otsego Lake to maintain its aesthetic character, its cold water fishery, and its ability to continue to serve as the symbol of our region. What we're doing is comparable to what's being done on the river and the Bay itself, except we're providing a baseline for as close to pristine conditions as we're ever going to find. Anybody in the Bay watershed can use this data as a reference. We contributed to a lake management plan, which was put together by a whole series of people and organizations and agencies that are involved in different ways. That has allowed everybody to agree on a plan, which is now easily funded, including hiring a full-time watershed manager. That's where I think we've made our greatest contribution, along with field education, which is vital for the future because we're teaching people about their natural resource legacies and the quality of their lives in a way that makes it tangible, alive, and very real."

MICHAEL J. OGBURN ~

Blacksburg, Virginia

Team Leader, Hybrid Electric Vehicle Team

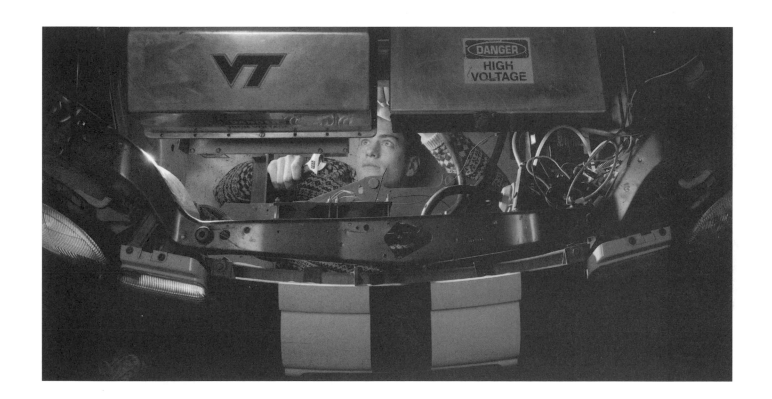

As a brilliant twenty-three-year-old graduate student at Virginia Polytechnic Institute and State University (Virginia Tech), with job prospects at several distinguished corporations, Mike Ogburn is a young man swinging the world by its tail. Or is that tailpipe? When not researching Fuel Cell Vehicle drivetrains, he is team leader of the university's Hybrid Electric Vehicle Team (HEVT), a student organization that has been an innovative pioneer in engineering hybrid electric and alternative-fuel vehicles. Their latest invention, fueled by electricity and a hydrogen fuel cell, is quiet, surprisingly spunky, and reduces carbon dioxide (CO_2) and nitrogen oxide (NO_x) emissions by two-thirds. The engine's only waste product is water. "Instead of a puff of exhaust smoke, there's a column of white steam," Ogburn reports. "We've actually drunk water straight from the tailpipe!"

This technology could significantly impact the Chesapeake region, since nitrogen oxide emissions contribute to eutrophication problems by worsening the lack of oxygen in Bay waterways. Motor vehicle exhaust, a mobile point source, accounts for about a third of these emissions in the Bay's airshed—the area that supplies most of the air pollution landing in the Chesapeake watershed. Regulators have proposed sharp cuts in emissions that could significantly decrease the amount of pollution entering the Bay. Reducing emissions is at the forefront of Ogburn's objectives. The HEVT has been the "winningest" team in the prestigious Future Car Challenge, taking first or second place in each of the four years of the competition. The goal is to convert a traditional automobile into a car of the future, one that gets eighty miles per gallon while retaining the safety, performance, affordability, and low emissions that consumers expect.

"Our goal is producing something that works and is usable by the average human being," Ogburn confirms. "It takes an amazing engineering effort to get this stuff to work right. Especially when you're in a competition where if you don't shoot for the moon you don't have a chance of winning." The team works in a corridor of padlocked bays where students devise such curiosities as robotic vehicles and a "personal electric rapid transit" (PERT) system that looks like something straight out of *The Jetsons* cartoon. Ogburn also has an office equipped with grease-smudged CAD computers, where he instructs students on automotive design and manufacturing.

In the HEVT electric car, he explains, "an inverter made of six monster transistors takes DC battery power and operates the motor. It drives almost exactly like a normal car except it whispers rather than revs, and it needs to be charged with magnetic induction through a plug-in device. A typical pure electric vehicle will cruise around town for about twenty miles at a time. It's a great errand vehicle." But, Ogburn notes, longer trips are impractical.

This is where hybrids come into play. A hybrid electric vehicle uses a small additional power source such as a gasoline generator or hydrogen fuel cell to recharge the onboard battery pack. Because this power source operates at its most efficient point, the vehicle's fuel economy can be as much as twice that of a traditional gasoline-powered car. The HEVT team uses a three-cylinder engine that runs continuously to provide enough average power to keep the batteries charged.

"So you floor it, the tires spin—this thing will lay about forty feet of rubber—and the batteries start to discharge. But then as you get off the gas and hit the brakes, regenerative energy comes back from the electric motor to slow the car down, saving brake pads and improving fuel economy at the same time. The engine and generator or super-clean fuel cell continuously pumps power back into the batteries. The computer automatically starts and stops the engine and keeps the batteries charged. In city driving it only uses the electric motor and turns the engine off. It allows you to creep along at five to fifteen miles an hour with electric and as you get up to highway speed the auxiliary engine kicks in. It gets fifty to sixty miles per gallon all around." Also geared toward today's niche market of urban commuter drivers, these hybrids are market-ready because they run on gasoline and don't have to be plugged in. "For commercial availability today, vehicles need to run on something that's *available:* gasoline or diesel," Ogburn points out. "You can't buy fuels like hydrogen, methanol, ethanol, and propane on every corner yet. But in ten to twenty years I expect to see some major changes in the forms of energy that drive our economy."

Ogburn's latest technology involves a twenty-kilowatt proton exchange membrane (PEM) fuel cell stack, an electrochemical device in which hydrogen and oxygen gas combine to produce electrical current. Fuel cells produce no air pollution, have no moving parts, and are highly energy efficient, several times that of conventional gasoline-powered engines and electric cars. Unlike batteries, fuel cells don't have to be recharged. "A fuel cell," Ogburn explains, "never discharges as long as the fuels—

hydrogen and oxygen—are available." Fuel cells can also be resupplied with hydrogen in a matter of minutes compared to the several hours needed to recharge the batteries in electric cars. Instead of the complexity of a crank shaft, cam shaft, and pistons moving in closely machined cylinders, the system has only a few moving parts: a water pump for cooling, an air pump or compressor, and valves to regulate those flows.

Ogburn believes hydrogen fuel cells are a "huge opportunity" as a future energy source. "It's the only automotive fuel that has the potential to push cars well and comes from a completely renewable source. Everything else produces CO_2. We're either going to run out of oil or oil derivatives, or we're going to run out of air to burn it with. The automakers foresee CO_2 regulation. The best way to get CO_2 down is to increase fuel economy or use new energy technologies such as fuel cells that run on a carbon-free fuel like hydrogen. You can only increase fuel economy so much because it still takes power to push a car, and we're addicted to transportation, so hydrogen looks like a very attractive option."

In addition to standard performance, safety, and consumer acceptability, "green gas emissions" is a new judging category in this year's Future Truck Competition, using a 2000 Chevy Suburban. "When cars burn fuel they put out emissions," Ogburn elaborates, "but we'll also be scored on upstream pollution such as emissions spewed out by the chemical plant that produces gasoline or the power plant that generates electricity to run the car."

Entrants are also required to demonstrate "things we're supposed to be good at as students, engineers, and people: convincing others that we're doing this for a good cause, and that our design is beneficial." One of Ogburn's slogans in giving presentations is "Education is our goal, and the world is our textbook." He attributes the team's success not only to academics but also to teamwork and dedication to the environment. "Besides serving as a walking electric-vehicle encyclopedia, and learning to be a good people manager, I've gotten myself on a save-the-planet kick," he acknowledges. "I've lived in the Blacksburg area all my life, and it bothers me to see smog from the Blue Ridge Mountain overlooks. The atmosphere makes a pretty bad waste repository. That's what got me interested in fuel economy. After working on our first fuel cell vehicle I saw the possibilities, and how much room there was for improvement.

"Lead-acid and nickel-cadmium batteries put chemicals into the watershed," he illustrates. "I don't see full-time hybrids with nickel-metal-hydride batteries as a long-term solution because they will eventually end up in the gullies, too. Electric cars only need an oil change about every 100,000 miles, and don't require coolant changes, so that stuff stays out of the watershed. Fuel cells have a chance to make a significant improvement to air and water quality. There are enormous challenges, but I think it's the only way we can satisfy our addiction to automobiles and not kill the planet. I don't want to work for a company that makes industrial products or doesn't do something that's going to make a difference. I've got myself stuck on making a difference."

WILLIAM ARTHUR EBERHARDT ⤺

Laceyville, Pennsylvania

Retired Environmental Engineer / River Sojourner

L IKE THAT OF THE SUSQUEHANNA RIVER ON WHICH HE HAS lived and worked for most of his life—a waterway that Susan Stranahan has said can "seize your soul as quickly as it grabs the prow of a canoe on a bright June morning"—Bill Eberhardt's current is unpretentious, steadfast, and determined. Both the river and the man bear a sinuousness of keen, businesslike fortitude mingled with peaceful serenity. Mirroring the river's natural propensity to flood, Eberhardt also has a penchant for spilling over boundaries by reaching out to others in his workplace and local community. Whether seated in his canoe or behind a conference table, he has devoted his life to providing award-winning leadership for the good of the river, the local environment, and those that live and work there. While some have called him a spiritual leader, he responds that he is merely being himself: "I'm stubborn, I tell people the way I see it, and I have consistent expectations—and high expectations."

In 1996, Eberhardt, who holds a Ph.D. in civil engineering, retired from the Procter & Gamble Paper Products Company (P&G) after a distinguished thirty-year career as site environmental manager at the company's Mehoopany Plant in Wyoming County. With its towers and pipe bridges, smokestacks giving forth billowy white steam, acres of tractor trailers, and ribbons of railways situated riverside against a backdrop of forested, hairpin mountain roads, mist-filled valleys, and jagged outcrops trickling with water, this working-class Emerald City cranks out daily payloads of paper towels, toilet tissue, and disposable diapers. Under the leadership of people like Eberhardt, public relations manager Joe DeMarco (center) and current site environmental manager Drew Hadley (right) the Mehoopany plant is a prime example of business endeavoring to integrate with the environment.

The Susquehanna River, the Bay's major tributary, delivers 50 percent of the fresh water to the estuary and has a long history of development along its banks, often providing industry with two important services: running machinery and removing waste. The river has served factories, tanneries, slaughterhouses, dairies, food processing plants, and America's first steel mill. Pulp and paper mills such as the Mehoopany plant are the largest freshwater dischargers of conventional, point-source pollutants and additives of any industry regulated by national effluent standards. Today, while the river faces the demands of businesses, agriculture, and residential development, Eberhardt reveals "there is a changing ethic that's pretty dramatic. We're seeing companies taking more environmental responsibility, farms building buffers, and communities improving sewage treatment."

P&G, a member of Businesses for the Bay (a voluntary pollution prevention program for industries and small businesses within the Chesapeake Bay watershed), has been a leader in this new standard. The plant was originally built in 1966 on the North Branch Susquehanna River. "We wanted to shield the plant from the river and make it reasonably aesthetic," Eberhardt explains. "Today's increasing knowledge tells us it's the right thing to do for ecological reasons as well." Currently, the plant employs about 2,500 people and, until last year, when it eliminated the pulping portion of its operation, was the single remaining pulping facility in P&G's vast, international organization and the only one of its type in the world to have eliminated chlorine bleaching from its operation. For thirty years, the plant's pulp and paper mill literally brought in trees at one end and rolled out finished products at the other. P&G requires large quantities of water to produce its products, pumping about six million gallons per day from the river. Wastewater treatment facilities recycle and reuse this water several times before it is filtered, purified, and returned to the river. "From the outset of the Mehoopany venture," Eberhardt asserts, "the protection and enhancement of the river corridor has been one of our primary goals."

Of the many important aspects of his work at the plant over the years, of particular significance to the watershed are waste reduction, nitrogen reduction, in-stream biological monitoring, and community outreach. In 1985, the plant was one of the five largest point sources of nitrogen in the Susquehanna River basin. By 1994, it had voluntarily reduced nitrogen output by 40 percent, an accomplishment that earned the plant the 1997 Governor's Environmental Excellence Award. Pollution control technology and efficient operating practices continue to help the plant routinely surpass federal effluent limitations, (it averages only 10 percent of allowable discharge). Eberhardt's team went one step further by voluntarily working with the Academy of Natural Sciences of Philadelphia to conduct annual monitoring of aquatic life in the river since the year before the plant was built.

A primary part of Eberhardt's and his associates' work concentrates on ways to "plan pollution out of the plant's processes, products, and packaging," including innovative reductions in residual and hazardous wastes, air emissions, water and energy use, and packaging. An out-standing example in this area is the on-site sanitary landfill. In 1986, the plant disposed of about 150,000 tons of material there. By 1992, the plant had achieved an 83 percent reduction in waste, and the company completely closed down the facility. "We were able to do this with no impact on our operations," Eberhardt reports. "This not only protected and improved the environment, but also improved our financial position by saving over $25 million per year through recovery, resale, and energy generation. This success came from being innovative with our byproducts and taking an approach that has turned our wastes to a business advantage." Today, over 85 percent of the unavoidable solid waste generated by the plant is used beneficially.

"We're all working toward being here for the long term," Eberhardt continues. "The way we succeed in that is by our broad business results—our effect on the community, environment, and bottom line profits. A good portion of our pollution prevention pays off, but not always. They're not all profit makers, particularly after the low-hanging fruit is gone. We realize that some things are beneficial even if they don't directly contribute to the short-term bottom line. Sometimes it's just right to do."

But there's a lot more to Eberhardt than strategizing and formulating budgets, technical papers, and flow charts. He takes P&G's environmental message beyond the walls of the plant with programs designed to bring people together in common understanding. "We will achieve more environmental gain by working as partners than we will working as adversaries. Waste minimization has been an extremely strong side for us," he acknowledges, "but we couldn't achieve these successes without tremendous employee involvement, a strong corporate ethic, and community and regulatory support. Our employees have a good set of values; they're the ones who go out and make it happen. We're very fortunate, too, to work for a company that cares. Those aspects will play forever as this plant continues to grow and face the future."

Nowadays Eberhardt has more time outside of the plant to spend supporting the river. His commitment to the Susquehanna has led to a commitment for the Chesapeake Bay watershed. He serves on several environmental boards, including the Citizens Advisory Committee to the Chesapeake Bay Executive Council. One of his favorite achievements is cofounding, with the Alliance for the Chesapeake Bay organization, the Susquehanna Sojourn. Hundreds of canoeists participate in this flotilla, which highlights the river's resources and its connection to the Chesapeake Bay through annual, one-week journeys down different portions of the river, with stops in riverside towns for educational activities, press events, and meetings with public officials. "We get people to come out and think about the importance of the river." Last year, Eberhardt and his wife, Audrey, paddled the entire length of the Susquehanna, 444 miles from Cooperstown, New York, joining the sojourn along the way, and continuing to its release into the Bay proper near Havre de Grace, Maryland. Because she once almost drowned, Audrey is leery of the water, but even she cannot resist the summons of the river and fellowship with its people. "Year after year, I'm like a supportive grandmother. Besides," she admits, "I'm afraid I'll miss something!"

Bill Eberhardt has contributed a distinguished body of work to both the public and private sectors of Pennsylvania's pollution control field. A recent award application stated that "No matter where you look—inside P&G, in the community, in government, wherever Bill has been involved—you will see and feel the influence of his vision, his principles, his integrity, his strong belief in people, and his tireless willingness to work side-by-side with others." Eberhardt acknowledges that "taking care of the environment cannot be done by one individual or organization on its own. If you are trying to do the right thing, you alone can't define that. You need to get others with you. And," he concludes, "if you believe in something, want to do it right, and have the technical knowledge to do it, and a company that backs you, you don't need regulatory motivation."

On an afternoon stroll through the woods, past his new, handmade Adirondack lean-to and along the side of his modest country home facing a stream, Eberhardt takes a fond inventory of the many trees he has planted over the years. With a hint of the local accent, he describes them as "beauty-full" and points out their colorful "burr-ees." Easily dragging his canoe down to the water, he pauses for a moment to carefully tend a recently planted seedling at the water's edge. "Yes," he gently cheers, "I think it's going to make it."

ABBY CHAPPLE ~

Largent, West Virginia

Mountain Mama

FROM WHERE ABBY CHAPPLE SITS, THE EAGLE FLIES BELOW. Chapple lives on a shale barren outside a town that teeters at the vertex where Virginia's northernmost point juts into the neck of the West Virginia Panhandle. Stratified shale, Indian trails, caves, and scrubby vegetation—flowering cactus, native wildflowers, lichens—characterize her sixteen acres of mountainside, named Glad Tidings. These mountains overlook four states, three branches of the Potomac River and their labyrinth of tributaries, and the country roads serenaded by singer John Denver. Chapple, once an avid sailor and skipper in Annapolis, Maryland, felt a distinct sense of belonging when, as a "flatlander," she drove through the state for the first time. When she and her third husband, David, moved here about five years ago, Chapple, redheaded and full of brassy verve, set to work learning about the community's history and watershed issues. Today, all a stranger to these parts has to do is mention Chesapeake Bay and folks know, "You must be lookin' for Abby Chapple."

Chapple was born in Manhattan and grew up on a nonworking farm in New Jersey. "We were known as 'fanny' farmers because we sat on our fannies instead of working the farm," she recalls. "But I spent my childhood walking around the woods by myself, so this place was like coming home." Before retiring, she worked extensively in public and private sector positions: in the furniture industry, as a White House appointee to the Consumer Product Safety Commission, in interior designing, and for fifteen years as home editor at the *Washington Star* newspaper. "I was a fledgling Martha Stewart," she quips. Today, she does consulting and desktop publishing from her home. "I'm actually just a pushy broad," she wisecracks. "I'm semi-retired. I'm semi-everything!" She is a devout Messianic Jew and is involved with several area organizations, including Friends of the Cacapon River (FCR). "I bring various governmental, industrial, and geographic perspectives to the table," she says. "Basically, I'm a researcher. I want the details, the statistics . . . I want to know why. Because I came from Annapolis, I can relate the experience of living downstream. When I care about something, I'm passionate about it. This area is primitive and I love it in these 'wild and wonderful' mountains."

If it weren't for these ancient Appalachian Mountains, West Virginia might not exist as a separate state. Originally part of Virginia, the boundaries for this remote inland region—the most mountainous state east of the Mississippi—were drawn following a rift between highland pioneers and their wealthier tidewater relatives. The region seceded from Virginia during the Civil War. "The history of West Virginia has always been out-siders taking out—mineral rights, coal, timber, hunting," Chapple ex-plains. Peppered with feuding clans, shotguns, rough characters, and the occasional Confederate flag, "It's a tough state with tough people." Once the capital of coal country, today the state draws thousands of recre-ational tourists to its ski slopes, hiking trails, and river rapids. Chapple lives in Morgan County, at the heart of the Chesapeake Bay watershed, where train whistles still blow in the distance across the Cacapon (mean-ing "healing waters." To pronounce it, Chapple advises, "think of a stut-tering neutered chicken."), the Little Cacapon, and the Lost Rivers.

Chapple's first introduction to community involvement in the water-shed came from a sign posted by the FCR at the Stonycreek General Store, the only market within twenty miles of town. Permeated by the sounds of the running creek, a jingling entrance bell, and sizzling fried eggs, the store is provisioned with stacks of firewood, racks of all-occa-sion cards, ammo, cans of snuff, flypaper, beer, and Spam. Chapple greets her neighbors as they come and go. "This is where I hang out," she says. "I shop here, post information here, people yell at me here!"

Chapple explains that in recent years the area has transitioned from a bedroom community of Cumberland to a retirement and recreational community for "weekenders" from Washington and Baltimore.

"When we bought our property, the real estate agents claimed the Ca-capon is the cleanest river east of the Rockies. That's hyperbole; but it is very clean. One of the reasons is there is so little development. But there are about fourteen hundred little houses between here and Berkeley Springs and about 70 percent of the Cacapon is platted for development. At one time the *Washington Post* gave away 100-foot 'picnic lots' with every subscription, so there are oodles of tiny lots. If they were to be de-veloped, it would be disastrous. The area has 'grown like Topsy'—hap-hazardly, without zoning or regulation."

Its population, too, is a gumbo of three groups that Chapple describes as natives, outsiders, and in-betweeners. Two years ago, when she became president of the FCR, a primary focus was to bring the three groups to-gether. During her tenure, membership has increased from eleven to eighty-five, with a mailing list of 350, and the group has been recognized for its outreach and educational efforts. "There is a mandate, a *necessity* for people to realize watershed connections—to connect the dots. Our work enforces that connection. One of my concerns is that the people who have lived here all their lives work with us and don't see us as tree-huggers and frog-kissers. The locals tend to take the river for granted because they don't have any basis of comparison to know how awful it can become. To me it's a learning experience—another master's degree."

Either alone or in collaboration with other groups, the FCR conducts baseline studies, stream bank surveys, and bio-assessment monitoring, as well as providing ecocamps for kids. It also advocates well testing, outhouse setbacks, and the establishment of buffers to support riparian vegetation and to reduce runoff. Erosion and sedimentation pose the largest threat to local tributaries. Soil dregs destroy spawning areas for fish and insect larvae and smother aquatic plants, which degrade the health of the river. Housing construction, lawns, and roads substantially increase runoff, and erosion increases with the removal of trees and native plants along the riverbanks, such as the endangered Harperella (*Ptilimnium nodosum*). Extreme sedimentation could potentially raise the riverbed, leading to higher and more devastating flooding.

Flooding from storms, heavy precipitation, and snowmelt is a significant concern. On the south bank of what is known as "Long Pond," the legendary "Noah tree" records high-water marks over the centuries, the highest almost forty feet (from a flood in 1951). Accounts of floodwaters sweeping away trees, trash, roads, riverbanks, and entire houses are common. While in many parts of the Chesapeake watershed waterfront property is the territory of the elite, along these rivers waterfront property often is subject to severe flooding. "It's expensive to run a road and utilities up the mountain," Chapple explains. "So the poorest houses are right on the river."

Many riverside properties are summer cabins used by out-of-towners. "We import suburban ideals and guess what?" Chapple asks. "We have to have a lawn. Then we mow right down to the river so there's no riparian zone to purify runoff and protect the river. People say they don't want to interfere with the view. Doesn't it matter that we're polluting the river? Are we going to bring golf courses, mowing, and pesticides . . . here? So it can wash into our rivers? No, let's not do that."

Chapple goes on to explain that, although farming is limited in the lower reaches of the Cacapon, the potential impact of this industry is great. "The Lost River and its tributaries have already been declared impaired because of poultry farming," she reports. "These factory operations require very little land to produce large numbers of birds and huge volumes of manure and other wastes that could have devastating consequences for our river. They take the chicken shit and apply it to the fields, which causes nutrients and antibiotics to wash into the water. Unfenced cattle trample riverbanks and dislodge soft alluvial soils. Agricultural fertilizers and pesticides also pose a threat. Any time we have a major flood, all that inundates the river."

Other factors contribute to the watershed's sedimentation problems. The area's logging history compounds runoff. "This area was completely logged at one point. There are no old-growth trees, which further increases runoff and siltation. That's one of the reasons the water level has changed and there's not enough shade and cool water to support trout anymore." Mud from rough-cut public access areas and dirt roads—crude, rutted remnants of horse-and-wagon days—also washes into the waterways. "Because of 'dirty' water, we've lost what are known as SAVs [submerged aquatic vegetation]," Chapple says, aptly pronouncing the acronym like *salves*. "Like the little plants that provide oxygen in fish tanks? Missing! Decreasing underwater vegetation is an indicator that we're losing the river. Especially when there are more tires in there than there are SAVs."

However, Chapple points out that "we are in the enviable position of being proactive, of possibly preventing what other watersheds are facing. We're trying to find real answers, not just knee-jerk, emotional responses. We're making little steps. If given a chance, the land will repair itself. For all of the bad stuff, isn't it a wonderful river?"

Despite Chapple's "pushiness," there is a decidedly contemplative side to this feisty lady. Relaxing at the ledge of her favorite cliff, she declares, "Being here is not unlike being on a sailboat. See the cloud fingers reaching for the mountains? Look at that river, isn't it worth saving? It not only has a historic past, but an exciting future. People around here know my name . . . I don't want them to know my name, I want them to think 'Cacapon River.'"

LLOYD (LOU) WELLS ∽

Hagerstown, Maryland

Inmate "Fishman"

A GANG OF FAT CATS LIVES BEHIND THE STATE PRISON BUILDING at the Maryland Correctional Training Center (MCTC) in Hagerstown, Maryland. When Lou Wells opens the back door, the well-fed felines—all an identical shade of gray, matching the slate roof of the stone barn that houses the institution's aquaculture program—amble out from nowhere in anticipation of fresh fish. "When we lose a fish from the tanks, I just toss it out the back door," Wells admits. The Hagerstown prison complex holds about sixty-seven hundred prisoners, but the prerelease program assigns only one man—dubbed "Fishman"—to run its aquaculture program. Wells, who is from Baltimore County, has been incarcerated for about six years on a conviction of armed robbery. "I started out in maximum security. Now I'm all the way down to prerelease. This is a step away from going home. As long as I keep earning ten days a month off my sentence, I'll be released in about ten months." That means the fish he's been raising since last summer will be released before he is.

Wells spends his nights behind bars and surrounded by a fence rigged with coiled razor wire. But seven days a week he works, mostly unsupervised, tending fish in a building constructed by past inmates from stone quarried at nearby Antietam Creek. "It's so much better to be away from the boredom of the jail and have some freedom. Here we get out, go to work—ain't no fences around us. Our bosses don't watchdog us; they're busy doing their own jobs. In some jails you're treated strictly as an inmate with a number. Here, you're treated like a regular person— given trust and a little responsibility, which will help on the street. But you have to stay out of trouble and work your way down the system to earn a spot like this." (The job pays $3.50 a day weekdays and overtime on weekends and holidays.) Wells has a mannerly demeanor and is conscientious about his daily duties. He delights in being splashed by feeding fish and watching the harvest grow. With its purposeful yet relaxed working atmosphere, wall hangings of fish, a pinup girl poster, and a sign by the back door that reads, "It's difficult to soar with eagles when you work with turkeys," this seems like any other workplace.

Initiated in 1994, the MCTC aquaculture project is a pilot program of State Use Industries (SUI), a self-supporting agency that provides structured employment and training for offenders to improve their employability while producing saleable goods and services. SUI offers thirty products and services, including furniture, meat, construction, and graphics. The Hagerstown complex operates thirteen SUI shops, which employ a total of 386 inmates and yielded $31.5 million in sales in its 1999–2000 fiscal year. The aquaculture operation is a cooperative effort between SUI and the Maryland Department of Natural Resources (DNR) to raise fish for stocking various waterways.

Wells explains that the program started out as "a PR thing" between state agencies. "DNR supplies the fish, we raise them out, and then we sell them back to DNR. They pay us about $1.25 per fish for some species and per-inch of accelerated growth on others. So if they come in at six inches and we sell them at fourteen, they pay us for eight inches. It runs ten to fifty cents an inch. The fish have the advantage of being in a controlled situation, so they grow continuously for about a year; whereas in a natural setting they don't grow much in the colder months. Now we're raising two thousand tiger muskies, ten thousand bluegill hybrids, and a bunch of catfish."

The program raises several species, including tiger muskie (a recent game fish hybrid of muskellunge and northern pike, which grows up to fifty inches), hybrid sunfish (a female bluegill crossed with a male green sunfish), striped bass, and channel catfish. Wells rears fish from small fingerlings to subadult or adult size. The operation has stocked more than five thousand fish in rivers, lakes, and ponds in Maryland. Most go into the Potomac River and Piney Run Reservoir in Carroll County.

Wells's job, performed amidst a racket of running water and humming motors, is a mix of biology, mechanics, and plumbing. "I learned most of it as I went along. It's passed on from one fishman to another. When the program started, they said to my boss, 'Here's a picture, can you build one like it?'" The operation is an efficient mishmash of holding tanks (some made from backyard swimming pools and livestock troughs), biofilters, settling units, PVC piping, inlets, hoses, and buckets. An automated emergency oxygen tank stands ready to oxygenate the tanks in case of a power failure. Metal supply cabinets hold fish food, filter beads, baking soda, and dechlorinating chemicals. A large scale, string mops, and a fridge sit against the building's periphery.

"This operation takes a lot of tinkering and tender loving care," Wells explains. "For almost a year, we raise these fish like babies—feeding them three times a day, keeping a clean environment, adjusting temperature, doing constant water quality monitoring. I clean the tanks and recirculate 30 to 75 percent of the water every three days, depending on conditions in the tank. There's another tank in the attic where I dechlorinate fresh water before it goes into the fish tanks. I do daily water tests for pH, ammonia, and nitrogen, and clean out the biofilters about once a week. If necessary, I add baking soda to adjust pH. It takes more than a box of baking soda to neutralize three thousand gallons of water—we buy it by the bucketful, but don't have much cause to use it. I'm also responsible for keeping inventory of feed, test kits, and salt, which we add to prevent diseases and regenerate the fish's protective coating."

Wells explains that the stone construction of the building allows for relatively cool temperatures all year. "We can only control the temperature by ten degrees, tops," he says. "In the wintertime we can generate a little heat using 6,000-watt tank heaters and electric strips; but for warm weather we only have one little chiller, which brings the temperature down a degree or two. These old stone barns only get to about eighty-five degrees even when it's one hundred outside, so that helps. We're basically dealing with the ambient temperature. We lose one or two fish a week. That goes up in warmer weather when there are more bacteria and viruses."

The inmate aquaculture program started out as a way of supplying fish to derbies for inner city kids and has expanded to stocking recreational areas. Tiger muskies also contribute to biological fish control by curbing overpopulation of suckers and yellow perch. "This work allows me to prove myself and at the same time contribute to Bay fisheries," Wells says. "The program helps get recreational fishermen out on the water, which gives people an insight on a different facet of the watershed. One big thing is, it gets kids interested in fishing. To a kid, catching a fish can be a turning point. If they don't turn into a lifetime conservationist, at least they're going to generate some income for DNR when they buy a license! I fished at Liberty Reservoir since I was about eight. I'd go out there a couple times a week . . . before I came here. Now I fish every day," he shrugs.

Some of these fish will be transported to their natural habitat next week. "It's sad to see them go," Wells admits. "But I'm anxious to see how much we make. We did good with 'em I think." The last task will be to tag the fish just before they're released so that DNR can track longevity, travel, and migration. Upon his own release, Wells expects to resume employment as a bricklayer. He also plans to get back to real fishing. "Maybe I'll even catch one of these someday," he envisions. "I'll help tag them, but *they'll* leave their mark on me and the fishing holes they'll be living in . . . not to mention those cats out back," he adds with a grin.

ALAN C. GREGORY ∽

Conyngham, Pennsylvania

Conservationist / Journalist

ALAN GREGORY GREW UP IN IDAHO, WITH STRONG FAMILY ties and "a deep connection to the land and preservation of its natural diversity." It's an ethic that has stayed strong no matter where he travels. For twenty-six years he has worked as a civilian and military journalist, and he is currently writing for a newspaper in Hazleton, Pennsylvania. He is also a lieutenant colonel in the Air Force Reserve and an active birder, butterfly-counter, and "frog watch" monitor. Passionate about environmental justice, he speaks of it deliberately, looking listeners in the eye with a steely blue gaze, occasionally breaking a boyish smile as warm as the heat from a coal-burning stove. While his ambition is to work as a full-time conservationist ("I only work at the paper because my wife told me I had to—to help pay for the house"), in his spare time, for over eight years, Gregory has fought a little-supported environmental battle in the Nescopeck Creek watershed.

This watershed's story is told through its coloration—"black water events" from retail coal preparation plants, orange plumes from iron hydroxides in mining discharge, and streambeds coated with "yellow boy," highly acidic iron oxide runoff from mining discharge that kills all plant life, leaving the water clear and barren. "When coal is removed from its underground seams," Gregory explains, "water penetrates the openings." When water and air come into contact with Pennsylvania's coal-bearing strata, a chemical reaction takes place that speeds up the normal course of nature. By the time the water leaves the mine, it's a potent mix of sulfates, acid, and iron hydroxides, plus aluminum, calcium, manganese, and ferrous iron. "The pH is lethal to aquatic life. Like a bottle of dilute sulfuric acid, it looks like good, clear water, but it's an environmental wrecking ball."

In this area, much of the affliction stems from acid mine drainage (AMD) discharged at the Jeddo Mine Tunnel, a relic of the heyday of underground mining. The tunnel mouth is located near Hazleton (population 23,000), a town that was literally and figuratively built on coal. This region has a long history of "clean water versus jobs" debates, and only recently has the clean water voice been validated. It is hardscrabble country. "The economy," Gregory explains, "is based on taking from the land, not living with it." He points out thousands of acres of stripped-out former coal-mining lands called "strippings"—seemingly endless wastelands where huge "culm banks" and pools remain to this day—that surround the city. "It's a town built on top of a quagmire of old mine shafts." For decades, this region's livelihood depended on mining coal from underground shafts and surface diggings. Businesses and houses—stacked like blocks on the sides of an Appalachian hollow, the Nescopeck Creek Valley—were inextricably tied to hard coal, or anthracite, which, in the United States, exists only in a 500-square-mile area of northeastern Pennsylvania. Approximately 7 billion tons of it has been mined from these hills since the eighteenth century. Today, drainage from abandoned mines is the major source of water pollution in the state, accounting for about half the total miles of degraded streams.

Construction on the gravity drainage tunnel began in the late nineteenth century, and the tunnel eventually drained more than thirty-two square miles. It was built by the Jeddo Mining Company to "de-water" deep underground mine workings from the Little Black Creek, Big Black Creek, Cross Creek, and Hazleton coal basins. The company rechanneled streams and dug out an enormous drainage system of tunnels and large haulageways, constructing what, at the time, was considered an engineering marvel. Today, Gregory describes the structure as "a dinosaur that survived extinction." More than a century of subsurface and surface mining activities has left a legacy of contaminated water. Raw sewage, heavy metals, hydrocarbon residues, and pollution from runoff also discharge here. The tunnel collects and discharges more than half of the precipitation received in the drainage area. All of the expelled material ends up in the Little Nescopeck Creek, which joins Nescopeck Creek, and eventually enters the Susquehanna River.

"Below the tunnel confluence," Gregory reports, "the Little Nescopeck is biologically dead. Because of tunnel discharge, unnatural rechanneling, and runoff, it's ten times the width it was three hundred years ago when it was a blue ribbon trout stream. Instead of continuing as a fairly narrow stream running placidly through the woods, there's an artificial confluence that is so strong it supports class-three white water rapids downstream!" Gregory reports that above the confluence the Nescopeck and Little Nescopeck retain a healthy aquatic ecosystem. "It's actually a cold-water fishery with salamanders, turtles, stonefly hatches, and native brook trout. We can surmise that similar conditions once existed in the entire Nescopeck Creek."

In 1991, Gregory and his hiking partner, Drew Magill, who grew up in the valley, began investigating the extent of AMD in local waterways. They cofounded a group called the Friends of the Nescopeck, a water-

shed association that seeks to restore aquatic life to Little Nescopeck Creek while conserving the remaining green landscape of the Nescopeck Creek watershed. "We don't have an office," Gregory allows, "we don't have tax status, we don't have bylaws, or officers. We're just a coalition of kindred spirits." Eight years later, after extensive research and legwork, the group was instrumental in the publication of a thick, bound report, prepared for the Pennsylvania Department of Environmental Protection. Filled with background information, technical data, graphs, and foldout maps, the report outlines a strategy for reducing the amount of contaminated water discharged from the Jeddo Mine Tunnel.

"Using aerial photographs, a backpack GPS [global positioning system] unit, and yellow 'Rite in the Rain' field books," Gregory explains, "we carried out field reconnaissance to pinpoint dozens of infiltration points [sites where water seeps down into the mine pool]. We did a lot of hiking, put a lot of miles on our cars, and spent a lot of money out of our own pockets." The group conducted weekly monitoring of twelve sites between the Little Nescopeck Creek and the Susquehanna River, testing a variety of parameters: pH, dissolved oxygen, fecal coliforms, and heavy metals. They iced down water samples in a cooler, took them to the airport for transport by courier to a lab for analysis, and transferred field data to a database. Since the final report was completed, the group only monitors once a month at the tunnel mouth, testing turbidity, pH, and alkalinity.

"It was just a small group of people that pulled together around a mission. We got very little support from the community and environmental groups," Gregory divulges. "There are many good people in Hazleton, but it's difficult to generate a groundswell of support for long-term environmental issues. People have been living with the scarred landscape for so long that they don't really know what the land could look like otherwise. People who live downstream don't fully grasp what's happening upstream," he adds. "We've tried to get Bay environmentalists to come up here and take a look. Our experience has been they're too busy lobbying and selling tee shirts and bumper stickers to get involved or just offer moral support by writing a letter to the editor. Even this far upstream, this watershed is directly impacting the Chesapeake Bay."

Surrounded by the land he now calls home, Gregory extends his arms and calls over the clamorous current of water rushing from the mouth of the tunnel. "Close your eyes and envision hearing water trickling down the slope from melting snow. It's running into the little stream down there, and that little stream has fish in it and is surrounded by natural habitat. Instead," he says, growing visibly angry, "this thing is a monster! It's a metaphor for the tunnel vision regarding economic growth in this area. Habitat? Developers just built a 600,000-square-foot warehouse on what used to be a pitch pine and oak forest full of natural diversity, full of life. They blitzed it with bulldozers. What we have is guys driving forklifts around for seven dollars an hour. That's not economic development!" he decries. "You want economic development? Then start living *with* the land. Reclaim minelands and build on them. Don't destroy a forest that should be preserved!"

Calming, he continues: "Conservation is about seeing the big picture. As part of an educational effort, we're going to be installing signs identifying the name of each creek and underneath the fact that the stream is dead because of AMD. That's going to be news to a lot of people. You have to inform people before they can emotionally support restoration work. We'd love to be able to change the signs so they just say 'Little Nescopeck Creek, Cold Water Fishery.'"

Gregory recognizes it's unlikely there will be fish in the Little Nescopeck in his lifetime. "It's physically and financially unrealistic. But that doesn't mean we won't continue to work toward that goal. We hope the report leads to real, on-the-ground efforts. The implementation phase comes next. The solution is to keep as much water out of the tunnel as possible—you don't have to be a chemist; you have to be a plumber. Then what's left can be treated at the mouth. We're investigating success stories from western Maryland, where researchers have had positive results using silos of alkaline lime kiln dust, applying a sealing grout made of ash from coal-fired power plants, and even raising trout in treated mine water. We also envision wetlands being used to treat the mine water before it enters the watershed. We plan to do the right thing with the bulldozers this time."

KHALIL HASSAN ⌐

Criglersville, Virginia

Retired Firefighter / Upstream Grassroots Coordinator

Tʜᴇ ʀᴏᴜᴛᴇ ᴛᴏ ᴋʜᴀʟɪʟ ʜᴀssᴀɴ's ʀᴇᴍᴏᴛᴇ ᴄᴏʀɴᴇʀ ᴏғ ᴍᴀᴅɪsᴏɴ County is long and convoluted, but the journey ends in breathtaking recompense—rivers flowing by mill wheels, brooks cluttered with stones and saplings growing right out of the streambeds, and cricks cutting little ledges in the land as they meander through cattle pastures and woods, all plaited from the palms of the Blue Ridge Mountains. "When I saw the river down there," Hassan recollects, "I said to myself, 'This is me, I gotta be here.'" In the years since, he has found a new identity not only for himself but also for the waters that enticed him, by strengthening the concept that this high country is entwined with the Chesapeake Bay via the Rapidan and Rappahannock Rivers.

This unassuming man, with an unexpected sense of humor, retired here in 1992 after serving as a firefighter in Washington, D.C., for twenty-five years. For the time being, he lives in a trailer (with a screen torn by snooping bears and a compost pile marauded by bobcats) while he builds a geodesic dome house at the end of a back road that passes a suspended bridge, continues through a "low water bridge" ford crossing, inclines and narrows to a dirt farm lane, then evolves into a crude, uphill driveway.

Hassan became involved in local volunteer work after a flood destroyed the first house he and his wife had lived in after moving to Criglersville. "We were strangers here—the local term is *come here's,* that's anybody who didn't come over on the Mayflower—but there was a strong outpouring of help from our neighbors. Once we got settled again, I felt I wanted to give something back."

It's not always easy for an outsider to make inroads. "Newcomers have to pass the litmus test. I'm a vegetarian living in beef country," Hassan illustrates. "There's no tofu at the Mountain Store! But once I got past that, it wasn't a problem. It's hard for me to go back to the city now."

Hassan chairs the Madison County Task Force for Sustainable Growth, which formed in 1997 because of a conflict with the county over a proposed development that was eventually defeated. "It's still fairly pristine here," Hassan says, stating the obvious, "but it's not going to last. Part of the problem is there are too many short-term solutions; there's not enough long-term thinking, in the public and private sectors."

The Task Force promotes awareness through regular forums and presentations on local issues. Sitting at a computer in a crowded corner of his trailer, Hassan edits newsletters replete with hand-drawn lampoons. Initially, the group's focus was on land planning, but it has expanded to other areas, such as water quality.

Though long considered one of the cleanest rivers on the East Coast, recent studies indicate that the Rappahannock River suffers from significant degradations in water quality. In 1998, the Virginia Institute of Marine Science (VIMS) released a sobering report on Virginia's Bay tributaries stating that "the extent of the Rappahannock's degradation was far worse than anyone's expectations." The Rapidan watershed is the primary source area for high sediment and nutrient loads entering the Rappahannock's mainstream. "The major concern is the prevalence of 'dead water,'" Hassan elaborates. This phenomenon is caused by high nutrient loads and poor flushing, and it results in oxygen depletion due to algae decay in the river's deep water. The shape of the river bottom prevents deep water from mixing with aerated water, so dead water lingers through the summer. Bottom dwellers like crabs, clams and mussels begin to die out, and there's a loss of habitat for many species of fish. Soil from erosion and runoff becomes suspended in the river and compounds the problem by blocking the light necessary for submerged aquatic vegetation, which Hassan calls "the centerpiece of a healthy estuary ecosystem."

Virginia's Tributary Restoration Strategy takes a cooperative approach to restoration that emphasizes local needs and viewpoints. Officials have identified impaired waters by the uses they either fail to support or only partially support. These degradations have been identified through vast water quality monitoring that is conducted by state agencies, universities, and citizen groups.

Stream cleanups and monitoring are ongoing activities for Hassan's group. "We (sometimes it's just me) started monitoring one of the streams through the Save Our Streams program. Part of the function of the Task Force is to train more people in monitoring techniques."

Healthy waterways support an abundance of macroinvertebrates, creatures that look like real-life versions of a child's rubbery "creepy crawlers." When water quality declines, these populations change in predictable and measurable ways because they have different levels of tolerance to pollutants such as toxic chemicals, nutrients from farms and lawns, fecal materials, and sediment. For example, mayfly nymphs, gilled snails, and water penny larvae are pollution intolerant; midge larva, clams, and sowbugs are moderately tolerant; and aquatic worms are pollution tolerant. By tracking these organisms, monitors can determine if a stream is improving, getting worse, or staying the same. "We establish a baseline of water quality by observing what can tolerate the toxic stuff," Hassan reiterates. "We use a kick-seine net to catch the critters. Then we sort and count them. Anybody can do it."

The Task Force is also involved with several local groups working to build a large, diverse corps of volunteers for conservation and restoration projects throughout the Rapidan watershed. One of the outreach initiatives is recruiting and training "Water Watchers," residents who make field notes and observations, determine causes, and initiate recommended responses. Occurrences these residents watch for include fish kills, algae growth, abnormal flows, and illegal dredging. "I record visual observations of a section of a waterway," Hassan explains, "looking at the condition of the stream bank: is there erosion, cattle, debris in the stream? Is it cloudy or clear? That establishes a baseline so that if all of a sudden the water is cloudy for a week, you know something's going on, either upstream, or at the site. If I observe anything unusual, I report it to the appropriate agency or watershed coordinator."

Hassan keeps a notebook on the front seat of his pickup truck, in which he makes regular entries about conditions on the Robinson River. On the rusty rear of his truck a bumper sticker reads *If the people lead, the leaders will follow.* "I never realized the enormity of it," he concedes. "We have people involved from several counties—Madison, Orange, Rappahannock, and others. I just spread the word—talking to people, posting flyers and notices in local papers, sending email. To me it doesn't seem like being a leader."

Wading through the river, Hassan sometimes traverses bedrock—large, broad rocks that are so strong they have been used to support houses and bridge pilings. "The bedrock is too deeply embedded to be removed mechanically or by nature. It's symbolic of an innate characteristic of the people who live here," he imparts. "All of us—natives and newcomers—have found our little piece of paradise. Every bend in the road, every twist on a footpath reveals yet another treasure that is only Madison. This is where we want to be. That steadfast devotion distinguishes the people of many unique places across the Chesapeake watershed, and will be a driving force for its future."

ANDREW JOHNSTON ❧

Lovettsville-Taylorstown, Virginia

EcoVillage Volunteer

THE VOLUNTEER SPIRIT OF PEOPLE LIKE ANDY JOHNSTON, WHO prefer hard work to accolades, often fuels the pulse of change. Johnston volunteers at EcoVillage, an innovative housing development in Loudoun County, Virginia. He is chairman of the volunteer committee and a member of the economic development committee. He conducts product research, recruits and supervises summer interns, produces a community newsletter, and obtained organic certification for the entire 186-acre site. He has been a focal point in the volunteer effort, working with the Virginia forestry program and acting as reforestation coordinator for the planting of more than eight thousand indigenous trees. Many of the volunteers are "future residents" of the community, but Johnston simply believes in the project. "Environmentally friendly development isn't just for the benefit of those who plan to live in a new community," he says. "This type of development is beneficial to the larger established community and the bioregion. Communities like EcoVillage can act as a catalyst to promote conservation, environmental protection, and sustainable business enterprise.

"As neighbors, my wife and I were intrigued by the EcoVillage community," Johnston explains. He was between jobs when they moved to the area and able to devote time to the project—he estimates $40,000 to $50,000 worth over the past three years. Previously, Johnston lived much of his life in the heart of West Virginia's coal country. "My God, the orange streams that I grew up with," he exclaims in a mild Appalachian drawl. "Dead—totally dead from coal mining discharges. As kids, we fished for carp and catfish down at the sewers because there weren't any game fish left in the river. We didn't think anything about it."

Today, Johnston's environmental outlook is quite different. "The EcoVillage property includes several streams and springs," he reports. "That means the property produces water that feeds Catoctin Creek [a state-designated scenic river], the Potomac River, and eventually the Chesapeake Bay. We place a high priority on protecting and restoring riparian habitats. We've initiated baseline water quality sampling and expect monitoring to become a regular activity as development continues."

EcoVillage adds a unique component to his list of community service work, which includes involvement in the local community association, watershed group, and middle school. In his professional life, he has a master's degree in counseling psychology and has worked with the mentally ill, the homeless, disturbed youth, and low-income populations. He is currently employed as Assistant Director for Community Services for Loudoun United Way, a position geared toward community development needs in northern Loudoun County.

Originally this area was part of the Great Eastern Piedmont Forest, until it was cleared for agriculture. Today, with more than forty thousand new units in the pipeline, Loudoun County is the third fastest growing county in the nation. Yet EcoVillage, sequestered by expanses of farm country and the outlying Potomac River and Appalachian Mountains, is not exactly easy to find. There are no directional signs and little more than dirt and gravel roads and a few farm buildings behind the nondescript entrance. Even so, with no model homes or splashy promotional campaign, future residents (which include the developers themselves, Grady and Tena O'Rear) not only have reserved all twenty-five lots in the first of two clusters of homes but are lending a helping hand to make EcoVillage a reality.

Even though site work is still underway, future residents have already fashioned a sense of community. They have cleaned out streamside dumpsites, removed barbed wire to facilitate wildlife corridors, relocated trees to make room for an on-site bridge, and investigated the possibility of their own organic community-supported agriculture program and community home school. Johnston explains that EcoVillage has attracted a wide variety of people. "We've got the 'techie' AOL folks, city commuters, growing families, and even '60s counterculture folks looking to fulfill a fading dream."

Ironically, what looks like just another subdivision road cut through the landscape is actually the result of eight years of careful planning. EcoVillage combines the cohousing model of people living together in a community with the ideal of sustainable development. The development plan incorporates clustered, energy-efficient homes with natural areas, agriculture, and community features such as two 5,000-square-foot "common houses" with kitchens, playrooms, libraries, laundry and storage facilities, workshops, and mailboxes. Johnston explains that cohousing neighborhoods combine the autonomy of living in private homes with the advantages of living in a shared community. "People live in their own homes, but may choose to share some of their meals in a common house," he says, "which also serves as a recreation and socialization center. Cohousing communities are designed, planned, and managed with a high degree of resident participation and offer a return to close-knit, safe neighborhoods."

EcoVillagers engage in constant "design charrettes"—brainstorming sessions involving various stakeholders. In the interest of affordability and environmental gain, they have decided on uniformity of architecture, sacrificing diversity of house design in favor of other forms of individual expression. Unlike those of most developments, the EcoVillage's covenants and restrictions address issues like trespass of solar envelopes and "viewsheds," invasive plants, and organic certification regulations. An expert design team has developed sustainable strategies such as passive solar heating, natural cooling, and geothermal heat pumps that will offer superior energy efficiency. Estimates of annual energy costs for a typical four-bedroom single-family home with a basement are less than one-fourth of those for a comparable, conventionally-built home—$134 for heating, $102 for air conditioning and $128 for hot water. The infrastructure will feature peripheral parking, extensive pedestrian paths, outdoor ground lights that preserve visibility of the night sky, and technologies such as low-water-use fixtures, floor planking made from center cuts of old fence posts, and "Eco Shake" roofing, made from recycled vinyl and sawdust and warrantied for fifty years. Clustering homes leaves over 85 percent of the land as open space, which the community will use for forest management, agriculture, and meadowland.

The developer is committed to restoring biodiversity and protecting wildlife and natural resources. A commuter rail station, carpools, bus transportation, and the Internet are intentionally accessible from the rural community, which supports home-based occupations and a localized, sustainable economy. Johnston's tasks with the Economic Development Committee, formerly chaired by his wife, include working on a proposal to purchase the Taylorstown General Store, within walking distance of the project. "We look toward preserving this national landmark and developing a way to keep it viable as a community resource," he explains.

No doubt, the nearby store will prove useful to EcoVillage residents, who will begin to take occupancy by the fall of 2001. When completed, EcoVillage will be one of the largest cohousing communities in the United States, comprising two distinct neighborhoods, each with twenty-five rural hamlet lots and a common house. Lots will feature one-

to four-bedroom homes—each with a carefully engineered southern exposure and fully equipped kitchen—built on about half-acre lots, with prices in the mid-$300,000s. Given the booming real estate market in the area, Johnston reports that such home prices are extremely competitive. He further explains that the EcoVillage design and construction process "will be used as a vehicle to model 'green' design projects and techniques that can hopefully be routinely made a part of the housing industry."

Johnston has also helped initiate a builder certification program through the EcoVillage Institute, Inc. (EVI), a nonprofit organization established to promote the development of communities that conserve ecosystems and foster social responsiveness. EVI plans to promote concepts such as land and water conservation and preservation, reforestation, the development of wildlife corridors, organic farming and gardening, the selection of nontoxic and low-toxic building materials, energy efficiency, "daylighting," and passive heating and cooling systems. In addition, it will emphasize air, noise, and light pollution-abatement techniques, for example, offering automobile alternatives through the installation of pedestrian, bicycle, and golf-cart paths and selecting ground lighting as opposed to overhead lighting. The U.S. Environmental Protection Agency has awarded EVI a grant to develop and deliver a Sustainable Community Builder / Developer Certification Program. The program will train all contractors working on the construction of EcoVillage to employ earth-friendly, energy-saving construction methods, which will then be offered to other contractors nationwide.

"I've volunteered in a lot of different capacities in my life," Johnston acknowledges. "What's been exciting on this project is helping the community understand something that definitely raises eyebrows. It's ironic," he adds, "that many of us crave a sense of community that we feel is becoming more scarce. We also want more environmentally friendly development alternatives. Nevertheless, when someone tries to create it, others look askance at it. One, more informal, volunteer activity in which I am constantly engaged is community education and stereotype-busting. I cannot tell you how many times I have had to explain to people that EcoVillage is not a 'commune.'

"As an individual," he continues, "I've planted my trees, but more importantly I've helped leverage a whole lot of other volunteers. This is a pilot project that can serve as a model for communities everywhere struggling with growth or just wanting to develop sustainable housing. Perhaps the most daunting problem facing 'green' development is how to integrate environmental goals and economic factors, particularly in areas like Loudoun County where land costs are at a premium. We believe that putting a high investment into planning is a key solution to this problem."

Standing in a field he is transforming from hay production to forest, Johnston recites an ancient Greek proverb: "'When a man plants a tree under which he knows he will never sit, surely civilization has come to that land.' EcoVillage is not a token effort of reduction of environmental impact," he concludes. "It is a profound shift that strives to restore nature, expand human potential, and create a lifestyle that nurtures the human spirit. It offers hope for future generations."

ANDREW McKNIGHT 〜

Mountville, Virginia

Singer-Songwriter / Engineer

Whether he is performing as a charismatic crowd-pleaser or alone by the rippling creeks of his beloved Shenandoah River Valley, Andrew McKnight's music is steadfast and hearty. An energetic, congenial man, who until a few years ago worked as a licensed professional environmental engineer with degrees in chemistry and engineering, McKnight has a strong sense of history and place, which is expressed in his lyrics—*this Old Dominion calls me like a lover tried and true.* His music is a diverse "mountain gumbo" of folk, blues, country, and old-time styles, and he has a unique ability to impact listeners with anecdotes in word and song, such as the story of a drought-stricken farmer's wife drenching her checkered kitchen dress as she dances in an overdue rainstorm or a married couple's fifty years of joy and hardship under the Shenandoah moon. "I do love a good story!" he says in a voice that reverberates with Virginia twang. Many of his songs are "naturalistic vignettes" featuring characters living close to the land or addressing such topics as the "chemical voodoo" of residual industrial waste and rampant land development.

McKnight lives alone near Middleburg, along the nation's first toll road, Snickersville Turnpike. The lay of the land looks very much as it did on the hot day in June 1863 when Custer fought the Battle of Aldie. With the Blue Ridge Mountains and rolling hunt country as a backdrop, garnished with "slave walls"—fences made of stacked-up river stones—and old tollhouses, the area has a charming, rustic character. "It's like livin' in a calendar," McKnight quips.

Yet, with the sprawling suburbs of Washington, D.C., looming close, Snickersville Turnpike, a rustic road as winsome as an a cappella folk ballad, is endangered by the "hard rock" prospect of widening and flattening its backroad pavement and historic humpback Hibbs Bridge (pictured). McKnight explains that Virginia's "onerous" Dillon Rule (a judicial doctrine that limits the power of local governments to exercise their regulatory powers, such as issuing zoning ordinances) casts a shadow of uncertainty on land use in the area. A crescendo of development—subdivisions, shopping centers, fast food joints, and a golf course—encroaches along the John S. Mosby Highway, a circumstance addressed by McKnight's "Letter to Colonel Mosby":

Colonel Mosby, I am but a simple man
But we are common in our love for Virginia's land
We'll protect it, we both do the best we can
Now it's my turn to make a stand

McKnight has refined a philosophy that combines the fervor of an environmentalist with an engineer's bent for problem solving. His engineering career focused on water- and air-quality management for a variety of industries and included a substantial amount of wastewater work at coal-fired power plants in the rural southeastern United States. One of his major areas of wastewater research was identifying the implications of adding ammonia to control airborne nitrogen oxide emissions from coal-fired power plants, a major cause of high Appalachian forest decline as well as ground-level ozone. "Much of my life is tied to coal country. My heart is really in Appalachia," he reveals.

"There's an intense geographical component to my interest. It's a mutual fascination. Folks livin' in the coalfield towns of Virginia and West Virginia relate to my characters and songs. My engineering work initially exposed me to fascinating little places that, against all odds—isolation, resource exploitation, public perception, commercialization—have retained their unique regional identity. A lot of that seems to be vanishing before my eyes as each town gets the same stores with the same facades. That's a tragedy."

McKnight believes heritage and tradition are "the number one endangered species of 'progress.' It's one thing," he insists, "to have progress that celebrates that legacy, and goes forward from it. It's another thing to obliterate it. Like one of my songs says, *If it smells like progress, well, that's just the smoke of our dreams.* Unfettered growth is as detrimental to the landscape as anything we can do. I believe the solution involves incorporating interactions of environmental and spiritual health. I'm not sure anybody has the one right answer, but we've been doing the wrong answers for too long. We've always been a rural nation. When we lose that, we lose something really important of ourselves. It's as much about protecting the *landscapes* that've been in our heritage as it is about preserving the heritage itself. When I think about what's happenin' downstream from me, it comes down to details like, 'Well, okay, this land is rural, but when you pave it over the amount of mud and pollution that runs downstream is unnatural and significant.' That land washing away is washing away a piece of us.

"We're replacing things that have tangible historical and cultural significance with things that are going to have absolutely none. A hundred years from now," he predicts, "these boxy modern-day housing developments are gonna go the same way as bell-bottom pants."

McKnight gave up his profession as an environmental engineer in 1996 to hit the road across the country as a guitar-toting troubadour. As an artist, he is drawn to issues of environmental injustice, such as a proposed (and defeated) Disney park in Virginia and thorny issues of mountaintop mining in West Virginia. "As an engineer, I've always felt that helping power plants meet regulations and improve wastewater treatment with economically feasible answers was something for the greater good. My songwriting reflects an understanding of balancing opposing perspectives, but also knowing what we're capable of dealing with successfully. I also am quite aware of when we hide behind somethin' to avoid detriment to the bottom line, and am not afraid to call it on occasion."

McKnight believes that a primary factor in the environmental future of the region will be its people. "The Chesapeake is a huge watershed," he acknowledges. "Lifestyles and geography vary greatly: in some parts there's clashes between the old and new, watermen vs. tourists vs. moneyed recreational boaters; in other parts it's rural vs. suburban, mountains vs. flats. It's a whole lot different here than directly on the Bay. The biggest impact that I hope to have is that people understand, through the use of water as metaphor, that apparent disparate populations are all connected to each other. The industrial chicken farms of the Potomac Valley are as much an issue as the ones on the Delmarva Peninsula; it's just that nobody talks about them because they're upstream.

"The future of the Chesapeake Bay is going to have a lot to do with awareness. Great progress has been made in understanding basic ecosystem concepts that are important to the Bay's survival. As people's awareness of interrelationships grows, it will translate from in-Bay indicators like submerged aquatic vegetation and rockfish, to things that are upstream and tangible, such as preserving green space to soak up runoff from development.

"If I succeed at introducing people to this perspective and conveying nature's preciousness, then I will have done my job. My role is, through the eyes of a character rather than dogma or preaching, to present a character's relationship to the landscape, then letting listeners extrapolate for themselves what their relationship is to their own landscape. It's easy for me to convey conviction about this, because I have a deep, spiritual relationship to the land. Ya'll need to drive the river road along the Shenandoah to understand *me*."

Between songs sung by the Hibbs Bridge, McKnight says that the life of a traveling musician, which takes him away from the river road, is often a paradox of being surrounded by cheering fans and being alone and pensive. One of his songs tells of the "lingering touch" of living along Chesapeake shores:

Eighteen hundred miles,
from the Chesapeake to this Great Divide
Eighteen hundred miles,
separate me from the truth inside
and I am lonesome, lonesome under western skies

"Being a good songwriter is a gift that is meant to be shared," he asserts. "I can use that gift and spiritual connection to communicate and enlighten people who might not be reached otherwise. That's where it all ties together—this place where I live and this gift that I have are not unrelated. Songwriters not only carry the traditions of the people and the land, we also help to create the future. Every now and then we all need to realize that we're makin' our own history—what we're doing today might be real significant. I hope the history we write about the Chesapeake Bay is going to be one of renewal, revival, and hope rather than the end of an era."

RUFUS S. LUSK, III ∽

Gaithersburg, Maryland

Ordained Clergyman / Business Executive

WHEN IT COMES TO PROMINENT CONTRIBUTIONS BY INDI-
viduals, Reverend Rufus Lusk has a supreme role model in Jesus Christ. "I strongly believe that all Christians are called to ministry," Lusk says. "Our work, be it the most humble or the most significant in the eyes of the world, can be offered to the glory of God and used to serve others. Every calling is an important calling." Besides being a pastor, Lusk is also a successful businessman. And in word and deed, whether from the pulpit, the sidewalk, the laptop, or the deck of the *Tempus Fugit* ("Time Flies"), his forty-foot charter sailboat, he promotes environmental stewardship in the Chesapeake Bay watershed.

Lusk grew up in Washington, D.C., and attended Georgetown University. In 1974, he graduated from Yale Divinity School and was ordained a clergyman in the United Church of Christ, a denomination descended from the Puritans and Pilgrims in New England. With a focus on community outreach, he served churches in Connecticut and New York before returning to the Chesapeake Bay region. In 1979, he left full-time ministry for what he thought would be "just a few years" to help his father run a struggling family real estate–information business that had been in operation since 1930. Under Lusk's leadership, the enterprise tripled its revenues and became nationally recognized as one of the most innovative and quality-conscious companies in the industry. Eventually he sold the company for $5.75 million. In 1997, he turned his attention to stabilizing and improving another family business, the 56,000-square-foot Port Towns Shopping Center at Colmar Manor (Maryland).

"We're only one-fourth mile from the District of Columbia," Lusk says.

"Yet you can go around the bend of the Anacostia River and feel like you're in a pristine West Virginia river. Because it's silted up over the years, the Anacostia is very shallow, especially in this area—at low tide you can see the bottom." He explains that two hundred years ago, the river was forty feet deep and four times as wide and, after Baltimore, the Port of Bladensburg was the second busiest harbor in Maryland. The "Port Towns" of Bladensburg, Cottage City, and Colmar Manor grew up around this port, which was a major interchange for tobacco and the slave trade.

Today, the Inner-Beltway vicinity is located in the Port Towns Enterprise Zone and the Anacostia Trails Heritage Area. There, the Port Towns Revitalization Project has been designated under Maryland's Smart Growth Initiative, which offers tax, hiring, and investment incentives to new and existing businesses. When the Port Towns Shopping Center opened in 1986, it was hailed as the "crown jewel" of Colmar Manor's revitalization. Lusk reports that about 2 million shoppers come through its stores each year and more than forty thousand cars travel this section of Bladensburg Road each day. "People might consider this type of real estate a strip center," he says, "but I think of it as a *neighborhood* shopping center. Our mission is to serve the community. Part of that is working with community groups and being an active, contributing part of the neighborhood. The center looks nice and is very clean and well maintained, which is not necessarily true of retail centers in many older areas. Many of our tenants are 'Mom and Pop' businesses that have been here for over a decade. The merchants know their customers by name. There's a small town feel to shopping here."

He goes on to say that his family has a long-term commitment to the neighborhood. "My wife and I recently made a decision to donate $10,000 a year for ten years to local civic and environmental organizations. It's a small amount, but we hope it will encourage other business owners to think about giving back to the community. We're vested in this area and enthusiastic about its future," he says. "Together with the residents and local government, we're working to rediscover our local heritage and restore the area and its environment."

The center has recently made many exterior improvements, including new banners, landscaping, a community bulletin board, and a bike rack. The Prince George's County Department of Environmental Resources (DER) has constructed a new sidewalk and pedestrian bridge over ad-

jacent Dueling Creek (so named because Washingtonians went there to settle matters of honor after dueling was banned in the District in the early nineteenth century) and installed a state-of-the-art storm-water management system, called a rain garden, to handle runoff from the center's parking facility.

"We have three acres of parking," Lusk explains. "Before we installed the rain garden, the runoff would rush into Dueling Creek, a tributary of the Anacostia River, which flows into the Potomac River and on into the Bay. When the county was looking for a demonstration site for rain garden retrofit of an older shopping center, we raised our hand and said, 'Great, we love it.' DER are the heroes in this project: They took the initiative, they built it, and they even paid for it. Can you believe my good fortune?! My place has been to give it a high profile and be a bit of an evangelist for the procedure."

DER's Programs and Planning Division has established partnerships with many organizations, including the State of Maryland, the U.S. Army Corps of Engineers, the U.S. Environmental Protection Agency, schools, and businesses, on an array of environmental issues. Programs focus on stream water quality, pollution prevention, revitalization of older communities, preservation and replacement of trees, restoration of the Anacostia River and its tributaries, and protection of the Chesapeake Bay. These partnerships and the cooperative programs that continue to grow out of them have enabled Prince George's County to be recognized as a national model for ecosystem management and restoration. With the rain garden concept—using nature to protect nature—DER has pioneered an innovative, attractive, and environmentally sensitive approach to reducing storm-water pollution.

Many human activities, from washing cars to fertilizing lawns, can turn rainfall into an environmental problem. Oil, chemicals, pesticides, sediments, and debris often run off lawns and impervious surfaces like driveways, streets, and parking lots into storm drains and ultimately into local streams and rivers. An acre of paved parking lot produces about thirty thousand gallons of runoff per inch of rain—sixteen times the runoff of an open meadow. In addition, warm runoff causes thermal pollution, while the velocity at which it hits a stream causes serious erosion, both of which harm plants and animals.

Rain gardens are based on the concept of *bioretention*, a water-quality practice in which plants and soils naturally remove pollutants from storm water. Digging down about ten feet, earthmovers are used to create rain gardens in low-lying areas by installing layers of soil, sand, rock, and organic mulch. Unlike traditional systems of curbs, gutters, and storm drains, which carry runoff directly to local waterways, rain gardens filter and reuse the water, reducing storm-water pollution while providing attractive landscaping. During the few days after a storm, the specially selected soils absorb and store flooded rainwater, nourishing the garden's grasses, trees, and flowers over the following days. Bioretention areas result in nitrogen and phosphorus reduction, erosion control, and habitat improvement. In addition, rain gardens are much more aesthetically pleasing and cost effective than curbs and gutters. Since the installation of the rain garden at Lusk's center, the DER has built a new one in a nearby light-industrial park.

Last year, as his business responsibilities eased, Lusk developed an interdenominational specialty in Interim Ministry, to serve congregations that are between permanent pastors, and returned to full-time ministry at Prince of Peace Lutheran Church in Gaithersburg, Maryland. "My task is to prepare the way for the next person. I'd heard about the Lutherans from Garrison Keillor," he quips. "When I got there, I was amazed that they smiled! They're a great group of people, and very caring. Prince of Peace has firm commitments to social outreach programs, including cleanups of local parks and streams. We're making the church as 'green' as possible—from big projects like our new education wing to little things like not using Styrofoam cups—we're constantly washing dishes! We have a lot of families who are very outdoors oriented and take a strong interest in nature activities.

"Environmental education is woven into Christian education and Scripture," Lusk continues. "In my work I touch on the whole theology of Creation and good stewardship. Stewardship is a big word in churches today. It indicates that we don't own the Earth, we're just caring for it, each with our own talents." He tells a story in which several people are counting snowflakes as they pile up on a branch. "They get to the 3,728,460th snowflake, and the next one breaks the branch. That's an interesting way to look at a lot of things," he reflects. "Ultimately, all those small actions of people mount up. It's astounding what one person can do when connected with others. Unfortunately, it's often most visible in its negative form—like the Anacostia River after a rainstorm when runoff deposits an unbelievable amount of debris in the river.

"Ultimately, nothing is lost," he affirms. "It just goes somewhere else! In the scientific world, that's called the law of conservation of matter. The environmental movement has forced religious communities to think more about stewardship issues. To a certain extent, the science of ecology itself came out of synagogues, churches, and other religious communities as they've meditated on God's Creation. Today, perhaps we're more conscious of the doctrine of creation than people in the past. Disastrously, religion is often seen as the antagonist of science; but the proper role is to let science *deepen* our amazement—science enhances our sense of wonder; religion celebrates it. We're really all fighting for and saying the same thing: Creation is a limited resource."

JOLINE P. FROCK ⤳
JOSEPH R. FROCK ⤳

Olney, Maryland

Longtime Recyclers / Low-Input Lawn Tenders

MARRIED FOR FORTY-FIVE YEARS, JOLINE (JO) AND JOSEPH (Joe) Frock have lived most of those years between the Chesapeake Bay and the mountain streams of western Maryland—entwined by the rippling currents of the Patuxent River and Rock Creek—in the suburban outskirts between Washington, D.C., and Baltimore. Today four-lane divided highways intersect their town, but the Frocks remember when it was just a crossroads in a sparsely populated countryside. Over the years, the family has explored the reaches of the Chesapeake watershed, from hiking along its mountain streams to boating on the Bay proper and catching crabs and clams on the rivers of Maryland's Eastern Shore. The couple has raised seven children while diligently working at their respective careers, he as an electrical engineer, she as a home day-care operator. They live in a modest, welcoming home and are often surrounded by children of all ages. To today's generation the words *ecology* and *recycling* are commonplace, but it wasn't always so. The Frocks are ordinary citizens who hold a longstanding, day-to-day environmental ethic that began over three decades ago "when people were just starting to think about ecology," Jo recollects. "It was a brand new concept. When we started talking about it, most people didn't know what it meant."

"It was really before the word *recycling* was coined," Joe adds.

"Nobody had even heard the word, much less how to go about doing it," Jo shrugs. "People looked at me like I was tetched!"

In the late 1960s, their only son, Scott, had a paper route from which he accumulated extra newspapers. "We heard about a salvage company (Montgomery Scrap Company) that would buy newspapers," Jo begins. "So we started saving the leftover papers. Then when Scott would go around each month to collect subscription payments from his customers, he'd collect old newspapers, too. Soon we added our neighbors. Then people heard about us collecting newspapers and they'd ask to be included. Before we knew it, we had about forty people we collected from. We outlined it all in writing with the participants. You have to understand, this was before Xerox machines, so we wrote out a note, using carbon paper, explaining what we were doing—where we sold the papers, how much we got per pound, where we sent the money. We donated the money to a fledgling grassroots recycling organization."

Once a month Jo and Scott collected papers in an old panel van named Obie (after the police officer in Arlo Guthrie's counterculture song

"Alice's Restaurant"). Jo clearly remembers, "We filled up the whole back of it with papers. I learned to pack that van to the gills! At the last moment I'd shove the papers back against the ceiling and slam the door shut. I did have to leave a little space in the front seat, though," she acknowledges, "because the twins [her youngest daughters] weren't in school yet, and they rode with me.

"The three of us would haul the papers to Montgomery Scrap," she continues, "where they'd weigh the whole thing—the whole Obie—with the newspapers and us in it. Then we'd drive off the scales, unload the papers (except Kristin, the younger twin, who was afraid to leave her seat), weigh again, and collect our money. It wasn't much, just a few cents per hundred pounds, maybe five dollars a load."

The family continued in this manner for several years before they "hit upon the idea that we could have paper drives," Jo relates. "I arranged for the scrap company to bring a dumpster to the elementary school once a month. The school sent a notice home with the students, and I wrote a little column on ecology subjects for their weekly newsletter."

"And we made a big wooden sign to put up announcing the monthly drives," Joe adds. "Every month we'd paint out the date and put in the new date."

Jo would "honcho the operation." She says, "I called it 'baby-sit the dumpster.' Because if I wasn't there, people would just toss the papers in, and a lot of space would be wasted. So I'd stack them up nice and tight."

Meanwhile, the Frocks were learning more about this new idea of recycling. Jo says, "We investigated ways we could recycle other things. I wrote to the wine companies that we patronized and asked them if they would reuse the bottles if we sent them back. They all said 'no.' They didn't have the facilities to do that then. We heard about a place in Baltimore where people could take back bottles and cans. We thought it was a great idea—don't put it in the trash anymore, but find a way to use it again. So we started taking our bottles to Baltimore, where they would smash them with these *pounders*. The recycle collection locations got closer and closer. Now and then we'd hear about a new one opening nearby. After a few years the county opened one next to the dump.

"That was a big step, because they got the first sorting machine," she recalls. "I took the day-care children with me to make drop-offs, and some of their parents would give me things to take along. The center had a catwalk so people could watch the machine. We saw the operation firsthand. We learned why you can't put in loose bottle caps and can lids or smashed cans. The sorter can't handle that—they get jammed in the crannies of the machine."

In the meantime, Jo was "leaning on" their neighbors to recycle. "I even offered to take their recycle stuff with ours. But people weren't very responsive. It wasn't until about five years ago, when the county started curbside pickup, that the neighbors really got started." And even then, some needed a push to make the change. "It was quite a chore to convince a few of them that it's really not that bad," she admits. "One woman said, 'I can't have that blue bin in my kitchen!' I showed her how we have it set up in our house, with the newspapers in a paper bag in the closet, and the bins outside. I showed her that it's just a different way to put out the trash, and that it's really not inconvenient."

As the Frock children got older, they, in essence, recycled these recycling principles. After Kristin (having outgrown her fear of the recycling process) graduated from college, she instituted a recycling procedure for the residents of her apartment house. She also helped pressure her employer, the owner of a busy, local restaurant and bar, to "get into a recycling mode." At first, Kristin, Jo, or Joe took the materials to the collection center. Then, after Kristin left the area, the restaurant owner delivered them herself. Now the restaurant has an extensive recycling policy that includes county-run curbside pickup of beer bottles and cans, a cardboard dumpster, and the reuse of pungent five-gallon dill pickle buckets.

This is one example of how, over the years, public and governmental awareness has changed significantly as waste disposal has become a major environmental concern. "Too much trash, no place to put it," Joe summarizes.

As a result of efforts such as those expended by the Frocks, most people no longer think that recyclers are a little crazy. The Montgomery County recycling program has continually expanded and reached a goal of achieving "50 percent recycled waste by the year 2000." There are extensive recycling guidelines, and eligible curbside pick-up items include newspapers, bottles, cans, plastics, and all paper.

However, Joe points out, "simply collecting materials is not recycling." Once collected, recyclables must be inspected, sorted, bundled, transported, processed, manufactured into usable materials, and eventually resold. The county recycling center, located in a 50,000-square-foot facility, employs thirty people and—rigged with a fleet of recycling trucks, a "tipping floor," bucket loaders, an infeed conveyor belt, a monster magnet, and a powerful baler—is designed to process up to one hundred tons of commingled containers per shift.

This cycle can be expensive, and reliable markets for recyclable materials are not always in place. In addition, there are environmental impacts from some recycling processes, as well as from transporting materials within the cycle. For a recycling program to be successful, both economic and environmental impacts must be considered. The county urges communities to foster recycling programs by cultivating reliable markets for recyclables and encouraging the active participation of both residents and businesses.

"Once recyclable materials are made into new products, then it is up to us again," Jo expounds. "As consumers, it's up to us to make wise purchasing decisions and to close the recycling loop by purchasing products made from recycled materials and reusing materials before discarding them. I tell people, 'you don't have a choice, you have to do this.' I feel that strongly about it."

"Sometimes," Joe interjects, "sound environmental practices call for action; other times inaction works pretty well, too." Sometimes, he clarifies, it's simply a matter of rethinking how we do things. Do I really need to buy that item? Can I live without it or make do with something I already have? And if I do buy it, where will it wind up when I'm done with it? Do I really want to spend the resources—time, money, fuel, and water—required to maintain my yard every week, whether it needs it or not? What are the implications (especially in highly developed and paved areas of the watershed, where erosion and runoff are intensified) of taking a weed-free stance? Does it really make sense to bag up the free, natural nutrients in yard waste into nondegradable plastic bags and ship them off to an already overflowing landfill?

In many suburban communities, grass clippings consume 25 to 40 percent of landfill space during the growing season. Americans use approximately 100 million tons of fertilizer and 80 million pounds of pesticides, and we spend more than $750 million on grass seed each year. Homeowners use ten times the rate-per-acre of pesticides used by farmers. Due to population growth in the Chesapeake Bay region, it is anticipated that about 750,000 acres of farmland and forest will be converted to residential housing in the next twenty-five years. According to the

Center for Watershed Protection, located in Ellicott City, Maryland, about a quarter of all homeowners overfertilize their yards each year; and only two in ten obtain a soil test to determine whether any fertilizer is even needed. The center recommends the following steps for "developing a watershed ethic" regarding lawn care:

- Apply no fertilizer or pesticides to lawns.
- Minimize turf area and avoid growing lawns in regions where the climate cannot sustain them without supplemental irrigation.
- Gradually replace lawns with native trees, shrubs, and ground covers.
- Cultivate lawns with the primary goal of absorbing runoff from roofs and other sources.

Joe concurs. "My philosophy is to cut as little as possible, never water, and leave the clippings where they fall."

"Lawn clippings represent nutrient recycling at its best," Jo confirms. "Healthy soil is the best defense. Besides, pest control can quickly become a never-ending cycle in a lawn. For those reasons, we don't do 'Frock's folly'—fertilizing and manicuring our lawn," she quips.

"The fact that I don't rake up the grass and all that jazz is the ecological part," Joe explains. "It's not only from an environmental standpoint, though, it's also from a laziness standpoint!" he confesses. "I leave the cut grass to wend its way down to the ground, decompose, and self-fertilize the grass. By not cutting as often, the roots are shaded, so in the long run, instead of turning brown, the grass stays greener in the heat of the summer without any watering or other effort from me. I also don't burn as much gas in the mower. It might not seem like much for one person, but if you've got millions of people doing it, it adds up. I'd rather relax on my lawn than mow it. Sometimes the best action to take is no action at all!"

"If we want to preserve this wonderful watershed for upcoming generations," Jo concludes, "we have to be aware of what we are and aren't doing. People make daily decisions that affect water quality in local creeks and rivers. Even if it's something small, like recycling newspapers or skipping the chemical fertilizers or just shifting your mindset, just as the little creek in my backyard eventually flows to the big sea, one person really can have widespread influence."

JAMES T. COTTLE ~

Chevy Chase, Maryland

Leisure Fisherman / Folk Artist

As a boy growing up in Sault Sainte Marie, Michigan, a small town near the Canadian border, Jim Cottle acquired a rudimentary and enduring attachment to the outdoors. In "the Soo," as it is called, ice fishing is a way of life, one that was originated by Native Americans who fished from teepees on the iced-over Great Lakes. Cottle learned to fish on frozen Lake Superior, perched on a stool in a stove-piped wooden shanty, dangling fish decoys into a hole cut through up to twenty inches of ice and snagging passing pike with a spear. "There's an attachment to the essence of nature that makes fishing much more than the pursuit of food or sport," he believes. "It's hard to match the beauty of a huge golden moon on the rise above the eastern horizon, the western skyline still aglow from the setting sun, as a boy heads home after a day in the shanty. With the snow pure and white around you and the crisp freshness of subzero temperatures adding snap to your footsteps, it feels good to be alive. Those sorts of boyhood scenes stay with you for a lifetime."

An intelligent man with a knack for integrating academia with an appreciation for the curiosities of everyday living, Cottle teaches language communications at the University of Maryland University College (UMUC) and serves as a private international language consultant, developing programs for and instructing students of English as a second language (ESL). He also gives lectures and demonstrations on fish decoy carving around the country, visiting places such as the Smithsonian Institution and National Museum of American Art in Washington, D.C., the Museum of American Folk Art in New York, and the Chesapeake Bay Maritime Museum in Maryland. "In my heart, I'm a teacher," he acknowledges. "I love introducing people to something new."

Cottle started carving fish decoys early on. "My dad was a carpenter," he recounts in a voice that retains his boyhood vernacular. Sitting in his workshop, painstakingly carving away shavings of sugar pine with a familiar, relaxed stroke, he demonstrates his craft. "These were all my father's tools. He died when I was in elementary school. Since I was the handy one, always doing something like tearing my bike apart, it fell on me to fix stuff around the house. Then I learned fish carving from my older brother." Cottle moved to Maryland over thirty years ago, and a few years ago he made some decoys for friends. Soon others were asking for their own pike, trout, muskie, and other lake fish decoys in the rustic, authentic style used by Michigan ice fishermen. Since waterfowl are the customary subjects for decoy art and collectibles in the Chesapeake Bay region, Cottle was surprised to discover the local interest in ice fishing decoys he carves in the basement of his home. "There's a universality," he deduces, "to human intrigue with the water and fishing."

Cottle has adapted his carving talents to the Chesapeake region by whittling plugs for rod fishing. These lures produce a wobbling action he describes as "imitating a crippled minnow." He makes up to ten at once. "I can spend a couple of hours and have lures ready for a fishing trip. I'm not afraid of losing them," he grins. "I know the guy who makes them! I play around with colors and know the ones that work."

Using his handmade plugs with debarbed hooks, most of the time Cottle practices "catch and release" fishing from his canoe or kayak, sometimes using a two-horsepower motor. "I usually stick to coves on lakes and fish mainly on the Potomac River and smaller Eastern Shore rivers like the Marshyhope, the Tuckahoe, the Blackwater, and the Monocacy in western Maryland. The Potomac River inside the Washington Beltway has some of the best fishing on the whole river. My little niche is between the beltway and Little Falls. The water is so rough most people fish from the shore. But I venture out into the running water. I can see the beltway overpass with trucks and vehicles speeding across it and wild water underneath."

It's an ironic picture: the solitary angler peacefully fishing in the wilderness on the fringes of urban development. "I can float along the Potomac and see nothing but rocks, water, and trees. Nobody out there with me except the deer and heron. There's an eagle that flies in that area."

On occasion, Cottle will do an eight- to twelve-mile float with his fishing partner on the Upper Potomac. To avoid the need to use two cars, he has devised an ingenious transportation system. "I take along my son's old twenty-inch dirt bike. I drop the canoe off at the boat ramp, drive my van down to the take-out area, take the dirt bike out of the van, and ride up the towpath to where my partner is waiting. I take the bike apart, put it in the canoe, and spend the day floating and fishing. At the end of the float, we load up and leave. Most people use two cars for such floats, but this eliminates the need for an extra vehicle. I get in some extra exercise, too."

Cottle promotes trails for hiking, bicycling, walking, and inline skating as forms of exercise and recreation. "Rather than getting out on the

Bay in a big cruiser, I put a high value on promoting simpler kinds of outdoor activity." However, he is dismayed by the unclean condition of many streams and trails. "Fishing line, worm buckets, beer cans, food wrappers, you name it. In Austria, my wife's homeland, we hike and ride bikes in the mountains. Very seldom do we see any kind of trash on the trails there. People are very aware of keeping the environment healthy. So many measures are legislated that the people have no choice but to be conservation-minded. You can't imagine the detailed sorting involved in the recycling. The citizens comply without complaining. There shouldn't have to be groups cleaning up the Potomac River, except when it floods. Individual actions really make a difference in this regard."

Cottle and his wife, Edeltraud, practice many sound environmental habits. "Because I teach through UMUC's distance learning curriculum, which uses voice mail and computer applications rather than a traditional classroom, I rarely drive to campus. Instead of thirty students driving individual cars to a classroom for a two-hour class, we're able to take advantage of technology to reduce transportation demands. Whenever possible, I take the subway, which eliminates another car on the road. I like to park in a nearby neighborhood, walk to the subway, work while I ride, and walk to my destination. Edeltraud and I put very few miles on our cars each year because we rarely run just one errand when we go out."

Cottle points out items in his workshop, from a tool chest converted from a dentist's cabinet, to his shop apron, that were made from leftover materials. "There's always a use for something in addition to the original one," he asserts. "I save the smallest wood pieces, containers, scraps of leather, rope, metal, plastic—anything I think I can make use of in my carvings. I've learned how to save paints and paint cleaners so I can get the most out of them before disposing of them. I freeze oil paints in little plastic film canisters that I save or beg from photo shops. If I keep paint thinner in a sealed container after using it to clean brushes, all the paint settles to the bottom and gets hard, leaving perfectly clean thinner on the surface that can be used again and again. My son used to tease, 'Dad only buys something as a last resort, if he can't make it first.' He's the same way now, so I guess I had some influence on him."

Sweeping up wood curls from the floor, Cottle concludes, "My whole attitude is that conservation starts right here—in my workshop, in my home, at my office. That's where the difference will be made. I recycle my paints. I use my turpentine till there's nothing but mud on the bottom of the jar. That's my little thing, but if 100,000 people do it, that's gallons and gallons of solutions not dumped down the drain." Dipping a set of freshly painted plugs into a tin of lacquer, he reflects, "The older I get, the closer I get to the things of my youth." Even though he knows most of his carvings will end up on mantelpieces, Cottle still tests his final products in a washtub to make sure they float, jig, and dance through the water properly before he'll sell any fish decoy. "Fish decoys are first and foremost functional objects used to attract large fish," he explains, "for the purpose of spearing them through a hole in the ice. If it doesn't work in the water, then it's just a fish carving." Carving has become more than a hobby to Cottle. It's about keeping a traditional American folk art alive and exploring the Chesapeake watershed he now calls home. "I love paddling in unfamiliar fishing streams, wading in river riffles, drifting up secluded coves. Catching fish would be gravy. But it's a darn good meal even without the gravy."

LORI SANDMAN ❧

Strausstown, Pennsylvania

Director, Environmental Quality Initiative

Lori Sandman's extended family still owns the farm in rural Berks County, Pennsylvania, where she spent her summers as a kid; but today a neighboring farmer runs the dairy operation. Sandman's own home overlooks the farm, yet she's not your run-of-the-mill "girl next door." Her cousins operated the farm for several years but eventually took jobs off the farm. "The depressed price of milk has driven a lot of farmers out of business," she explains. "For decades, while production costs have steadily increased, the price the farmer gets for fluid milk has stayed the same." She goes on to say that a big part of why many farmers are struggling is the disparity between the farm and the consumer.

"The poor return to farmers, coupled with environmental pressures, are very difficult issues to overcome. My family lived that struggle and I felt that declining profitability needed to be addressed. I helped establish the Environmental Quality Initiative [EQI] to create financial incentives to keep farmers on the farm. There's a lot of work and effort that goes into farmland protection, but I feel strongly that if we don't put some effort toward *farmer* protection—to keep the farmers in place—all that conserved farmland isn't going to be worth much."

This outlook stems from beyond a local perspective. As a girl, Sandman, whose father was an airline pilot, learned about nature in faraway places like Australia and Guatemala. "We traveled often and lived overseas so we could learn about other people and places. My mom's favorite saying is 'drink from every side of the cup.' For many years, we lived in the Florida everglades in the winter and spent our summers on the farm. While in Australia, I learned to love the water and appreciate the natural environment during ferry rides across Sydney Harbor to school. One of my greatest memories was experiencing the amazing diversity of the Great Barrier Reef and the rainforests. This changed the way I saw myself as part of the natural world."

Sandman worked her way through college in part by milking 100 cows three times a day. She graduated from the University of Vermont's College of Agriculture with a degree in molecular biology and biochemistry and subsequently conducted research and development in molecular genetics and biochemistry at Harvard and Dartmouth Medical Schools and Hershey Medical Center, researching leukemia and the impact of coal mining on lung cells.

In the early 1990s, Sandman moved back to Pennsylvania, where agriculture is the largest industry in the state and dairy farming is the biggest portion of that industry. She took a job with the Chester County Conservation District working with a diverse set of farmers and writing Pennsylvania's first nutrient management plans. "Pennsylvania had the foresight to encourage environmentally sound agriculture *before* regulation applied even more financial pressure on farmers who were already going out of business. We showed that nutrient management planning can encourage sound, performance-based economic return." Sandman is also a certified crop advisor and is approved by the state as a nutrient management specialist and forest stewardship consultant. In 1995, the Dairy Network Partnership (which has since become EQI) hired Sandman to manage operations. This multiagency collaboration focused on encouraging on-farm environmental management. The partnership's work resulted in the development of an incentive program designed to build a bridge between food producers and consumers. From cow pies to pie charts, from rustic milkhouses to bustling, brightly lit dairy cases, Sandman's work, based from a home office (with her two young children often nearby), takes her to barnyards, processing plants, retail stores, and corporate boardrooms.

Incorporated in 1999, EQI is a unique collaboration of diverse organizations: the Chesapeake Bay Foundation, the Pennsylvania Association for Sustainable Agriculture, Pennsylvania State University, the Rodale Institute, and the EPA. The objective of the partnership is to develop financial incentives for farmers to implement best management practices. "The core belief is that environmental performance can and should be rewarded in the marketplace where the farmer's goods are processed and sold," Sandman explains. "We developed the EQI seal and the 'Your choice makes a difference' slogan as a way for consumers to use their grocery dollars as an incentive-driven vote for a sound environment. The mark identifies products that return a portion of the purchase price to farmers who have achieved excellence in environmental management. It is cause-related marketing with environmental protection as a farm product."

Historically, government cost-sharing programs helped pay for water quality protection on farms. Although progress has been made in reducing agricultural impacts, they still contribute significantly to non–point source pollution, and direct regulation is likely to be implemented. Regulations typically mandate requirements without consideration of the financial impact on farm production. Sandman explains that money spent to meet these requirements often turns into "sunk" costs that may protect the environment but earn no return for the farmer. Dairy farmers typically respond to sunk costs by bumping up milk production per cow or increasing the number of cows milked, following the dictum of "get bigger or get out." An alternative to cost-share or regulatory approaches is a market-based program recognizing that farmers can add value to their production by providing environmental protection to shared resources, such as groundwater and surface water, along with the milk they produce.

Trained EQI staff use a comprehensive "scorecard" called the Environmental Farmstead Evaluation to rate participating farms. Evaluation categories include barnyard, stream, and drainageways, pesticide storage and handling, milkhouse waste, home sewage, and well condition. "Farmers are very willing to make these changes," Sandman recognizes. "But implementation can be costly. Often there's no way to recover the costs of improvements. We're working to offer the farmer a budget of sorts to offset the cost. Once they reach that threshold of excellence, farmers receive a bonus of fifty cents per hundred pounds of milk shipped. A farm with a herd size of sixty-five to seventy cows could qualify for a bonus of about $7,000 a year. If, for instance, a farm invests $20,000 in a manure storage system or animal-access lanes, it could recover the investment over a three-year period."

In 1999, the program introduced a new brand, Chesapeake Milk, sold exclusively in Fresh Fields / Whole Foods markets in the Mid-Atlantic region during a one-year test market. Stores offered whole, reduced fat, and fat-free versions in an attractive half-gallon container featuring a picture of a waterfront farm and the slogan *A Glass a Day Protects the Bay.* "Chesapeake Milk is a vehicle to get consumers familiar with our ecolabel as a seal of environmental excellence," Sandman explains. "We made history as the first product to return a portion of the consumer dollar to farmers for their efforts in environmental protection. Milk is a good prototype product because there are distinct pools of farmers that ship to a given processor or co-op." However, the idea is for the EQI mark to be transferred to other new and existing products.

"These products will be part of an emerging group of transition products—those between conventional and organic foods, in their pricing, but also in what they represent to the consumer. So that between the EQI item and the one next to it, I'll choose this one because it's supporting environmentally sound farming. What you're purchasing is the *process,* not the product. It's not that the product inside the carton is necessarily differentiated. It may not be qualitatively different from other products, but the EQI reward—your nickel—pays farmers who have demonstrated environmental excellence."

Sandman reveals that "engaging the rest of the players in the food system—from the dairy processor / cooperative to the consumer—is the biggest challenge. Many do not perceive the potential environmental disruption associated with milk production as a shared responsibility. It is a major task to convince everyone in the food chain that we all—not just the farmer—must think of environmental protection as a valuable farm product we're willing to pay for." She points out that, while surveys reflect that 48 percent of consumers are "overwhelmed and unconcerned" about product choice, 52 percent are environmentally motivated. "The marketplace is changing," she says. "Today, 'green' consumers are mainstream. There's a great deal of interest in this type of product, and supporting environmental decisions with the grocery dollar."

Now that Chesapeake Milk is through with the test-marketing phase, Sandman is expanding the product to other markets by first researching various points in the system—the processor level, retail managers, community groups, public meetings, and consumer opinion. "We want to convey the message that all consumers have the opportunity to *choose* to support products that make a difference in their communities and their environment. We want to improve the economics of farmers so that younger generations will remain on the land and farms will remain in our communities. Maybe more importantly, I am a mom. I would like my children to inherit productive soil, clean water and air, and a deep respect for nature. I want to show them that preserving our natural resources is a responsibility that connects us—to each other, to our communities, and to the natural world. By supporting sound agricultural practices, consumers' decisions can really impact their community. Widespread adoption of this type of program by food processors, cooperatives, and retail chains can provide a real solution to agricultural pollution issues."

BENJAMIN K. SYMONS ∽

Bethesda, Maryland

Aqua Eagles "Stream Team" Club Member

Thanks in part to hundreds of young citizens like Ben Symons, an excitable student at Westbrook Elementary School and "Stream Team" member, Little Falls Dam now has a fishway, which allows fish such as American shad, the largest member of the herring family, to return to historic habitat upstream. The school's fourth grade curriculum, designed by teacher Sandra Geddes, includes extensive Chesapeake Bay, stream, and watershed studies. Fifth graders like Symons can voluntarily continue that focus by joining Geddes's extracurricular Stream Team club. Outside her classroom stand three large racks of knee-high, horizontally hung waterproof boots, bought with funds from the Westbrook PTA and the Chesapeake Bay Trust, for the many field trips her students take around the Bay. "We've been on boats," Symons recounts, "released shad and horseshoe crabs, planted underwater grasses, worked alongside watermen, done stream monitoring, and gone to outdoor camp—you name it, we've done it."

"Each year's focus is different," adds Geddes, who has been teaching for thirty-three years and prefers to take a backseat to her students. "We might work on expanding our annual 'Stream Fest' or on letter-writing, trying to get legislative changes. One year we had a Stream Team rap group that performed with local folksinger Tom Wisner in a performance that was part of a video program, 'Waterway to the Bay.'" Like sunlight on water, her eyes flash with enthusiasm as she says, "We go with the flow."

Symons has moved up to what he calls "the fifth grade penthouse" on the upper level of the school building, but he often returns to Geddes's room, which teems with students' work, especially science projects: growing submerged aquatic vegetation (SAV), raising baby horseshoe crabs, and monitoring inverted two-liter bottles containing brine shrimp that will be fed to freshly hatched baby shad. For about ten days in early May, the eggs grow in a "full shad system"—two blue tanks (shad are thought to like the color blue) rigged with pumps, filters, valves, tubes, "bioballs" (ridged plastic spheres that trap bacteria), and plastic bottles filled with ice. "Water circulates between the two tanks," Symons explains. "The top tank is where the shad live. Water circulates over the ice bottles in the bottom tank to keep the upper tub temperature below seventy degrees Fahrenheit. Bacteria from the bioballs also flow into the upper tank. Fortunately, these are not germs—they're good bacteria that help clean the upper tank.

"The eggs are very fragile," he cautions. "If you so much as touch them with a net in their aquarium, they will die. Students measure pH in the tank and do daily tests for temperature, nitrates, nitrites, ammonia, and salinity. We do demonstrations for every class in the school using presentation boards and a microscope hooked up to a television. The eggs hatch and grow very quickly, so there is something new to see each day. It's amazing!" But, he is quick to point out, "we can't keep them for a long time because they imprint on where they were spawned so they can return there to lay eggs. We want them to imprint on the Potomac River; we don't want them looking for a blue bucket!"

Westbrook Elementary is part of a pilot aquaculture project to raise shad larvae and release them in conjunction with an extensive shad restoration project in the Potomac River. In 1995, the Interstate Commission on the Potomac River Basin (ICPRB) began working with the U.S. Fish and Wildlife Service, nonprofit organizations, and citizen volunteers to restock the river with shad. In 1996, the ICPRB incorporated the Chesapeake Bay Foundation's "Schools in Schools" program into the shad restoration project to allow local students to raise shad fry. So far, the project has released more than 10 million fry into the river.

"We were the first elementary school to be part of this adventure!" Symons exclaims. "On the day of the release, we transfer the fry into a bucket with a bubbler attached for oxygen, and take them down to the Potomac River. First we let them acclimate to the river temperature, and then everyone scoops shad into a cup. Even though they've grown a lot, they're still very tiny—just two eyes and wiggle!" Wading at the shoreline, their bright clothing and bare legs reflecting in the river water, students return the shad to their natural environment. They commemorate the event by making big signs that say *Bon Voyage* and *We'll miss you*, or by planting shad bushes (so named because they bloom at the same time that shad migrate) at the release site.

Geddes's shad-raising started about seven years ago when a colleague mentioned an upcoming release. "I replied, 'What are shad?'" she recalls. They quickly arranged a carpool and brought about half a dozen students to observe the release. Geddes met Jim Cummins of the ICPRB that day. "He invited us out on the river," she continues. "For a few years, I just took a couple of youngsters and we went out from sunset until midnight to catch the tide, put out gill nets, and help Jim and a local waterman collect and mix shad eggs and sperm."

"It looks like applesauce," Symons says. "When we return to the dock, Mr. Cummins places about 400,000 eggs in plastic bags, adds oxygen, and packs them in Styrofoam containers. The eggs have already grown to the size of pearls, and fill nine liter containers."

"It's wonderful!" Geddes adds. "It's just been in the past couple of years, through the 'Schools in Schools' program, that we've been able to include the whole club."

"We learned that shad are anadromous fish," Symons says. "This means they ascend rivers from the sea in order to breed. They are born in freshwater rivers such as the Potomac and spend their first summer there. Then they gather in schools and travel to the ocean to mature for three to six years before returning to the same rivers where they were born, to spawn and complete their life cycle. After spawning, those that survive the journey migrate back to the ocean."

In his presentations, Symons explains that until the 1930s, American shad was the dominant fish in local waterways and the most important commercial species in the Chesapeake Bay. "Because of their scrumptious roe and delicious meat," he tells audiences, "shad have been called 'poor man's salmon.'" He goes on to report that shad was an important food of Native Americans and early colonists and that, during the Revolutionary War, George Washington saved his troops by feeding them shad. Farmers even used shad as fertilizer for their fields. There appeared to be an endless supply. However, because of pollution, dams, loss of habitat, and overfishing, they have gradually disappeared. Since 1963, the shad population has declined by 94 percent in Maryland and by 82 percent in Virginia. In 1980, Maryland declared a fishing moratorium and Virginia followed in 1994.

"Blockages like dams sometimes stop shad from returning to their spawning grounds to lay their eggs," he continues. "This is a major problem. If they die before they spawn, soon there will be no more shad. Notches need to be cut in dams so that shad can swim back upstream to spawn."

"Together with ICPRB, we've been working for years on getting the fishway in Little Falls Dam," Geddes says. "The dam spans the Potomac about one mile northwest of the District of Columbia. Stream Teams have written many letters to legislators. Four years ago we went to Annapolis to present our work to a group of policymakers, encouraging them to support the project. This year we finally reached that mile-

stone—the Army Corps of Engineers modified the dam to allow upstream fish passage." These fish include not only American and hickory
shad but also others such as striped bass, herring, sturgeon, blueback,
and resident species like large and smallmouth bass, bluegill, pickerel,
various catfish, and minnows. For the first time in decades, a route has
been opened to about ten miles of prime spawning and nursery habitat
between Little Falls and Great Falls. "The children and I really believe we
had some part in bringing that about," Geddes declares.

This event is also a result of Maryland's Fish Passage Program, which
stemmed from the 1987 Chesapeake Bay Agreement to restore the health
of the Bay and seeks to restore migratory fish species to levels as close
to historic levels as possible. Since its inception in 1988, the program has
completed fifty-four projects, reopening over three hundred miles of historic fish passage. Experts say the new fishway will make a huge difference. The $1.9 million project will allow millions of shad fry, stocked in
the upstream area since 1995, to someday return to their natural spawning grounds.

In October 1999, Symons and Geddes attended the Little Falls dam-
breaking ceremony. Symons, confronted by a barrage of reporters and

cameras, gave a speech in which he said, "When I was in first grade, some Stream Team kids made a speech over the P.A. system. This was the first time I heard about the fish called shad. Last year, when I was in fourth grade, I got to make the brine shrimp hatchery to feed the shad. This year, Stream Team will fish for shad, do presentations, and train teachers who are new to shad. I'm glad that the notch will finally be made in Little Falls Dam so that all the Westbrook shad will have the opportunity to get back home to reproduce."

"It was pretty cool shaking hands with so many important people," Symons acknowledges. "Especially when [Montgomery County Executive] Doug Duncan introduced me as 'a dad to the shad.' I got to take the old part out of the dam model and replace it with the new fishway piece. Everyone applauded, which was really fun." Symons was congratulated by a crowd that included (pictured, left to right) Dr. Mufeed Odeh of the U.S. Geological Survey, Representative Constance A. Morella, U.S. Army Corps of Engineers Brigadier General Stephen Rhoades, Maryland Senator Paul S. Sarbanes, Governor Parris N. Glendening, and Secretary of the Interior Bruce Babbitt.

"The children here are very committed to science and the environment," Geddes confirms. "They're eager to do projects. We believe in and live our program each day and feel strongly that any stream program is a Bay program. Impacting our Little Falls stream—planting trees in our backyard or learning about local ecology—will make a difference. It's a lot of fun to be out on the Bay, but we don't have to be in the Potomac River or the Chesapeake Bay to make a difference."

Reading from the shad tank display, Symons brings his presentation to a close. "We cannot save the shad alone," he urges. "We need your help. If we do our part, the shad will once again be abundant in the Potomac."

ROBERT E. BOONE ∽

Bladensburg, Maryland

Cofounder, Anacostia Watershed Society

A FIT, STRAIGHT-SHOOTING MAN WHO GRACEFULLY BALANCES acumen with yoga and meditation, Robert Boone is intimidated by few things. From dealing with garbage, raw sewage, and lawbreaking polluters to calling to task the EPA, Boone has fought to protect the Anacostia River for over a decade. In the late 1960s, he left his profession as a therapist and psychology professor in Manhattan, grew his hair down his back and his beard to his belly, lived in a teepee, and played music in Woodstock, New York, before studying Eastern philosophy in India, Pakistan, and Afghanistan. "Traveling home," he recalls in a subdued voice tinged with a southern accent, "I began to notice how people were disregarding the very basic life sources that sustain us. I saw it everywhere. When I was sailing from Jamaica to the U.S.," he continues, "I came across a sandbar island that was knee deep in plastic—trash that had washed out into the ocean or been dumped by cruise ships and naval vessels. It was outrageous—that just set it off for me."

Eventually Boone moved to the Washington, D.C., area, which he describes as a "policy and paper city. It's not really a 'doing' city," he adds. "I'm a 'doing' person, so maybe that's one reason I've been successful here. I'm not a talker or a paper shuffler; I don't have a lot of patience for those kinds of things."

In 1988, when Boone cofounded the nonprofit Anacostia Watershed Society (AWS), the Anacostia River—fouled with pollution and strewn with debris—was known as "the forgotten river." The Anacostia, a tributary of the Potomac River, provides the backdrop for a diverse environmental, economic, social, and cultural region. The watershed, spanning Montgomery and Prince George's Counties and Washington, D.C., is densely populated, with a total area of 170 square miles and eleven subwatersheds. Its tributaries range from boulder-strewn channels to meandering streams flowing through flat alluvial plains.

"Along its course," Boone outlines, "water quality can change from excellent to poor, income levels from wealthy to impoverished, and land use density from sparse to fully urbanized." The river has suffered from centuries of poorly managed agricultural activities, urbanization, and neglect and today supports only a fraction of the aquatic species it once held. "Despite its presence in the heart of the nation's capital and its pivotal role in U.S. history," Boone laments, "it is recognized as one of our most endangered urban rivers."

The AWS has a direct mandate to "heal the river." The organization

brings together people from all walks of life with the goal of attaining "a swimmable and fishable Anacostia River" (the minimum designated use under the Clean Water Act). Since its inception, the society has added more than 1,200 members and four full-time employees. It has racked up an impressive set of statistics: over 20,939 volunteers have planted over 9,552 trees, stenciled over 820 storm drains with the words "Don't Dump, Anacostia River Drainage," involved 6,310 inner city youths, and removed 283 tons of debris, including 6,974 tires.

"Our efforts present an opportunity for residents to reclaim their rightful stewardship," Boone maintains. "We're very proud of the work we do and most of the credit goes to our many volunteers. It's unbelievable the junk they've dragged out of this river over the years," he reports, standing beside a huge heap of freshly amassed, soggy trash crowned with a muddy microwave oven. However, he notes, "The District of Columbia gets a bad rap. A lot of debris, as well as chemicals like chlordane and PCBs [polychlorinated biphenyls], washes down from upstream. More than half the trash we collect in D.C. is running off the streets and parking lots upstream in Maryland."

Boone goes on to explain that the National Park Service's ownership of 95 percent of the Anacostia shoreline in Washington has compounded runoff problems. "The park service has focused on making it *look* nice," he expounds. From the late 1880s to the early the 1950s, the U.S. Army Corps of Engineers drained wetlands, channeled the river, and built levees. They removed all the trees from the riverbank so the water would efficiently flow out. And it does. But as developers paved over the Lower Anacostia, this engineering created flood conditions. While the paved area provides an efficient storm sewer, it has just about destroyed the ecology and wildlife of the area.

"Basic stream ecology," Boone elaborates, "calls for trees and vegetation on the banks. This keeps the water cool and shaded. The warmer water gets, the less oxygen-carrying ability it has. We've measured water coming off the parking lots in the summertime at ninety-five degrees! Also trees along stream banks restore habitat for birds and add to the food chain for fish and insects. The Corps is slowly allowing us to plant trees and reclaim wetlands. We're slowly bringing it back."

While a large part of Boone's pursuits is in the trenches, there is a strategic aspect to his work. The AWS is a strong advocate for local environmental issues and has acted as plaintiff in several lawsuits, including one against an automobile recycling operation on Lower Beaverdam Creek. Under cover of what Boone calls a "dysfunctional" neighborhood, for years the company had been dumping pollutants into the waterway and depositing fuel tanks and tires on the lawns of residents, showing blatant disregard for the creek and its inhabitants.

"This is our worst industrial site," Boone reports, "visually and environmentally. They drained antifreeze, brake fluid, and oil onto the ground, which washed directly into the stream when it rained. When they dragged cars across the stream to the processing plant, pieces would rip off and get left behind. At one time they would receive and dismantle stolen cars for parts."

One day in 1991, Boone, dwarfed by the junk metal canyon and followed by three lawyers, led the way through the squalid entrance and into the operation's office, where he confronted its owners. "They're not your favorite people, but we have to deal with them," Boone contends. "They'll break the law until they get caught. There were a number of times," he concedes, "when I was concerned about my welfare." When the AWS finally got the automobile operation in court, the prosecution rested on three concerns, including violations in waste disposal, material storage, storm water management, intermittent fires, and late-night explosions. In 1998, after four years of litigation, the AWS won a pollution abatement settlement in which they and the state instituted cleanup requirements such as an upgraded, regulated storm-water runoff pond, jersey barriers, stream-bank grading, vegetated buffers, and increased inspection and reporting of potential explosives.

Gazing over the unsightly car graveyard, Boone points out that "we don't think about where our old car goes when we get that shiny new one. Cars totally dominate our lives today," he laments. "Car habitat is what we have in our culture! A few short years ago, people thought we could pave our way out of the traffic problems in this area by building more roads. Most people now realize that's not the case. Otherwise, we're going to become another Los Angeles. The answer," Boone advises, "lies in quality public transportation. The Metro [Washington, D.C., subway] is good, but it's about a third of what it ought to be.

"This city," he continues, "has more environmental groups than any other city in the world, but look at the Anacostia! Many Washingtonians feel like they live in their head, or on an airplane, not in a watershed. One-point-two billion gallons per year of sewage enter the river in Washington, D.C. When we get heavy rains, sewage—straight from the toilets of the Halls of Congress, the Supreme Court, and the White House— discharges directly into our river at nineteen points south of RFK Stadium. None of the District of Columbia's waters are in compliance with the Clean Water Act," he decries. Last year the AWS initiated a lawsuit against the EPA for its failure to establish crucial pollutant limits for District waters.

While it may seem like an uphill battle, Boone, behind a desk with an eight-inch stack of papers skewered on a phone message stand, works tirelessly. "The Anacostia is not the forgotten river anymore," he declares. "We've motivated a lot of people to realize that individual actions make a difference. By relating to people and overseeing government programs, we have set a standard to represent the public. As this nation's capital, the whole world is emulating us; we have a moral obligation to lead the planet, in a conscious, skillful way, out of the nosedive we're in."

As a result of renewed community interest and support, Boone concludes, the Anacostia River "can rightly be called an example of modern watershed management, a national model for stream restoration, and a living laboratory for ecosystem management within a minority community. With proper stewardship, individually and collectively, the river can be renewed by turning around years of neglect and restoring not only the water column but the river mystique that is part of the soul and pride of a river community."

CAROLINE SUZETTE PARK ∽

Washington, D.C.

Staff Attorney / Graduate Teaching Fellow

Tʜᴇ ɪʀᴏɴʏ ᴏꜰ ᴄᴀʀᴏʟɪɴᴇ ᴘᴀʀᴋ'ꜱ ᴡᴏʀᴋ ɪꜱ ᴛʜᴀᴛ ꜱʜᴇ ʀᴀʀᴇʟʏ ʜᴀꜱ the chance to enjoy the natural resources she strives to protect. As an attorney and clinical fellow at Georgetown University Law Center's Institute for Public Representation (IPR), working from an office in downtown Washington, D.C., Park spends most of her time up to her eyeballs in law books, case studies, and environmental impact statements. A spitfire of energy, knowledge, and passion, this petite, approachable woman speaks with clear-sighted confidence.

Park grew up in Philadelphia, the daughter of Korean immigrants who became naturalized citizens; she loves birds, plays the piano, and has studied French, Spanish, and Russian. Environmental work is important to her because it integrates Christian stewardship principles with her practice of law. "My faith is probably the most important thing in my life," she imparts. Her interest in the environment began when she conducted five years of mercury toxicity research for high school science fairs. "It sounds more complicated than it was," she admits. "I watered pea plants to see whether acid rain and other elements, like selenium, would affect the uptake of mercury in the plants. I was really fascinated by mercury because I had read about huge poisoning problems in Japan and the Great Lakes region. Law school seemed like a good way to use my communication and research skills and pursue my interest in the environment."

Following graduation from the Law Center in 1995, Park worked as a trial attorney for the Environment Crimes Section of the U.S. Department of Justice, investigating violations of federal environmental and criminal law. "That was exciting and there was lots of travel," she recounts, "but I wanted to do more work in the local community." In 1998, she returned to the Law Center to represent citizens and groups in natural resource and environmental matters as part of a curriculum to earn her masters of law degree in advocacy. She points out that "most fellows aren't in this for the degree. It's a chance to work with students in a clinical setting, have direct contact with clients in a pro bono context, and learn how to do informal and formal teaching. At IPR we deal with the 'meat and potatoes' of environmental work: trying to protect natural resources through federal statutes such as the National Environmental Policy Act (NEPA) and the Endangered Species and Clean Water Acts. Since we provide free representation, IPR is a tremendous resource for the community."

A pioneer in clinical legal education, Georgetown University Law Center has the largest, most diverse clinical program in the country. The campus swarms with students from across the country who flock, like legal lemmings, to study in the center's fourteen clinics. "It's a huge place," Park corroborates. "You have to find your niche."

Established at the Law Center in 1971, the IPR is both a public interest law firm and a clinical education program with a two-fold mission to educate students in the practical art of "lawyering" and to provide legal representation to underrepresented individuals and groups. The staff works in three project areas: civil rights, communications law, and environmental law. It includes three senior attorneys who are members of the Law Center faculty, along with five graduate fellows who work closely with eighteen second- and third-year students.

"The Institute offers the very highest level of professional training and a variety of advocacy opportunities," Park explains. Under the day-to-day, hands-on supervision of IPR senior attorneys and graduate fellows, students develop their oral and written advocacy skills and benefit from ongoing participation in decision-making about cases. Since most issues taken on by IPR involve novel legal questions, there is a good deal of policy debate, research, and collaborative work, as well as consultation and work with other public interest groups and outside lawyers. "We do an intensive, almost microscopic review of the students' work," Park explains. "It's not uncommon for them to do six or seven drafts of everything. It's hard!" she admits. "It's difficult to be patient with the process.

We're trying to attain our clients' goals, meet deadlines, and make this an educational experience all at the same time.

"Environmental law is very complicated. Based on the law, we determine whether we can pursue arguments based on our client's goals. Many of our clients are very savvy about environmental conservation and ecological issues. Some are also quite familiar with the law and we engage them at a high level of legal discussion. Other clients have a more general understanding of the law, and we'll walk them through our analysis step-by-step. At times I might have to say, 'I know this is your goal, but this is the limitation of the law. This is what we can accomplish for you. These other goals are not things we can argue for.' That's where the activism and political networking comes in to play. The law can't be the sole solution. It has to work in conjunction with community and local support. It's not always easy to say that to a client."

Park explains that, under NEPA, prior to engaging in major actions a federal agency must conduct an intensive environmental review. An agency first prepares a draft environmental impact statement and solicits comments from other government agencies and the public through written responses and public hearings. After considering those comments, the agency prepares a final statement and may solicit further comment before issuing a final Record of Decision. Groups that participate in the administrative process can file lawsuits to challenge the agency's decision. "However, as attorneys, we need to analyze whether there is a basis for filing a civil lawsuit," Park continues.

"When we're commenting in front of an agency, we have leeway to make broad arguments in support of our clients' positions. But filing a suit in court requires a whole separate level of analysis. There are procedural hurdles, such as statutes of limitations and standing [a Constitutional requirement that a party be sufficiently injured to bring a case]. Then we have to ask, 'Even though we commented on this before an agency, are these things that a court would entertain and render a favorable decision on?' We have to do a cost-benefit analysis of sorts for our clients to see if litigation will effectively bring about the desired results."

Park handles approximately four projects per semester. Currently, she and student Lori Reimherr represent the Anacostia Watershed Society, the Sierra Club, and other groups in seeking to ensure that the National

Harbor and Woodrow Wilson Bridge projects comply with federal environmental laws to the fullest extent. The National Harbor is a proposed 534-acre resort planned for Smoot Bay, an important eagle and fish habitat located seven miles south of Washington, D.C., on the banks of the Potomac River. In 1998 and 1999, the National Capital Planning Commission, a federal land-use and planning agency, issued draft and final environmental impact statements for the project. Park and a student submitted extensive comments on both documents.

The Woodrow Wilson Bridge carries Capital Beltway traffic across the Potomac River between Alexandria, Virginia, and Oxon Hill, Maryland. The proposed bridge expansion involves replacing the bridge centerpiece and upgrading four interchanges in a five-mile area, including two that will provide access to National Harbor. "Right now it's a six-lane drawbridge," Reimherr explains. "The Federal Highway Administration (FHWA) wants to double the size to twelve lanes. It only needs to be eight lanes to match the size of the existing beltway, so FHWA is proposing to build a drawbridge that's wider than the existing freeway."

In November 1997, the highway administration issued a voluminous final environmental impact statement and Record of Decision approving a new $2 billion facility featuring side-by-side, movable-span, twin bridges with a seventy-foot navigational clearance. In the early part of the year 2000, highway administration officials issued a 600-page draft supplemental environmental impact statement that documented further environmental impacts of the bridge that they had discovered as they refined the twelve-lane design. "The Sierra Club asked us to comment on that supplement in support of the position that the alternatives discussed were not broad enough," Park explains. "The club wants to see an integrated tunnel-rail alternative." Citing a phenomenon called "induced transportation demand," whereby wider roads attract more cars, the Sierra Club contends that bridge expansion alone, without the integration of mass transportation, will offer minimal congestion relief.

In 1999, Reimherr, coached and mooted by Park, testified on behalf of the Sierra Club at a large FHWA hearing with regard to the supplemental draft. "It took a lot of nerve for Lori to get up there and do that," Park discloses. "The key to effective oral advocacy is to boil your points down so it's not full text. If you try to read full text you'll freak yourself out."

Park believes that advocacy, education, and awareness will play a significant role in the future of environmental protection. "Unless somebody thinks a resource has value on a personal level, they're not going to fight to protect it. If one individual changes their mind, it can have a meaningful impact. In large projects, it's public opinion that provides momentum. If people don't rally around issues, is the government necessarily going to do it? Maybe not. They could be allocating money somewhere else. It's a patience thing. I'm not going to change the world overnight, but at least I can make one step wherever I have the opportunity."

SAMUEL WALTER DROEGE ✍

Davidsonville, Maryland

Natural Home Builder / Scavenger

IT'S NOT UNUSUAL TO FIND SAM DROEGE EMBARKING ON SUCH curious pastimes as building straw houses, dumpster-diving, bargaining with bulldozer operators, and lumberjacking. An enterprising, well-spoken wildlife biologist with a deliberately simple lifestyle and a flare for frugality, Droege lives in a one-room octagonal hut stashed away amidst a landscape of countryside estates. He uses solar-powered electricity and an open-air shower and kitchen (sans refrigerator) overlooking a garden, an orchard, and 550 acres of farmland accessible only by a bumpy, overgrown dirt driveway.

The structure's only purchased materials include the tin roof, sliding glass door, and straw bales. Droege scavenged windows, wiring, electrical outlets, a ceiling fan, and the brick floor. He constructed the structure with roughly eight tons of adobe made from chopped straw, sand, and clay, which was smeared by hand and trowel over the straw bales on both the exterior and interior sides. "It's actually quite fun to do," Droege reveals. The bales provide an R40-50 insulation rating, which, combined with the stucco and scavenged R20 insulation in the ceiling, makes for an interior temperature fluctuation of only a degree or two during the day. "There's a tremendous amount of mass in the walls and floor," Droege explains. "With the solar gain from the panels and south-facing windows, it's like a big flywheel."

The use of natural materials makes for tactile surroundings and a dim décor. Dark brick, clay, and wood absorb light from the glass panes. "I like darker spaces," Droege admits. "If it were painted white it would be glowing," he says, "but paint and plaster hide the natural materials, and I find it refreshing and comforting to be so directly surrounded by such things. Most people want big windows and smooth, painted walls. Society as a whole leans toward absolute perfection—machined, glossy, flawless. To me it's better to use clay made from the land right outside. How could you not like that?"

Droege, in collaboration with others, has completed several other structures, including a log cabin and private schoolhouse. Rather than listen to descriptions of floor plans and color schemes, visitors touring Droege's buildings hear explanations of wood species—hemlock, pine, cherry, red oak, walnut—and stories about the origins of the building materials—solar panels funded by a demonstration grant, wiring from deconstructed houses, trees cut during power line clearing, pipes from a construction dumpster, bricks indented with handprints of the slaves who made them when the farm was a tobacco plantation.

"In terms of philosophy," Droege expounds, "scavenging and dumpster-diving are near the top of the list of direct environmental actions we can all take. What better thing to do than rescue something from being transported to the dump, and simultaneously save the energy and materials necessary to produce it new?" Droege explains that this idea has manifested itself in a number of ways, from shopping at thrift stores to tearing apart houses slated for demolition. He recently purchased a portable sawmill, which allows him to cut lumber and beams from logs that would otherwise be chopped up or sent to the chipper.

The farm is scattered with stockpiles of wood and other stuff that may look like junk but are actually accumulated building materials. These include a huge stack of timbers from an abandoned shipping dock, ten thousand fiberglass ceiling tiles from a renovated office building, an assortment of solar devices, vats of quick lime plaster, and "barter items."

He began his first undertaking, a 1,900-square-foot log house, twelve years ago. "I made mistakes, but it's a very forgiving type of construction. There's no model that says it has to be square or smooth and specific," he says, pointing out marks left by woodworking tools on exposed beams. "I just started doing it, learning from books, friends, trial and error, and it became more and more complex." He erected the last stage of the house using wooden pegs and dovetailed mortise and tenon joints. "This was more complicated. I worked as an apprentice with a timber framer."

The structure also sports a patchwork of building materials, including recycled solar panels with backup from a generator ("a quirky one that I got out of an RV"), an old freestanding bathtub, castoff ceramic tiles, and walnut beams from a neighbor's fallen trees. Droege salvaged many of the logs from trees cut during clearing for roads and power lines. Others he harvested from the farm's woodland—not to make room for the house but from careful thinning of the forest.

"We oriented the house so that only one or two trees had to be removed," Droege explains. "The woods are right outside the windows. A normal house would have had heavy equipment dig out a foundation and clear twenty feet on either side, which results in a grassy patch abutted by an edge where the forest has healed itself." In contrast,

Droege's house rests on hand-formed concrete pilings, and he used a tractor to haul the logs.

"I wanted as little disturbance as possible. The canopy keeps light out," he illustrates, "which keeps other vegetation from growing up. Weeds and grasses can't grow, so there's no maintenance or mowing. Essentially," he sums up, "this house is *in* the forest instead of surrounded by it—a component of the woods, rather than a thing that is stuck inside a hole in the trees. Most houses bring in exotic species and alter the thermodynamics by having an unnatural open space. The idea here was to leave the land as-is, with minimal impact."

Droege's out-of-pocket expenses were about $20,000, a large portion of which paid for utilities—well and septic systems and a phone line. Because he now has a sawmill, he estimates he could build a similar home today for about $3,000 plus utilities. "When you get into the scavenging world," Droege discloses, "almost everything can be found. It's rare that you have to buy something, even big-ticket items."

Droege's buildings reflect a joining of construction techniques and environmental mindset. "Most people," he believes, "live in communities where they're isolated from their neighbors and perceive they don't have the time and information to be hands-on and develop these kinds of swaps. People build what they see on the street or in a magazine. The reason my buildings are always on demonstration tours is people are starting to think about this as an option. We're on the cutting edge."

Droege's savvy dedication is ingrained into his daily life. "The Chesapeake Bay watershed is where I live and this is how I behave. As with this type of construction, a lot depends on what frame of reference you use. Part of my consciousness is observing the consequences of me being alive, and the decisions I make. It just makes sense to recycle, to reuse. This is a way to demonstrate—to do and to live—the ethic that I feel is very important. It would be far easier to do traditional building, rather than learning how to harvest a tree, do timber framing, use a tractor and chains, get a skidder in and out of the woods. But these types of techniques have low or reversible impact. Recycling renders more benefits than cutting down forest because a tree in a forest does useful things even if it's rotting. I think that way subconsciously all the time, and try to live that. I enjoy living like this; it's not a burden at all."

ELIZABETH S. HARTWELL ⤿

Alexandria, Virginia

Volunteer Activist

At age seventy-four, after thirty-five years of staunch citizen activism, Liz Hartwell now resides in an assisted-living apartment a stone's throw from the banks of the river she spent a lifetime loving and defending. Confined to her bed and bound by the thin tubular shackles of a permanent oxygen machine, the fire of youth and courage still blazes through her frailty. With a smile that could melt butter and uncontainable candor, her speech, though labored and interrupted by the debilitating coughs of emphysema, retains the charm of a gutsy southern lady. "I have absolutely no regrets. I have had the most wonderful life that you could *evvuh* think of." To this day, it is not unusual to find her straining to see and gripping a pen in her arthritis-ridden hand, in order to write letters about environmental issues and fax them to the outside world from her nightstand. She has impelled decades of widespread "branches of results" and has meticulously pasted together a tower of scrapbooks, now piled over eight feet high in her entry closet.

From 1965 to 1988, Hartwell was a firebrand for campaigns against dozens of threats to her local environment, most of them on the Mason Neck peninsula in southeastern Fairfax County. "I moved to Mason Neck in 1959. When I started as an activist I was the typical, pardon the expression, '50s housewife'—the girdle, the seams on the hose, the high heels, the garden club . . . the whole bit. I knew how government works, but I didn't know anybody or anything about conservation. It was obvious that I needed to learn from other conservationists and to generate publicity. I just jumped in—it was free spirit!"

Hartwell led a successful citizens' crusade to preserve over five thousand acres of the peninsula. In early 1965, upon learning of a rezoning application for the development of a "satellite city" on the most ecologically valuable land on "the Neck," she began the battle to save that area. She decided that not only should the development be defeated but as much of Mason Neck as possible should be preserved. The peninsula's nesting and roosting eagles (listed as endangered under the U.S. Fish and Wildlife Service Endangered Species Acts of 1966 and 1973) would be the key to her effort.

The next month, in typical feisty fashion, Hartwell drove her car, uninvited, behind an official forty-mile bus tour headed by then-Secretary of the Interior Stewart Udall, who had been charged with implementing President Johnson's mandate to make the Potomac a "recreation and conservation model for the nation." Her writing career was launched when her account of the tour, "Journey with Udall," was published on the front page of a local newspaper. Over the years she made numerous telephone calls and sent countless letters, telegrams, urgent notices, and invitations to join the Conservation Committee for Mason Neck (CCMN), becoming a well-known and respected correspondent of several high-ranking government officials.

Nine months after "Journey with Udall" was published, Hartwell's persistence paid off. Zoning was denied for the proposed development in favor of the preservation of Mason Neck. Over the next two years, Hartwell spearheaded a grassroots effort, largely through letter writing, to ward off other proposals for development (subdivisions, an industrial exposition, the Outer Beltway, sewage treatment plants) and rescinded park bond referendums. "All these crises," Hartwell reports, "had the hoped-for conclusions." In October 1967, the county approved the Lower Potomac Master Plan, which removed the Outer Beltway and established much of Mason Neck as parks and a refuge.

These victories, however, did not end the ongoing struggle for the preservation of the tract. "Many of these battles were extremely complicated," she relates. "But all except one, in which citizen action came too late, ended in victory." Soon Hartwell was a well-known David in an arena of Goliaths, and several battles were waged as a result of insider tips. Articles were written about her under such titles as "The Mason Neck Story: What One Person Can Do," "The Lady versus the Bulldozers," and "Commander in the War on Mason Neck."

Her attention-getting methods went on to include helicopter flights to show eagles' nests to officials, making a movie to gain the support of various organizations, and conducting boat tours of the Neck's waterways in her Boston Whaler, often towing her canoe (for everyone from government officials to conservationists, reporters, and "just plain citizens who wanted to see eagles"). Hartwell gained tremendous support because of these tours. Over time she personally obtained the support of many national, regional, and local organizations through membership, action alerts, and attendance at hearings, seminars, and planning sessions. "Comparatively few of these organizations actually joined the CCMN," she recounts, "but the unfailing response to my action alerts was invaluable."

Hartwell served on countless boards, councils, and advisory committees, and she has won numerous conservation awards. Included among her remarkable record of accomplishments are:

- halting a 100-foot tower planned by the U.S. Army for "meteorological" experiments involving aerosol spraying of zinc cadmium sulfide (1968)
- preventing a landfill on what is now the Featherstone National Wildlife Refuge, across Occoquan Bay from Mason Neck (1969)
- persuading Fairfax County to ban the pesticide Dieldrin (1969)
- pushing through passage of a Maryland law making it a criminal offense to dredge sand and gravel from tidal waters or marshlands of Charles County, a decision that was upheld by the U.S. Supreme Court (1970–71)
- blocking a proposed resort conference center on an island in Belmont Bay (1971–72)
- writing, with the George Wythe School of Law at the College of William and Mary, the Virginia Wetlands Bill and playing a major role in its passage (1972)
- exposing secret plans to construct an airport and sludge incinerator on nearby Ft. Belvoir (1973 and 1980)
- organizing a coalition that forced an alternate route for a proposed natural gas pipeline to run from Cove Point, Maryland, across the Potomac, and through the length of Mason Neck (1974–75)
- effecting a unanimous vote by Fairfax County for subsidized sewer rates and against the construction of a proposed interceptor sewer (1978–79)

- forestalling construction of an enormous marina directly across the Potomac from Mason Neck at the mouth of Pomonkey Creek (1979)
- leading a successful lobbying effort to persuade Congress to appropriate $3 million for acquisition of 355 acres of privately owned inholdings next to Mason Neck National Wildlife Refuge (1982–83)

In 1999, the U.S. Fish and Wildlife Service announced its intention to remove the bald eagle from its list of endangered and threatened wildlife. As a result of Hartwell's leadership, today Mason Neck is the site of the 2,277-acre Mason Neck National Wildlife Refuge, the first refuge in the United States established for the protection of the bald eagle; the 1,804-acre Mason Neck State Park, Northern Virginia's first state park; and the 1,002-acre Pohick Bay Regional Park. A plaque at the entrance to the State Park Visitor Center reads, IN APPRECIATION OF ELIZABETH HARTWELL WHO LED THE CITIZEN CRUSADE TO SAVE MASON NECK, 6 NOVEMBER 1987. "The eagles won the battles for Mason Neck," Hartwell proclaims. "I was simply their spokesman. There are eight active eagle nests now that produce eaglets," she beams. "So you see, sometimes a little rebellion doesn't hurt at all."

Liz Hartwell has not been out of her room for almost two years (although she confides that she immediately began devising an "escape plan"). A bald eagle statuette and large encased butterfly collection are remnants of a life once led outdoors. "I caught all those butterflies myself. They are sixty-four years old, I'll have you know. And they still have their color!"

Of the voluminous missives of this captivating woman, perhaps the most succinct is found handwritten on a small notecard—about the size of an eagle's egg—clipped to a stack of correspondence, which simply reads, "As promised, Liz."

RAY R. WEIL ∽

College Park, Maryland

Soil Scientist / Agronomist

RAY WEIL, A SOIL SCIENTIST AND AGRONOMIST SPECIALIZING in soil fertility and ecology, is an internationally recognized leader in soil research and education. Weil is a slight, debonair fellow who grew up in Detroit. His life's work has been "to open up the world of soils to students, farmers, and environmental professionals." He is so dedicated to this goal that he's even willing to be photographed buried in soil. Weil has held professorial appointments in the Agronomy Department of the University of Maryland in College Park since 1979. From serving as a Peace Corps volunteer in Ethiopia to managing a 500-acre organic farm to holding numerous consulting and peer review positions, Weil's extensive career has embraced academia, consulting, and service. He participates in educational programs, for instance, shown here giving an on-farm presentation to visiting dignitaries, in joint consultation with the World Bank and the Chesapeake Bay Foundation's Clagett Farm. He has authored or coauthored more than one hundred publications, including *The Nature of Soils,* an internationally used textbook that has a long-standing reputation as "the Bible of soil science."

Despite Weil's impressive credentials, his expertise can be summed up in the simple concept of "listening to the land. If we take time to learn the language of the land," he advises, "the soil will speak to us." Soil is a complex mixture of eroded rock, mineral nutrients, decaying organic matter, water, air, and billions of living organisms, most of them microscopic decomposers. "In any ecosystem," Weil points out, "whether your backyard, a farm, a forest, or a regional watershed like the Chesapeake, soil's role is critical, not marginal."

Weil's textbook outlines five key roles of soils in an ecosystem:

1. Medium for plant growth and support. Properties of the soil often determine the nature of vegetation present and, indirectly, the number and types of animals (including people) that the vegetation can support.
2. Regulator of water supply and purification. Soil properties are the controlling factor in Earth's hydrologic system.
3. Recycling system for nutrients and organic wastes.
4. Habitat for living organisms of unimaginable numbers and diversity.
5. Engineering medium. In human-built ecosystems, soil not only is an important building material but also provides the foundation for virtually every road, airport, and house we build.

Creation stories from around the world teach that to be human is to be a creature of the soil. Yet, Weil cautions, "As human societies become increasingly urbanized, fewer people have intimate contact with the soil. Individuals lose sight of the ways they depend upon this practically non-renewable resource for their prosperity and survival." Formation of new soil is a very slow process. In temperate areas like the Chesapeake watershed, it takes two hundred to one thousand years, depending on climate and soil type, to renew one inch of topsoil. Worldwide, soil is eroding on farmland at seven to two hundred times the natural rate of soil renewal. "And," Weil adds, "because soils will continue to supply nearly all of our food and much of our fiber, while biofuels [produced from organic matter such as wood, dung, and liquid ethanol] will be increasingly important, our dependence on soils is likely to increase in the future. We're seeing early signs of this trend in soybean-oil based inks, cornstarch plastics, and wood alcohol fuels."

Walter Clay Lowdermilk, Chief of the Soil Conservation Service of the U. S. Department of Agriculture, once said, "A civilization writes its record on the land." Weil agrees. "The art of soil management is as old as civilization itself," he points out. Indeed, soil erosion may have been a factor in the decline of past civilizations, including early Middle Eastern nations and the Roman Empire. G. Tyler Miller, Jr., has called modern land mismanagement "the Great Terrain Robbery." "As we move into the twenty-first century," Weil advises, "new understandings and new technologies will be needed to protect the environment while producing food and biomass to support society."

Weil says that in the 1970s and 1980s, most point-source pollution was "largely taken care of by regulations and permits. So the remaining pollution is mostly non–point source [large or dispersed land areas such as cropfields, streets, and lawns that discharge pollutants into the environment over an expansive area]. The number one problem with the Bay is runoff of nutrients and sediment. We need to keep the land out of the water. The study of soil science has never been more important. Soil management really determines water quality. About 80 percent of the pollutants entering the Chesapeake Bay today are coming from the land, and most of that is from agriculture."

The Chesapeake Bay watershed is one of the richest agricultural regions of the earth; its fertility is comparable to the valleys of the Nile, the Ganges, and other great rivers. "Virtually all the water that goes down the rivers into the Bay has actually moved through the soil," Weil explains. "On the way, it can either pick up pollutants, or the soil can remove them. Soil has a large capacity to remove nutrients as well, but the problem in some areas of the watershed is that we exceed that capacity, which results in overfertilization of the rivers and the Bay."

Weil explains that, compounded by the industrialization and structure of modern day agriculture, this oversupply of nutrients, particularly phosphorus, is the basis for algal blooms and possibly responsible for outbreaks of *Pfiesteria* as well. "Traditionally," he says, "there was a reasonable nutrient balance on a farm. Most of what was grown was produced from the resources *on* the farm. The farmer didn't need to add much fertilizer because he was cycling the nutrients from his own crops to his own animals, and back again. The poultry industry is importing feed to raise millions of chickens on the lower Eastern Shore, in what are referred to as concentrated animal feeding operations. And the feed manufacturers actually *add* phosphorus to the chicken feed. The chicken needs phosphorus for bone development, but it can't digest the form of it that's in the corn and soybeans in commercial feed. So most of the natural phosphorus ends up in the manure, not in the chicken. A wild chicken would get it from eating insects and grass. The poultry industry overcompensates by adding a lot of digestible calcium phosphate, the excess of which also winds up in the manure. The trouble is, all this phosphorus comes from outside the farm."

He explains that crops used to manufacture chicken feed sometimes come from as far away as Iowa. Because the crop is exported, the farm where the feed is grown is depleted of its phosphorus and has to import more, which comes from mines in Florida. The nutrient from Iowa is shipped to southern Maryland chicken farms as part of the poultry feed and then spread on fields as manure. "Of course," Weil says, "it's way more than they need because the crop wasn't produced on the farm in the first place, and it's not economical to ship the manure back to Iowa, so all this excess phosphorus becomes concentrated in a few counties. It's an inherent imbalance.

"Maryland is a leader in nutrient management. For the past ten years we've been trying to limit manure in the Chesapeake watershed to control nitrogen inputs, which are much more mobile because the soil can't hold onto them. But we didn't focus on phosphorus. It turns out, if you put on the right amount of manure for the nitrogen, there's way too much phosphorus. Soil has a high capacity to hold phosphorus, but the soils are getting saturated, which means when it rains there's phosphorous runoff. In nature, nitrogen and phosphorus are scarce, so it doesn't take a lot to upset the balance in water. In the long run, these [*Pfiesteria*-related] problems may be the wake up call to change this juggernaut of unbalanced concentration."

Poultry farms on the Delmarva Peninsula produce over 800,000 tons of poultry manure each year. Weil believes it would be more sensible to subsidize the shipping of this manure, which is valuable as a fertilizer, and to have a more dispersed poultry industry. "I think phosphorus should be managed on a watershed basis," he says, "with an import permit showing how it will be removed from the watershed. This would be a strong incentive to disperse the industry."

However, Weil admits, farmers can't afford to experiment with their livelihood. "That's the purpose of the university. There have always been innovative farmers willing to work with us. Most farmers want to do the right thing to protect the environment and the Bay as much as is economically practical.

"For instance, the *no-tillage system* has been a revolution to farmers," he states, "and Maryland has also been a leader in that. Fields have been plowed for centuries, but it's not natural. Cultivation degrades the soil and exposes it to erosion. *No-till* not only prevents erosion and runoff but also saves the farmer time, energy, and expense. A cover crop is essential to *no-till* farming. It's only been in the last few years, partly because of government programs trying to protect the Bay, that cover crops have been subsidized."

Environmentally sound farming goes beyond subsidies. "A farmer has got to be an ecologist," Weil states. "The best way to do that is with diversity and rotation, trying to make use of the natural processes and resources that are on the farm—the plants, soils, sunlight, and rain—rather than having to import them. When the farmer does that he makes more money and increases sustainability."

Weil believes that the Chesapeake Bay "certainly has been recovering. If we can fix the agricultural problem, it will be good for everybody. The development side is more discouraging, because it's harder to manage. Maryland's *Smart Growth* philosophy of making cities desirable places to live by funneling resources into the urban areas is a good first step. We can keep building on that in ways that reduce development's negative effects on the Bay.

"However, our appetite for developing land is a lifestyle issue. That's a tougher problem. It's not just the *number* of people. People today expect more—more land, a larger house, increased mobility. Many people are not willing to accept responsibility for their lifestyles. But people change, and get educated. Fifty years ago if someone drove around in a big car and tossed tin cans out the window, people thought they were cool. Today, perceptions about gas guzzling, recycling, and litter have changed that status. We're doing that through environmental education.

"I live in an old house on a small lot near campus. I bicycle to work. That's my choice. I'm happy to let the farmers keep the rural area, and I'll visit it," he says with a knowing smile. "Being aware of those choices, and teaching people, not just farmers, to 'listen to the land' is essential to restoring the future of the Bay."

ELIZABETH A. GIBBS ✑

Richmond, Virginia

Mother / Advocate

ABOUT EIGHT YEARS AGO, LIZ GIBBS LEFT HER PRACTICE AS A housing authority lawyer to be at home with her young daughter. Today Gibbs has three daughters: Alex, ten, Caroline, eight, and Juliana, who was adopted at birth eighteen months ago. Gibbs and her husband, also an attorney, live in a large, "lived-in" house in the wooded hills of an established suburban community. Working from her station wagon (with a BAYWTCHRS vanity tag), a cluttered kitchen, or the computer down the hall, she good-humoredly juggles errands, baby bottles, meetings, a phone that rings off the hook, piano lessons, school projects, public hearings, bedtime stories, and caring for Diana, the fifteen-year-old, lovable but incontinent family dog ("We're full-service here," Gibbs calls out as she cleans the soiled dog crate). An easy-going, assured parent, she easily shifts from motherhood to witty, well-spoken advocate.

"I've always been interested in environmental issues, and when I left my job, I had more time to read the paper. All I was getting from the newspapers was frustrated. I understood enough to know that there were problems, but I didn't know how to help solve them. I wanted to join a group working on issues in the political arena and on the educational front," she says.

At that time, the Chesapeake Bay Foundation (CBF) had just established an activist group affiliated with its Richmond office. "They were organizing a grassroots network and one of the first meetings was just a few days later, two miles from my house. It was kismet!" Gibbs became the advocacy chairperson for the Bay Watchers, a volunteer group today known as the Bay Savers. "I knew my passion was advocacy," she recalls. "It also fit into my life because I had young children and I couldn't be taking off on weekends, but I *could* stay up late at night on my computer and write or get ready to go to public hearings. When I first joined, I felt like a fish out of water. Most folks had some direct, visceral connection to the Bay—a house on the river or having grown up in the area. I didn't have that kind of a connection. CBF had professionals—attorneys and scientists—who devoted their lives to their work. I was impressed by how effectively they worked within the system, so I joined up mainly for the advocacy. I was a new kind of member for them."

A short time later, George Allen became governor of Virginia. "That offered lots of fodder!" Gibbs exclaims, referring to Allen's attempts to revamp the state's environmental programs in favor of economic growth. "Allen and Becky Norton Dunlop, his chosen acolyte who headed the Virginia Department of Environmental Quality (DEQ), weren't enforcing laws that were already on the books, much less adding new ones. Allen's slogan was 'Virginia: We're Open for Business,'" Gibbs recalls. "And 'regulation' was a very naughty word. His administration's claim to fame was going to be bringing in big business from around the country. Politicians are shortsighted—it didn't matter if policy made sense in the long run."

As advocacy chairperson, Gibbs's first major conflict involved a 1995 attempt by Allen's administration to "cut a deal" with two shipyards on the James River by secretly eliminating the strict limits put in place by the General Assembly in the 1980s on release of TBT (tributyltin, a pesticide added to boat hull paint and one of the fourteen most toxic chemicals in the watershed). "This was an issue that drew people out because we felt that the DEQ was intentionally thwarting the public will. They were taken by surprise by the public outcry."

At a public hearing in Norfolk, Virginia, Gibbs said, "I've come from Richmond this evening as a taxpayer, a mother of two young children, and a citizen of the Commonwealth to give you my views on what the role of the DEQ should be in the lives of Virginians." She went on to describe that role as assuring that public communities, rivers, air, and the Bay are not degraded for present and future generations, "and to do so in accordance with our will. As holders of a public trust, that's your job, that's your duty to us.

"Unfortunately," she continued, "the reason I feel compelled to be here, is that I don't think you're doing your job very well." She chided the DEQ for making "hopelessly lopsided" decisions behind closed doors "without even a hint of public scrutiny," decisions robbing the public of the right to protect their air, health, and "exceptional waters" and to challenge the issuance of pollution permits. "How protected do you expect us to feel by the job you're doing? You can take that first step— tonight—toward really doing your job, if you'll just listen to what the public is telling you—listen to all these people who took the time to come here and talk to you, and then go back to your offices tomorrow and don't let that message be ignored any longer. This is our system and we have spoken. The good governor may have hired you to carry out his agenda, but you work for us. We need you. Please hear us."

Gibbs received a standing ovation, and the next day the local newspaper, the *Virginian-Pilot*, reported that "the Allen administration got an earful from a small but feisty crowd at City Hall: Stop messing with the environment."

As a result of the hearings, TBT standards remained intact and the Virginia Conservation Network asked Gibbs to speak at a press conference. "Things can really snowball!" she exclaims. "Once you get yourself out there and make some points that other people relate to or support, opportunities build on themselves. The more you do, the more you're able to do."

In 1996, congressional republicans tried to cut funding and limit the powers of the EPA, and Gibbs was invited to make a statement before the Democratic Task Force on the Environment. "Many speakers addressed specific, close-to-home issues," she recalls. "I was more of a generalist— 'We have to have EPA oversight, because look at the gaps states like ours are willing tolerate!' Pollution knows no state boundaries, and if we don't have somebody overseeing the big picture, we're going to have a 'race to the bottom' in terms of rules and regulations."

At the microphone in the Longworth congressional office building in Washington, D.C., Gibbs voiced her support for the EPA. "The message I've come here to bring is very simple: don't give up your oversight of our nation's environmental policy. Today, as a result of the federal Clean Water Act, the quality of water in Chesapeake rivers is vastly improved. I'd like to give you a citizen's perspective on what it's like to live in a state whose government has broken faith with the people on environmental policy. What we've come up against is an ongoing assault on the very foundation of democracy—that is, the participation by the public in its own governance."

Shortly afterward, the CBF wrote the legislation for the Water Quality Improvement Act, which the Virginia General Assembly passed in 1998. "That was quite a coup. There was a huge grassroots effort in which environmental organizations urged their constituent members to make their feelings known to the General Assembly. And it worked—our representatives got lots of phone calls, postcards, and letters, which turned that issue around. The power of people who finally figure out they can make a difference is amazing. With education and communication, democracy works!"

Today Gibbs has stepped down as advocacy chairperson to work on the CBF's President's Advisory Council and serve as president of the PTA. "When I first started with my daughters' PTA, I was the legislation chairman. That is my true passion—learning about issues and getting people involved. It was very similar to my work with Bay Savers."

She is also a volunteer speaker, talking to ordinary citizens about personal responsibility. She emphasizes the importance of "doing simple things, like not overfertilizing, keeping your car tuned up, and not using household toxins. People have to make their own personal choices. You don't necessarily have to use cloth diapers (I didn't!) or get rid of all your toxic cleaning supplies; just get rid of one or two. Change in moderation does count.

"But in addition, try to see the big picture—become aware of the issues, read the paper, call your government officials. It's also important that we understand the basic concept of a watershed, and how what people and industries do upstream can affect water quality miles away. I'm teaching my kids about the whole system, that one thing affects something else. I want to leave them a legacy of stewardship and advocacy, so that working on a public hearing speech is a normal activity. Let me tell you, if I can do it, anybody can do it! I don't have a background in environmental science. I have a background in being *interested* in protecting the environment, and that's a big difference. I grew up having a healthy respect for nature, and I want to help protect it for my children. We can't escape the connection between human health and well being and that of the natural environment that supports us."

Between homework, dinnertime, and preparing for a sleepover, Gibbs concludes, "I'm lucky to be able to stay at home and do this. If you don't have that luxury, you can do smaller pieces. I've worked on many issues and put in many hours, but I could not have done that without the support of my husband and family. There were plenty of people who did something once a month—came to meetings, went to hearings, planted trees. You don't have to go to public hearings; you can volunteer at school to help a child learn to read. There's always a place. We need all of those pieces to make an educated populace that can make a difference."

MARLENE MERVINE 〜

Bridgeville, Delaware

Wetlands and Land Preservationist

IMAGINE THIS: A MAGICIAN ASKS FOR VOLUNTEERS AND CHOOSES a fair farm girl, a dainty granny, a feisty dancer, a smart schoolmistress, and a quirky tree hugger, deposits them into a big box, ties it with a snug green bow, taps the box with his magic wand, waves it in the air, and voilà!—out steps Marlene Mervine, a concoction of them all. For over a decade, Mervine, sparked by the magic of the river near which she has lived all her life, has dedicated her talents to protecting Delaware's Nanticoke River watershed. "On some stretches of the river you can go for *miles* and just see woodland and wetland in either direction," she says. "It is so exciting!" She grew up on a farm along Marshyhope Creek. "Oh my," she laments, "in those days wetlands were for filling. I shudder to think about how people impacted the environment without knowing what they were doing." Today, this gentle lady has put her love of the Nanticoke watershed in action through wetland preservation and land conservation.

The Nanticoke River flows southwest from central Delaware through the Eastern Shore of Maryland to Tangier Sound and the Chesapeake Bay. The upper portion of the Nanticoke is the largest watershed in Delaware, occupying nearly 316,371 acres in Kent and Sussex Counties, about one-third of Delaware's land surface. Extensive unbroken forests line the river and distinguish it from other tributaries to the Bay; 38 percent of the watershed is forested, and it contains the largest continuous pine forest remaining on the Delmarva Peninsula. Freshwater wetlands border nearly all the major streams, accounting for 22 percent of the land surface. Diversity of habitat enables the watershed to support an abundance of plants and animals, along with valuable commercial and recreational fisheries. Several threatened and endangered species are common in the Nanticoke watershed, and, together with the neighboring Blackwater River watershed, the Nanticoke supports 35 percent of all wintering waterfowl that use the Atlantic Flyway, a migratory route that follows the east coast from Mexico to Canada. Despite threats from agriculture (approximately 43% of the land in the watershed supports about 1,300 animal production farms), development, and industry, the Nanticoke is one of the Bay's last unspoiled rivers, listed on the Nationwide Rivers Inventory because of its undeveloped nature.

"The Nanticoke is one of the last rivers on the whole East Coast of the United States that is this undeveloped," Mervine confirms. "In some places it looks virtually the same as when Captain John Smith made his explorations." She goes on to explain that the reason the river has been protected through the years is because its meanders and marshy ground precluded considerable amounts of settlements and commerce. Even today, the extensive wetlands have contributed to a relatively slow rate of development in the corridor. "It's a superb river for recreation, nature study, and simple solitude," she imparts. "We're so incredibly blessed to have the Nanticoke in this condition."

Mervine, an upbeat grandmother who lives within view of Collins Pond, an old mill pond and tributary of the river, went back to school at age thirty-eight and was past fifty when she settled upon her career. "I finally figured out what I wanted to be when I grew up!" she spouts. She worked in banking for twenty years and did volunteer watershed work for over a decade before she had the opportunity to convert her volunteer work into several part-time jobs, including coordinating the Delaware Adopt-a-Wetland (DAAW) program and serving on the board of directors and staff of the Nanticoke River Watershed Conservancy (NRWC). Slight and soft-spoken, she is at once fervent and diplomatic. "Land-use decisions and activities related to industry, agriculture, overfishing, and development are causing some of the problems our river and wetlands are facing. But I'm convinced that if we all work together we can find solutions."

In the late 1980s, Mervine became a member of the Governor's Advisory Board for the Nanticoke, a small group formed to gather information about protecting the watershed for the future. She says it was "a small thing that has evolved into something much larger. Today, there are several environmental groups along the river that support each other and have become an important force in protection of the river. Most of them evolved from that board."

Another member of the advisory board, Dot White, a poultry farmer and retired chemist, was influential not only personally to Mervine but also in unraveling the ecological role of wetlands to a watershed. "I was so inspired by her!" Mervine exclaims. "Her farm lay in the upper reaches of the Nanticoke watershed and produced a variety of byproducts that she knew were potentially detrimental to water quality. She started doing research and concluded the most efficient, natural way to reduce toxins was through wetlands, which was a new concept to this area. In the process," Mervine recounts, "she observed that, despite their benefits, wetlands were disappearing. She was a one-woman campaign for wetland preservation and devised a plan to have volunteers 'adopt' wetlands. After she organized the program, Dot asked me to help administer it." After White suddenly passed away, Mervine took over the program. "Dot was such a wonderful example of one person making a difference," Mervine says. "She was just a little farmer in Sussex County and through her efforts we now have well over sixty sites adopted and three thousand people faithfully working in the program."

Mervine explains that the marshy places she calls "wonderlands" were once regarded as mosquito-breeding waste areas to be filled and utilized to greater advantage. But, she continues, educational initiatives such as DAAW have raised public awareness of their unique biological diversity and importance in slowing erosion, purifying water supplies, acting as buffers against severe storms, and providing wildlife habitat. Mervine explains that the DAAW, under the Division of Fish and Wildlife of the Delaware Department of Natural Resources and Environmental Control and various county coordinators, is composed of volunteers. Participating groups include corporations, small businesses, schools, 4-H and scout clubs, civic organizations, bird clubs, river preservation groups, land trusts, and individuals. "We encourage activities ranging from clearing trash and water-quality sampling to enhancing habitat, completing plant and wildlife surveys, and conducting educational activities. My goal is to arrange adoptions for a large majority of Delaware's remaining 223,000 acres of wetlands."

However, Mervine cautions, "the wetlands program is excellent, but there are no legal teeth in it. At any time the landowner can decide to develop." This is where her work with the NRWC comes into play. The conservancy is committed to preserving lands with exceptional wildlife, scenic, fishery, recreational, or agricultural values. "I am their one and only staff," Mervine admits. "My work with the conservancy is the most important thing I do. We have rampant development coming across from the beach areas. I'm not saying all development is detrimental, but there comes a point where we have to preserve some part of what has shaped and molded us as people—some part of what our forefathers have handed down to us that has made southern Delaware a unique and wonderful place. It is now, while the Nanticoke River is still largely unspoiled, that we must preserve its places of special beauty and natural value. I work with landowners placing easements on or donating portions of their land for the protection of the river. The pressure to put land to other uses often conflicts with conservation. The critical scenic and wildlife lands owned by individuals will only be preserved if economically feasible conservation alternatives to development can be provided. This year, the Delaware legislature created a tax credit for persons who donate land or create easements. There is already a federal credit program in force, so we now have two tools to help with land preservation."

A recent NRWC easement acquisition is on the Chapel Branch Nature Area, at the confluence of the Chapel Branch tributary with the Nanticoke. The DuPont Corporation, one of Delaware's major industrial concerns, owns this 192-acre property. "DuPont had planned to timber the land to raise funds for a plant project. Several of us on DuPont's Citizens Advisory Board were very concerned. Through a series of initiatives, we were able to offer DuPont the same amount they would have received from the timber in return for a permanent conservation easement, leaving for future generations the lovely nature trail its employees had developed. It's a very valuable property for us. Chapel Branch is one of the streams along the river which has not been dammed; its free-flowing waters provide prime spawning habitat for shad and other fish." Once harvested from shad barges indigenous to the area (such as the one pictured), shad is a critically depleted species here, for which restoration efforts are underway. Mervine continues, "We have over a mile of fragile shoreline, with thirty-seven acres of wetlands that are now protected. The rest of the parcel is upland forest and streamside area. This is a special area for migrating songbirds. We're thrilled to have it!"

Brochures of the nature area outline forty-two stations along the nature trails, including information on such topics as the "fallen tree with bricks in roots," many plant and animal species (some endangered), local prehistoric animal life, and the historic role of white oak and Atlantic white cedar trees in local shipbuilding from colonial times to the mid-twentieth century. The conservancy will erect a kiosk depicting "a trail through time," the evolution of the property from old-growth forest to a Native American seasonal site to cleared farmland, a peach orchard, an industrial site, and its eventual return to old-growth forest.

"Everything is connected," Mervine concludes. "We must ask ourselves what sort of activity will take place on and around this river over the next several decades and beyond—and how can we plan for and maintain a balance between increased pressure from man and preserving this unique and vulnerable ecosystem? The protection and conservation of this river relies on combined efforts of individual landowners, private organizations, and government and nongovernment agencies. One person, one property, one land conservation program can make a difference. It's a basic instinct to protect the land you love. I'm very concerned about the future quality of life here for my grandchildren and Delawareans at large. Whatever I do will forever be a gift to Delaware."

BILLY W. MILLS, JR. ⌒

Walkerton, Virginia

Riverkeeper

ONE EVENING TEN YEARS AGO, BILLY MILLS CAME TO VIRGINIA'S "Middle Peninsula" on a lark and fell for the place hook, line, and sinker. "I owned a successful landscaping company in the mountains of Albermarle County [Virginia] when I got roped into running the slide machine for a talk about conservation easements. The next day, a local guy showed me these rivers and I saw bald eagles. It made my heart jump! I pulled up stakes and moved here, never looking back." As a "refugee from business," Mills lived on his sailboat and took a low-paying job as a technician for the Soil and Water Conservation District, which allowed him to make inroads with local landowners. Soon he attracted the attention of a conservation group called the Alliance for the Chesapeake Bay. "My job was to spawn a river group," he recounts. A robust cross between crusader and clown, Mills flows with genuine zeal for "his" rivers. This zeal, perhaps more than anything else, has spurred his success in sidling up to and uniting this old-line Virginia community.

"When I got here, there were already fledgling conservation operations trying to take root," he recalls. "I suggested that instead of a 'divide and conquer' strategy, we make a consortium. We started out, not as alarmists, but by talking about barbecue and beer—by integrating ourselves, and letting the residents figure out the benefits of conservation for themselves. I learned how to work a community, to take the germ of an idea and bull it through. I do what I do by evoking people's attachment to Chesapeake Bay."

Officially formed in 1991, the Mattaponi and Pamunkey Rivers Association (MPRA) today has a diverse grassroots membership including volunteers who contribute over twenty-five thousand hours of labor annually, participating in water-quality monitoring, stream assessments, educational trips and presentations, river cleanups, and river sojourns. A local newspaper has described Mills and his supporters as *Riverkeepers*, a term that originated in Old England, where Riverkeepers were charged with protecting public waterways and tributaries against poachers and polluters.

"This is a river-based local economy, and the whole community has bought into the conservation effort. After ten years of getting residents and businesses involved, we're having a hard time finding anything to clean up! Now we're working on converting river cleanups to river stewardship and maintenance of a treasured resource."

Tined by the confluence of the Mattaponi and Pamunkey Rivers into the York River, this watershed has been named "the most pristine freshwater complex on the Atlantic coast" by the Nature Conservancy. Rich in natural resources—mature timberland, bountiful wetlands, and hundreds of creeks and streams—it remains largely unspoiled. Both rivers have excellent water quality, deep channels, and strong currents that remain free flowing, with no dams or impoundments to block passage during spring spawning runs. "It's a mesmerizing place," Mills proclaims. "Most riverfronts have been bulkheaded, shore-lined, and built. Because of extensive marshland and swamps, ours hasn't. These rivers support valuable communities of endangered plants and aquatic species, and special freshwater tidal habitat." Indeed, the diversity of wildlife is among the most spectacular on the Eastern Seaboard, and local customs are deeply rooted in hunting, trapping, and fishing, traditions originated by the area's first known inhabitants: the Pamunkey, Mattaponi, and Rappahannock Indians.

Native American habitation dates back over ten thousand years. The region served as a significant trail crossroads and was the heart of the Powhatan Confederacy, which was ruled by the powerful Wahunsonacoch (known by the English as Chief Powhatan, father of Pocahontas, or Pocahuntas) and dominated Indian culture and civilization during the rich Colonial-era history. Although changing lifestyles and dwindling resources have caused many members to leave the area, remnants of the Algonquin tribes remain, including residents of the Mattaponi and Pamunkey Reservations. Mills has managed to gain the confidence of this segment of the local population. "I've established a long-term relationship built on little successes," he confides. This relationship represents a unique cross-cultural alliance hinged on reciprocity for the benefit of the future of the river, or *yeokanta*. Joint endeavors include shad recovery and participation in the Chesapeake Bay Gateways and Water Trails initiative, a system of interconnected water and land sites throughout the Chesapeake watershed that improves access to the water while conserving and displaying cultural and natural resources.

"Water trails existed long before roads," Mills points out, "and often were more prevalent than walking paths." When he began working with the county government on leading a community effort to establish modern water trails to help attract ecotourists, his indigenous neighbors became an integral part of the project. The eighty- to 100-mile-long Algonquin Trace will include the Mattaponi and Pamunkey Rivers and the entire York River, and it will consist of more than thirty permanent reserves showcasing natural and cultural resources while celebrating and interpreting the legacy of the region's indigenous people. "The focus period is pre–seventeenth-century tidewater Virginia," Mills outlines, "on the eve of the dramatic and pivotal 'first contact' between Native Americans and Virginia Company explorers and settlers. It's a story untold."

The trail is scheduled to be running by 2002 and complete by 2007. Mills and MPRA volunteers will break the trail by building and maintaining landings marked with informational signs and kiosks constructed of indigenous materials, which present lore about the trail and its vast aboriginal past. "One side of each kiosk will be an orientation—geographical, ecological, historical—to that section of the river trail; the other side will have an interpretation of something Algonquin." Stations, each named for a tribal settlement that was either directly on the site or close to it, include such diverse locations and topics as: villages and "king's houses" at Cantaunkack and native plants for dyes and colors at Oquonock, both on the York River; copper as valued currency at Matchutt, on the Mattaponi River; and trapping methods at Accosumwinck, on the Pamunkey river.

"Our idea is to get people off the interstates and onto our waterways for *exploratory* recreation." Stops range from the most basic "Rest and Relax" site, with a dock and kiosk exhibit, to the "Rest, Relax, and Explore," which adds a land-based connection such as hiking, biking, or motor vehicle trails, to the ultimate "Rest, Relax, Explore, and Camp Overnight" site, which provides family tent-camping facilities with fire rings, precut firewood, trash receptacles, and a privy or composting toilet. "Put a family out in a marsh at night to camp under the stars," Mills waxes, "and you've got a defender for life."

Shared preservation of this region is undeniably tied to its resources and native past in ways that extend beyond recreation. Each spring, as they have done for thousands of years, American shad make their annual run up the Pamunkey River. Recently, Pamunkey Indian tribal members, such as 100-year-old former chief Tecumseh Deerfoot Cook and his son, Assistant Chief Warren Cook (shown, with Mills, on back cover photo), direct descendants of Powhatan, have added a new twist to their age-old tradition of catching shad. Since 1918, the Pamunkey tribe has been hatching shad eggs and returning them back to these rivers. "We maintain a philosophy that if we take fish from the water, we should put them back," Cook confirms. In 1998, with the support of Indian, state, and federal funds, the Pamunkey shad hatchery was renovated and tripled in size to expand the replenishment process.

With tribesmen working both sides of the afternoon slack tide for over a month, drift-netting in a "reach" of one to three miles, the catch begins. In days gone by, shad runs like this would have brought in about one hundred spawning females a day. Today, if all goes well, the men will capture only about a dozen egg-laden females; they will then use strong hand pressure to force out a pinkish, syrupy mass from the underbelly into a bucket (a lethal event for the poor female). Males are similarly squeezed to release sperm, or milt, to fertilize the eggs. The reapers take this concoction to the hatchery, a pier-side field station with rows of holding tanks and a convoluted piping system. Here the eggs are hatched, raised, and tagged according to a schedule marked on a yellowed wall calendar (unused except for several springtime weeks that are brightly scrawled with red, time-sensitive notations).

Around day sixteen, hatchery workers release inch-long fingerlings back into the Pamunkey. This year's stock yielded more than 7 million "fry," which the tribe then helped to monitor as part of a new focus on the river's overall fish stocks. Rearing shad is something the Pamunkey Indians have done faithfully for almost one hundred years, and, as a result, the York River system maintains a good run of fish.

"It is their conservation ethic that laid the foundation for a working partnership between the Indians and the state and federal governments," Mills expounds. The tagging effort will help the state evaluate the contribution of the Pamunkey hatchery on American shad populations throughout Virginia waters. However, by Pamunkey standards, the ultimate measure of success will be increased numbers of shad—echoing an earlier time when their ancestors declared, *namaske,* or "fish are plentiful."

Such folkloric ideals seem possible on the waters of Billy Mills's adopted home. "Paddling alongside bird and riverine mammal populations, peering into the complexities of marshes and estuaries, and camping on the delicate, watery edges of sensitive areas all require a heightened appreciation and awareness of the immediate surroundings," Mills concludes. "Certainly more than is required to pitch a tent or park a trailer next to a picnic table, near a sewered restroom and asphalt parking area. We honestly believe if we help people enjoy what we enjoy about our watershed, that will help protect it. If we create a new generation of Bay-*lovers,* that will keep Bay restoration alive."

MARC S. CRUZ ∽

Accokeek, Maryland

Community-Supported Agriculture Shareholder

IN THE EARLY 1990S, MARC CRUZ—A MASTER MECHANIC WHO works as the foreman of a Mercedes Benz repair shop, wants to quit smoking, and has recently come to love eating vegetables—built a home on the southern tip of Prince George's County, where he now lives with his father. Just up the road, the Accokeek Foundation, an educational nonprofit organization established to preserve land (specifically Piscataway Park) directly across the Potomac River from George Washington's Mount Vernon, was investigating Community-Supported Agriculture (CSA), an unconventional approach to farming. CSA farms connect families and farmers, build a sense of community, encourage stewardship of the land, eliminate costly long-distance distribution systems, and keep food dollars in the local economy. Although Cruz grew up on a small farm in Iowa, he, like most of his neighbors, had never heard of CSA. Today, as one of the original shareholders in the Accokeek program, not only is he gobbling up fresh, certified-organic produce for thirty weeks a year, but he is also one of the program's biggest supporters. "I've learned so much in the five years I've participated. It's a tremendously intelligent way to use land. It's raised my awareness about issues of land use and environmental protection, and the workings of food production."

The Robert Ware Straus Ecosystem Farm demonstrates ecologically sensitive practices while producing high-value, wholesome crops. It also serves as an outdoor classroom for educational programs that blend history, ecology, economics, research, and responsible land management. The operation avoids using all harmful pesticides or chemicals. As a result, it positively addresses a crucial regional issue: reducing the flow of pollution into the Potomac River and Chesapeake Bay. A solar-powered trickle irrigation system that draws water from the river is a central, sustainable feature of the site. As a public education project, the farm benefits thousands of schoolchildren and adults throughout the region by demonstrating proactive measures to protect the land and river. The program is also developing an agro-forestry area in the Potomac River buffer zone, where workers have planted trees with economic value; agro-forestry allows the program to "farm" in fragile soils without further plowing.

The CSA initiative involves an innovative agricultural system in which consumers prepurchase a "share" of the farm's harvest. In return, shareholders receive a weekly supply of fresh produce. "It's a unique way to reconnect with the food production process," Cruz imparts. The arrangement is mutually beneficial since it provides guaranteed, up-front operating income to the farmer and assures quality produce, grown in an ecologically sound manner to the consumer. Because the concern of marketing the harvest is eliminated, CSA programs also permit the grower to concentrate on efficiently producing high-quality crops. Modeled after farms in Canada, Europe, and Japan, CSA farms first appeared in the United States in the mid-1980s. Today, about one thousand farms in the United States use the CSA model.

"We all share in the benefits and the losses," Cruz outlines. "It doesn't leave one man out there alone without any support." Unlike the traditional monoculture farms of Cruz's boyhood, CSA farms generally grow a wide variety of crops to help fight pests and protect against production losses. "Farming in Iowa is a completely different thing," Cruz confirms. "It's a highly mechanized production of phenomenal amounts of grain. By contrast, the methods used here take a completely different approach, both in the field and from a 'community supported' point of view.

"I've learned, firsthand, about techniques such as crop rotation, raised beds, double-digging, using straw mulch, composting, and cover crops [nonfood crops intended to prevent erosion, bolster soil tilth, and provide habitat for beneficial insects; to decompose and provide nutrients for the next crop; or to improve soil quality by 'fixing' nitrogen from the air into the soil]. I had no idea that Brussels sprouts grow up the side of a stalk. Most of the time, you get them and it says 'Birdseye' on the box!

"The people who work here are so passionate about what they do that shareholders can't help but learn from this experience. I enjoy being linked to the local landscape, which means I can purchase fewer vegetables that are shipped from faraway places. It makes it easy to practice the adage 'eat fresh, eat local, eat in season.'"

Debates about farming methodology and tenets aside, on weekly pickup days on this lush, secluded plot of land, when rows of boxes appear, which workers (who have been picking since dawn) hustle to fill with freshly washed, mouth-watering vegetables, fruits, herbs, and flowers—each carefully packed carton looking more like a centerpiece than a produce delivery—there can be little doubt that this farm has a good thing going. The seven-acre "hidden field," as it is called, bears not only the yield of its harvest but also—shared with osprey and heron at the riverside, turtles among the spuds, and deer outside the solar-powered deer fence—an undeniable feeling of repose. "There are no atheists in the furrows," Cruz epitomizes.

Beds are heavily laden with a certified organic bounty: everything from asparagus to watermelon to summertime standards such as beans, carrots, tomatoes, sweet corn, and squash to more adventurous offerings like artichokes, Hakurei turnips, pac choi, leeks, okra, Swiss chard, and music garlic. "We've even had purple beans and blue potatoes!" Cruz reports. "They're very tasty; you get over the color real quick!"

During times of bare ground to sprouting seedlings to staked rows of ripe harvests, shareholders are encouraged to ask questions and walk the fields. They are further involved in the process through weekly *Field Notes*, a newsletter chock-full of lively status reports, anecdotes, occasional soapbox articles, and recipes (e.g., Hakurei turnip sandwiches, sautéed garlic and Brussels sprouts, and chocolate chip pumpkin cookies). "These help me know what to do with the things I don't recognize!" Cruz admits.

While all this may look and sound idyllic, an enormous amount of planning and backbreaking labor goes into this operation. It is especially difficult because for the past three centuries this land had been used to grow tobacco, a crop that wears out soil quality, and earnest CSA production began only in 1995. The staff uses an array of techniques to gain maximum productivity from the natural limits of this "born-again" tobacco field. Shareholders are urged to participate in keeping soil fertility in a cyclical versus linear mode by returning waste from their kitchens to the farm's compost. "I bring a bucketful from home every week and toss it in the bin. It breaks down and becomes natural fertilizer instead

of 'linear export' away from the farm into the landfill. There's not a lot of topsoil here," Cruz explains. "It's mostly compacted clay, which is difficult to till when it's wet and causes erosion because it sheds water. Over the years, the transformation has been unbelievable. The program has made a lot of progress, and it continues to improve."

Cruz goes on to explain that organic growing requires a holistic approach. "It's not a quick-fix mentality." For pests, the farm crew—which consists of four full-timers (including a year-round farm manager), four summer interns, seasonal "harvest helpers," and a "spirited bunch of volunteers"—institutes an integrated pest management strategy. They may try several different methods, such as crop rotation, providing habitat for "beneficials" (creatures such as bluebirds, bats, and insects that feast on harmful pests), or installing "reemay" (a tentlike "floating row cover" barrier of spun polyester that prevents pest damage and protects plants from frost) before considering spraying organic pesticides. "Sometimes," Cruz points out, "the best action is no action." For instance, he explains, certain plants have a threshold level where the bugs can eat their fill without significantly impairing production. Or insect control by "omission," such as delaying the second planting of carrots to allow the life cycle of the carrot maggot to pass.

"I know the amount of effort that goes into this farm, because I've seen it in action. The link between humans and the land is a key to productivity. Everybody who's a part of the share program puts money and/or time into it. I help out if they need a mechanic. A few weeks ago, I was hammering trusses up on the roof of the new barn. This is truly a grassroots movement of people coming together around food and in support of the farmers who produce it.

"Mercedes has a motto: 'the best or nothing.' That's why I've worked for them for twenty-two years. It's the same attitude here—going the extra mile. This is an example of farming for the future by demonstrating an understanding of how to take crops from land while the soil is being regenerated. If this country's bountiful food production is to continue, we need to train a new generation of farmers to interact with the land. The growers here like to say they are growing *people* as well as crops. It's just a good feeling—people protecting the waterways and shaping the land, and the land feeding and shaping people at the same time. As a whole, we're able to accomplish a lot more than one person ever could."

LOUISA ROGOFF THOMPSON ꝏ

Ellicott City, Maryland

Volunteer Naturalist

Louisa Thompson, a retired clinical psychologist and insightful naturalist, believes that "in the next century, the greatest threat to our native plants and the wildlife species that depend upon them may well come from other plants." Although this may conjure up images of the needle-jawed Venus flytrap, many of the plants Thompson is referring to are quite familiar and can be found in our own backyards. Thompson is an expert on Mid-Atlantic native plants and participates in many regional educational programs. In conjunction with the Maryland Native Plant Society and Maryland Cooperative Extension Service, she developed and coordinates a demonstration stewardship project at Patapsco Valley State Park, located along the rocky slopes of the Patapsco River gorge in Howard and Baltimore Counties. She is also developing a training and technical assistance program for coordinators of similar projects that underscore the harmful effects of nonnative plants variously called alien, introduced, or exotic.

Thompson defines *native* as indigenous to a specific region, delineated by geological characteristics as well as climate. She goes on to explain that several thousand nonnative species have been brought to North America in the past three centuries. Some were brought intentionally, for their medicinal, ornamental, or food value. Others stowed away in soil, crop seed, packing material, or ballast. Native Americans referred to the lawn weed plantain as "the white man's footprints." The majority of these outlanders came from other continents, but a few have spread from other parts of the United States.

"Most are well-behaved," Thompson allows. "Several hundred, however, have no natural controls here. They are highly invasive, and significantly reduce the number of plant and animal species on any site they invade, even deep in forests and undisturbed ecosystems."

According to the Weed Science Society of America, invasive plants already infest more than 100 million acres in the United States, with control efforts and losses costing more than $20 billion annually. Surprisingly, many are popular, even beloved, landscape plants and trees. These include tree of heaven (*Ailanthus altissima*), popularized in the novel *A Tree Grows in Brooklyn,* Japanese honeysuckle (*Lonicera japonica*), a sweet-nectared vine that winds around the trunk of a host plant and eventually kills it, and such favorites as English ivy (*Hedera helix*), Vinca, Periwinkle (*Vinca minor*), and various mints. Other well-known noxious stranglers include kudzu (*Pueraria lobata*), called "the vine that smothered the South," and the wetland-choking common reed (*Phragmites australis*). The most invasive nonnative weeds bear aptly disconcerting names, such as mile-a-minute vine (*Polygonum perfoliatum*) and bull thistle (*Cirsium vulgare*).

Ironically, some invaders, such as Russian olive (*Eleagnus angustifolium*), multiflora rose (*Rosa multiflora*), and crown vetch (*Coronilla varia*), were formerly endorsed for erosion control and wildlife value. A number of ornamental plants once recommended for water gardens or moist garden soils have spread to riverbanks, floodplains, and wetlands. "Purple loosestrife [*Lythrum salicaria, L. virgatum*] is a very recent introduction," Thompson illustrates. "It's quite beautiful and a great butterfly plant, but it has no natural enemies and has taken over millions of acres of wetland in this country." Nonnatives are also pervasive along the river bottom, where they are spread downstream by floods, leading to economic problems such as the redredging of channels.

"Large patches of celandine buttercup [*Ranunculus ficaria*], Mexican bamboo [*Polygonum cuspidatum*], multiflora rose, and Wineberry [*Rubus phoenicolasius*] predominate in the Patapsco flood plain," Thompson relates. "Some are beginning to gain a foothold in tributary streams and trails high above the stream where springs and seeps keep the soil moist. They're extremely adaptable and difficult to eradicate once established," she advises. "Up to ten years of repeated treatment may be needed to remove Purple loosestrife or phragmites."

In areas where nonnative plants have taken hold, Thompson's prescribed control measures range from simply pulling up seedlings or cutting off spent flowers ("deadheading") to mowing and controlled burning and, when all else fails, using various corn-based and glyphosate (e.g., Roundup and Rodeo) herbicides. Depending on the situation, other tactics might include "girdling" a tree by cutting through the bark and growing layer (cambium) or a combination "hack and squirt" approach.

Thompson executes these maneuvers by leading the volunteer stewardship effort at the park. From April through November, volunteers—"adults and older teens who love the park"—gather monthly, armed with heavy gloves, tools, and blue flag markers, to combat exotics. "It's really an ethic, that we're responsible for these places we're using," she believes. "It's also an opportunity to see ecology in action. We work in teams to remove invasive plants and perform erosion control measures."

Thompson demonstrates identification and removal techniques to resist a targeted exotic plant with minimal environmental damage. In May, her teams pull Garlic mustard (*Alliaria petiolata*) before it sets seeds. In June and July, they pluck shallow-rooted Wineberry, bag the fruits, and hang the plants in a tree to prevent rerooting. In early fall they wield grass whips to lop off the tops of Vietnamese stilt grass (*Microstegium vimineum*). Later, when they can identify Norway maples by their golden yellow leaves, volunteers mark them for removal.

There's more to it than weeding. "We record the location and size of invasive plant infestations, eroded areas, and evidence of deer browsing. We're working on mapping the entire trail system. Several of our volunteers are birders, entomologists, and butterfly enthusiasts. We enjoy learning from each other by pooling our knowledge of wildlife and of the history and geology of the park to better understand what we observe. We take soil samples and consult Soil Survey information to help with species identification. Now and then we make a rare find—a magnificent, endangered white walnut [*Juglans cinerea*] tree with dramatic brown and white striped bark, loaded with nuts, or a zebra swallowtail butterfly [*Eurytides marcellus*]. We keep records and photographs of our interventions and monitor changes over time, to see what's most effective."

Teams see firsthand how the stranglehold of these plants impacts an ecosystem. "Exotics bulldoze their way into an ecosystem, but they don't hold the soil as well as the natives, and they don't fill all the different niches that provide for the needs of its many species of plants, animals, insects, and microorganisms. For instance, most invasives tend to be much denser than natives are. They grow in a *tangle,* which reduces available space, light, and ventilation, and changes the *structure* of the habitat. A bird will only nest in a particular, usual configuration. It wants to be a certain height off the ground with a certain density of cover. If it doesn't find it, it will not nest. And when unbalanced competition replaces many species with few, a system that produced food year round is replaced by much narrower food production. Allowing this change in diversity to occur unchecked is unhealthy for any ecosystem.

Thompson has developed a comprehensive list of recommended native shade and ornamental trees, hedges, shrubs, ornamental vines, ground covers, wetland plants, and alternatives to bamboo. Before planting an exotic species, she urges residents to consider the following:

- Does it naturalize or self-sow? How far does it spread? Does wind or water spread the seeds? If so, don't plant it unless you are prepared to remove all seeds, every year.
- Is it a wildlife food plant? If so, wildlife will spread it to woods and wetlands. These are plants to *avoid*. Plant natives instead.
- Is it a rapidly spreading ground cover? If so, don't plant it adjacent to open space.
- Is it low maintenance—hardy, tolerant of drought or flooding, shade-tolerant, pest-free? If so, it has no natural controls here. Do not plant if it can spread out of the garden.
- Does it have the ability to kill or suppress growth of surrounding plants by shading them out, chemically poisoning them, or outcompeting them for food and water? If so, you don't want it in your garden anyway!

"We don't understand ecosystems very well," she concludes. "It's difficult for humans to understand anything as complicated as an ecosystem, which has hundreds or thousands of components. If you take one out, you don't notice the difference. But we're getting to the point that we're taking out hundreds."

Is it a losing battle? "Maybe!" Thompson admits. "But I think that with proper education, it wouldn't have to be. Because if we lose this battle, we all lose. Each of us has a responsibility to protect the local ecosystem that cleans our air and water, stabilizes the soil, buffers floods, and provides food and shelter for innumerable species besides our own. That doesn't have to be an overwhelming prospect. I encourage people to study the ecology of their own backyard."

RANDOLPH L. ESTY ⤳

Queen Anne, Maryland

Town Mayor

RANDOLPH (RANDY) ESTY HAS BEEN THE MAYOR OF QUEEN Anne, Maryland (population about 250), for six years. "Technically," he says, "my title is President of the Town Commissioners, but a town's chief elected official is usually referred to as Mayor. I was chairman of the Planning Commission for three years and a commissioner for two years before I was elected president."

Esty has lived in Queen Anne, which is nestled between Queen Anne's, Talbot, and Caroline Counties, since 1986, when he retired from the Navy Exchange. Although he has lived in such places as Pennsylvania, New York, and Japan, and traveled on business to Hong Kong, Korea, Taiwan, and the Philippines, he and his wife, Rae, chose the Chesapeake Bay area for retirement. "We knew we wanted to live in a small town on the Eastern Shore. When we drove through Queen Anne, it was love at first sight," he declares.

"The main work of the commissioners is to maintain the town's landscape and infrastructure, and to make this a nice place to live. We work with the road and utility departments," he continues, "and we're working on a revitalization project, including sidewalk improvements. I'd love to bring back the shade trees that once canopied Main Street. I remember when the sun never reached the street because of those beautiful trees, which have since succumbed to Dutch elm disease."

Esty hopes the town will be included in Maryland's Rural Legacy Program, a component of the *Smart Growth* Initiative, which seeks the involvement of local governments in order to group properties into large areas, designated greenbelts, greenways, or natural resource corridors, to permanently protect them from development. "The program prevents sprawl by preserving the state's rural and agricultural heritage," Esty explains. "It gives small towns incentives to reestablish the sense of community that's been lost with suburban modernization."

Established in 1835, Queen Anne was once a bustling community. The Pennsylvania Railroad and the Maryland, Delaware & Virginia Railway Company each had a junction and central stop at the Queen Anne granary, complete with a rest stop and market. While trains no longer whistle their way through town, the granary, with its tall silos protruding from expanses of agricultural land, still operates today.

"This town was *the* transport center for grain in the late 1800s and early 1900s," says Esty. "The Eastern Shore was a hub of wheat and flour production. Grain and seed were hauled to the railroad by water, up the

Tuckahoe River from the Choptank and the Chesapeake Bay. There hasn't been much change in the character of the town, and that's how we'd like it to stay."

But that doesn't mean Esty doesn't see room for improvement. Last year he introduced curbside recycling, a rarity in the area. The State of Maryland pays for two sorting receptacles (at $3 apiece) for each of the town's sixty-five houses, and town taxes pay the monthly $129 pickup fee to a local recycling company for weekly pickups through the town.

"I pursued this project because I care about the environment, and so do the townspeople. We felt many elderly residents would recycle if it were more convenient than taking the items to a drop-off center. Basically, it's just a different way of putting out the trash."

Esty also arranges for a large dumpster to be placed in the firehouse parking lot for the week following the annual town yard sale. "That way," he says, "people have a place to properly dispose of what they don't sell. We've made these services convenient and affordable, so it's worked here. It's a visible way for the town to contribute to environmental stewardship."

Visibility also plays a role in another of Esty's community efforts: litter control. For the past six months, he and Rae have regularly gathered litter from the town's streets, between Norwich Creek and the Tuckahoe River.

"It started when we began walking for exercise," he explains, giving his belly a pat with both hands. "We were passing all this trash, and figured we might as well collect it while we walked. We could clean up the town and maybe it would be infectious—maybe others would see us and join the effort, or at least become more aware of the problem. We didn't realize what we were getting into!

"We'd go a couple of hundred feet and our pails would be filled. Even our litter pails came from litter! You can't believe the stuff we've seen on the roadside: whole bags of garbage, clothes, furniture, televisions, tires, a guitar, the kitchen sink. You see a lot of the same stuff again and again: beer bottles, soda cans, cigarettes, fast food waste. We have a little joke about who's been through town, like Beercan Man, Sister Sodapop, and Charlie Cheeseburger.

"Some corporations combat the problem through litter policing programs, where businesses contribute to litter pickup operations in the vicinity of their stores. That's all well and good, but it doesn't get to the root of the problem."

Litter is the result of careless attitudes and sloppy waste handling. Violators are difficult to catch. "It's the same ones again and again," Esty reports. "Some people just don't care. We can go out and clean up a stretch of road, and the next day it's littered again—'litter, back by popular neglect.'"

Litter-strewn lands and waterways display an undeniable example of the degradation of common-property resources, a situation that biologist Garrett Hardin termed the "tragedy of the commons." Each user reasons that the small amount they use or pollute is not enough to matter. But the cumulative effect eventually exhausts or ruins it for everyone.

Litter is more than an eyesore in the Bay watershed. In natural water bodies it is a hazard to birds, fish, turtles, and marine mammals that mistake it for food. Nationally, as many as 2 million seabirds and more than 100,000 marine mammals die each year when they ingest or become entangled in fishing nets, ropes, and other debris dumped into the water or discarded on beaches. Boating over refuse can cause engine damage. Synthetic chemicals from litter pollution are transported into the ocean and could contribute to the toxic load in bottom sediments, which find their way into the human food supply.

According to Keep America Beautiful, there are seven primary sources of litter: household trash, dumpsters, loading docks, construction sites, uncovered truck loads, pedestrians, and motorists. Litter is blown by wind and traffic or carried by water. It moves until trapped by a curb, building, fence, or shoreline. Once litter has accumulated, it invites people to add more, encouraging apathy.

Each year, highway departments spend millions of tax dollars and many hours picking up litter, as do local, state, and federal governments. Visitors are a large source of litter, but at the same time, they expect cleanliness. In general, clean communities have a better chance of attracting new businesses than those where litter is common.

"Our county and state governments have inmate litter crews and Adopt-a-Highway programs," Esty says. "But they can only do so much within the constraints of their resources. A lot of times it seems like a losing battle. Of course, it would be fair if the litterbugs were the ones cleaning up, but it just doesn't work out that way. The key is to focus on prevention, as well as cleanup. It's a battle that has to be fought through awareness and better public trash-disposal systems. Changes have to begin at home and at school, through education, setting a good example, and economic incentives, such as returnable bottles."

In 1964, 89 percent of all soft drinks and 50 percent of all beer in the United States were sold in refillable glass bottles. By 1995, such bottles made up only about 7 percent of the market and only ten states even had refillable glass bottles. The disappearance of most local bottling companies has also led to a loss of local jobs, income, and tax revenues.

"Because of rising landfill fees," Esty adds, "there are some areas that have no public trash pickup. Higher levels of government should provide for trash removal and make litter prevention a priority."

Esty is a member of the Maryland Municipal League and Annual Mayors Conference, which give local input to state government officials. "I don't mind saying this," he remarks. "Some elected officials are indifferent to environmental issues if it doesn't mean more votes. Others really help us. It depends on their agenda."

Esty believes that public and governmental understanding has improved the health of the Bay watershed. "I see a trend toward more awareness of human impact on our surroundings. There are small examples right here: the town is recycling, and gives away seedlings every Arbor Day. We're advocating the dualization of Route 404 [widening of the nearby two-lane highway, heavily traveled by beach-bound tourists, to four lanes], which will impact safety and our local environment. And we're considering a community composting program.

"It wasn't long ago that some toilets in town emptied directly into the creeks and rivers. Even now some wastewater is grandfathered out of the regulations and is still disposed this way. You see washing machines that empty right out into the street or into the old railroad bed. But we are learning that these practices need to be changed, and for the most part they've been eliminated."

Esty observes Queen Anne's tree-dotted Main Street from the front porch of his large, rambling house. "I care about this town and the environment," he says. "I'm doing what I can to be involved. In a town like this, rather set in its ways, with a small population and a large portion of elderly people, it's hard to get people involved in new ideas. And those who are wind up involved for a long time. But the town is in complete agreement with my message. In community-oriented conservation, a little leadership can go a long way."

BILLY FRANK LUCAS ↝

Smoketown, Pennsylvania

Pequea-Mill Creek Project Leader

IN SOME PARTS OF THE CHESAPEAKE BAY WATERSHED, SIGNAL flags wave from floating masts across miles of water; here in Amish country, washday brings a similar sight as bright solid-colored laundry flaps in the breeze across acres of farmland. Almost every house has a loaded clothesline pulley-strung from the second story window across a rustic farmyard. As Frank Lucas makes his rounds to the farms that predominate in this area of Pennsylvania, he shares the road with horse-drawn buggies and children walking to one-room schoolhouses carrying old-fashioned lunch pails. Lucas heads the Pequea-Mill Creek Hydrologic Unit Area Project in south-central Pennsylvania, which implements a wide range of agricultural practices such as barnyard management, contour farming, and stream bank protection. He works hand-in-hand with men whose farming methods—mule-powered plows, windmills, and manual labor—seem antiquated, but who are making modern changes to improve water quality in local streams.

Originally from Oklahoma, Lucas moved east in the 1960s. He has a small office on the second floor of a building next to the local firehouse, but most of his work is done in fields and pastures. His down-to-earth manner and sincere, shirt-sleeve dedication have helped him gain the trust of local "plain" farmers, who tend to be leery of their "English" or "fancy" neighbors, especially those connected to government. "They don't think of me as the government," Lucas says. "I work really hard not to be a bureaucrat. I get dirty just like the rest of them. If you won't work, they're not going to work with you. You can't wear a tie and say 'follow my instructions.' You have to show them."

Roughly parallel to each other, Pequea Creek and Mill Creek coil through this pastoral landscape, Pequea Creek flowing directly into the Susquehanna River and Mill Creek into the Conestoga River, which empties into the Susquehanna. Together the two creeks drain about 135,000 acres, or 22 percent of Lancaster County. Although there are some poultry and swine operations in the watershed, dairy farming, with fifty-five thousand milkers, is the dominant agricultural enterprise. If these two watersheds alone were to constitute a state, Lucas says, it would rank 36th in the nation in terms of number of dairy cows—all of which produce byproducts that translate into significant non–point source pollution, such as sedimentation from eroded, hoof-trampled stream banks and nutrient-rich pasture runoff.

The Pequea-Mill Creek Project began in 1991, to reduce the impacts that had choked the life out of Lancaster County's most intensely farmed watershed. A multiagency coalition, the initiative includes nearly twenty environmental organizations, comprising one of the most diverse partnerships ever created in Pennsylvania. As project leader, Lucas has been involved from the outset, working an area that includes about one thousand small farms, 75 percent of which are Amish. He advises local landowners on important components of barnyard and stream management, such as integrated crop management and installation of barnyard runoff controls and manure storage facilities. He also coordinates an active information and education program focusing on farmer participation and involving the private sector in water quality efforts, which includes pasture walks, field days, and video presentations. The project's main effort has been fencing stream banks to keep livestock out of the water and to prevent erosion.

Since 1988, various groups have worked with Pennsylvania farmers on streamside fencing, but the idea of completely overhauling long-degraded streams is radical. Lucas admits that at first even he was skeptical. "In the late 1980s, the game commission people started discussing streamside fencing, which at the time was an off-the-wall concept. They decided to do it, my boss wanted to do it, but I did *not* want to do it. I'm a voice in the wilderness on rotational grazing, and I wanted to work on that. My boss thumped my chest one morning and said, 'I want you to fence streams.' So I combined the two programs, which worked really well."

Lucas's efforts have resulted in over fifty-five miles of single-strand, solar-powered electric fence lines running on either side of local streams, five to ten feet from the shore, to keep cows out of the water. Assisted by community groups and agencies, Lucas has also planted vegetation along shorelines to stabilize banks, improving nutrient and erosion control. "The Amish landowner might liken it to a barn raising," he remarks, "with a lot more paperwork." Supporters have also helped install concrete crossings so cows can ford streams without tearing up the bottom. "If you don't have a stabilized crossing, you wind up with a big muddy mess because you're crossing fifty cows all at one place," he explains.

While he's no fan of fencing along bigger waterways, where flood waters, debris, and ice invariably will wash away his hard work, Lucas acknowledges, "It's really great on small tributaries. We've found if we work on the little streams, the big ones will take care of themselves." Because every vertical foot of erosion from a stream bank equals about 165 cubic yards of soil washing downstream, this work will ultimately lessen nutrient and sediment loads being delivered to the Bay.

"When you talk to a farmer," Lucas divulges, "he could care less about the Chesapeake Bay. He wants to know 'What's in it for me?' Herd health is my sales pitch." Fencing benefits cattle by reducing their contact with waterborne bacteria and diseases carried downstream from the droppings of neighboring herds. Wet, dirty conditions also contribute to mastitis problems, to the tune of $180 per cow per year. "I tell them," Lucas continues, "'There's nothing in that stream that's good for your cows and there's nothing your cows do to the stream that's good for the stream. If you let a thousand-dollar cow drink out of that stream, you might as well take $1,000 and let the wind blow it away. You're taking that kind of chance.' We have several veterinarians telling farmers that their cows ought to be drinking the same water they drink at the house. Given a choice, cows will drink from a hose source or trough; they won't drink out of the stream."

Lucas and other partners also propose to restore the region's trout fishery. Fostered by dam removals, allowing water to flow freely and leave a gravel rather than silted bottom, which provides spawning areas, cleaner streams could mean trout fishing in the future. The success of the Pequea-Mill Creek Project is dependent on the cooperation of Plain Sect farmers. Lucas uses enticements like duck-nesting boxes, bluebird houses, and, especially, the idea of trout fishing to attract Amish farmers to streamside fencing. "We think that will be a carrot to get other farms fenced," he says. "They love to fish and really miss it."

These watersheds are littered with limestone streams, which, when they're clean, provide prime trout habitat. "Many of these streams have been degraded for so long that few residents remember when they were pristine," Lucas says. He is in the second year of overseeing a hatchery built near Leola. Henry Beiler, the Amish man who owns this farm, has agreed to manage the nursery in return for Lucas stocking the streams of farmers who have volunteered in the fencing project. From October to April, Beiler raises 2,000 two- to six-inch-long trout fingerlings in two concrete raceways that are protected by screened lids and a chain-link fence. Each tank is about seven feet wide, fourteen feet long, and two feet deep. Gravity flow feeds stream water into the raceways, pushing it through 1,299 feet of four-inch pipe. An additional 125 feet of pipe carries the overflow back into an unnamed tributary of Mill Creek located on Beiler's property. This is the first trout nursery of its kind. "We have one stretch of about eighteen contiguous farms that we're going to stock this spring," Lucas reports. "These are rainbow trout. They're easy to grow, but they're not native here. Our ultimate goal is to have naturally reproducing, native brook trout in these streams.

"Everything that we would like to happen is beginning to happen," Lucas relates. He reports that insect populations are becoming pollution intolerant and, because of greater amounts and varieties of shoreline vegetation, the streams are no longer unnaturally wide. The resultant increase in velocity helps clean the silt out of the center and expose the gravel bottom that trout like. "What we're doing is a thousand times better than a big fund-raising picnic or even filter strips and forest buffers," Lucas proclaims. "A guy with a fifty-acre farm isn't going to give up one hundred feet on either side of every stream. We're not interested in fly-swatters and bumper stickers. You can make all the magnets you want, but the Amish don't even have refrigerators! I call those 'feel good' practices. They don't accomplish much. Stream-bank fencing has a much bigger impact on the Bay. It's amazing how quick these streams clean themselves up once you get the cows out."

Robert Frost wrote that "good fences make good neighbors," and in the case of Lucas's water quality efforts, these words have proven true. "We've made a dent, but we still have a long way to go," he concludes. "I'm confident that one farm at a time, strand by strand of fence, our work can become the norm. Thirty years ago, people wrote this whole area off. Now people are hopeful. I tell them, as long as I'm around, I'll help maintain these fences, whatever it takes."

CATHERINE CLUGSTON ∾

Cordova, Maryland

Realtor / Poultry Grower

CATHERINE CLUGSTON HAS MADE A LIFETIME CAREER OF SELL-ing real estate along the Chesapeake Bay. "I've sold marinas, businesses, development property, homes, and farms. Selling is my forte," she says in a soft-spoken yet assured voice. "I've also become good at growing chickens," she adds. For the past five years Clugston has operated two poultry farms, raising approximately 1.2 million chickens per year. "I don't see them as expendable. We care for our chickens as living creatures. When I moved here from Annapolis, I saw an opportunity to merge two things that I do well by specializing in poultry farm sales."

According to Delmarva Poultry Industry, Inc., the Delmarva Peninsula has long been recognized as the birthplace of the commercial broiler industry. The largest agricultural enterprise of the area, Delmarva's broiler industry is the backbone of the local economy and provides premium markets for thousands of acres of Delmarva-grown corn and soybeans used to feed the chickens. Delmarva is the sixth-largest broiler production area in the country, producing about 8 percent of the nation's broilers. Sussex County, Delaware, is the top broiler-producing county in the United States, and several Maryland counties are also among the national leaders, making this region the nation's most concentrated broiler-producing area. The Bayside broiler industry consists of about twenty-six hundred contract growers, ten feed mills, fifteen hatcheries, twelve processing plants operated by five integrated companies, and two independently operated further-processing plants. These companies process and market approximately 12 million broilers each week. Poultry growers own and operate sixty-one hundred broiler houses with a combined capacity of 124 million birds. Each weekday more than 150 tractor-trailers loaded with dressed poultry leave Delmarva, headed to Mid-Atlantic and northeastern markets and other export locations.

Recently the poultry industry has become unexpectedly controversial in Bay ecology and politics. Concern over nutrient-laden poultry waste stems from the finger-pointing premise that it is directly responsible for recent outbreaks of *Pfiesteria piscicida* in Chesapeake rivers, which were first detected in 1997. Clugston defends the environmental practices of poultry growers and points out that they are inaccurately portrayed as the sole culprit in a complex, often misunderstood industry. Processing companies such as Tyson and Perdue, known as "integrators," contract to supply hatchery stock, feed (mostly corn and soybeans grown by local field farmers), fresh litter, and heating fuel. The growers then raise flocks in grower-owned and operated chicken houses. When the birds are fully grown, the integrator transports them via tractor-trailer to processing plants and then on to wholesale and retail markets.

Most poultry farmers do not have enough acreage to fully utilize the fertilizer their flocks produce. "There's high demand from field farmers who want our waste," she explains. "We trade it in exchange for them hauling it away. It's free," she adds, "while a chemical is expensive. There is economic as well as environmental incentive."

Farmers also use poultry compost, in addition to manure, as fertilizer. Across the industry, about 3 to 6 percent of each flock die prematurely, requiring growers to dispose of large numbers of dead animals. For example, an operation that raises 1 million chickens per year will also yield thirty thousand to sixty thousand carcasses annually. Properly composted poultry carcasses contribute to the ecological cycle by reducing waste and producing a valuable, natural fertilizer.

Clugston feels the public is misinformed in its perception of farmers haphazardly overusing nutrient inputs. "We're very conscious of the fact that our farms affect the Bay watershed. We follow nutrient management plans. The farmer isn't putting any more fertilizer on the field than is practical or desirable. Crop farmers put our soiled litter into a dump truck, and immediately apply it to the fields where it's *needed*, when it's time to fertilize."

Government agencies regulate and monitor economic and environmental factors of the industry. "The grain farmers apply manure to their fields with the government's blessing," Clugston reveals, "because the government encourages farmers to use a natural product, as opposed to a synthetic product." Yet recent public alarm has led to calls for restrictions on poultry-based nutrients introduced into the watershed. "It's called *Pfiesteria hysteria*," Clugston says, "and it threatens the well-being of the watershed, as well as the chicken farmer's livelihood. Nature doesn't operate in hysterics, and neither should we."

Reactionary public outcry has led legislators to consider heavy regulation of the poultry industry. "If government targets this as the industry that needs to shape up or ship out, the integrators *will* ship out. Perdue threatened to take the company off the [Eastern] Shore and move south. It's a fact: they could do it. Any of [the integrators] could do it."

Clugston fears that the *Pfiesteria* issue might cripple the poultry industry without solving the Bay's problem. "The average grower already worries about doing their job well enough, without having to worry about the whole industry shutting down. They're thinking, 'This is the farm where we grew up and have always lived, what are we going to do now, we've got all these buildings out back, what are we going to put in them?' If the integrator leaves, the growers are left out in the cold.

"Unless they form their own cooperative, which was the way it was done years ago," she offers. However, while implementing a co-op might offer growers more say-so and security, growers would be in competition with integrators, and providing integration services for thousands of chicken houses would require a large capital investment. "Perhaps as difficult a hurdle," Clugston suggests, "is that a co-op would require all of the growers getting together to make it happen."

That's a tricky proposition in a fragmented industry filled with extremely independent farmers. "Because the integrators settle up the pay for the weekly catch [the rounding up of chickens ready for market] on a curve basis, we are in direct competition with each other," Clugston explains. "There's no incentive to share information, because it sharpens your competitor's edge and makes you more vulnerable."

Clugston feels that improving grower unity will strengthen agricultural sustainability in the region and help clear up misconceptions. "Many people don't understand the intricate infrastructure behind the poultry industry. For instance, the integrator is paying for the feed and litter. That's where the big dispute comes in over *Pfiesteria*, because so many farmers say, 'Hey wait a minute, when the litter goes into the building it belongs to the integrator; when it goes out it belongs to us. The food that goes into the chickens belongs to the integrator; but when it comes out, it belongs to us.'" Shrugging, she asks, "At what point does it change ownership? In the intestine?"

Closing the gaps and opening lines of communication would benefit the farmer, the industry, and the environment. "Many of us feel we've been silenced, without much of a voice to stand up against being convicted by politicians and public perception in an issue where the media is selling fear."

Biosecurity, which addresses precautions against the transfer of poultry disease among farms by manure carried on boots, tires, and so on, is another worry. A large sign posted at the entrance to Clugston's

chicken houses warns STOP: THIS IS A BIOSECURE AREA. NO ENTRY WITHOUT PERMISSION. CHECK IN AT OFFICE.

"We're also dissuaded from meeting because of disease," Clugston notes, "which is a big isolating factor. A lot of growers are afraid to get together—they're not used to talking to one another. While there are farming and industry organizations, there's no central forum, no networking specifically for chicken farmers.

"Most publications take a broad approach that can be politically or technically oriented, and far-removed from a grower's day to day experience," she clarifies. "I'm working on publishing a newsletter, which will appeal to growers on their own level. It will narrow down the issues and be a vehicle for sharing and education. I care about the environment and the farmers. This would present ideas in a nonthreatening way, and make a positive impact by improving communication between farmers, integrators, legislators, and environmentalists."

Clugston sees this as a critical time for bringing these groups together. "People are more sensitive to the environment. Poultry farmers are painfully aware of their impact on the environment. But the poultry industry is often forced into action by regulations that are costly or create competitive imbalance between states. Regulations are merely a quick-fix if we're not looking deep enough for the *cause* of problems," she cautions. "We have to look beyond the surface, at the combined effect of many years of sloppy behavior: overtilling the fields, accumulated runoff, metals from Baltimore found in the Pocomoke River, overfishing. And when you talk about fishing, you also talk about *too many* of one kind of fish in the Bay. It appears that *Pfiesteria* only becomes toxic when there's an overabundance. So maybe it's nature's way of getting rid of too many fish. If you talk to watermen, the older ones will tell you, 'Hey this isn't the first time this has happened, it happened a hundred years ago, it happened fifty years ago. It's nature's way of dealing with the problem.'

"Environmental regulation can have positive results, but it can be overdone. Overregulation can be detrimental to our economy. I'm concerned about the economy of the Eastern Shore, as a Realtor, poultry farmer, and person who lives here. We're driving people away. I know a lot of residents don't want to see more people move here, but we're all going to be out of a job if we're not open to some development and to wise use of the land. For instance, master plans and restrictions on zoning and critical areas allow development to occur where it's appropriate."

Yet Clugston has a positive outlook for the future of the Chesapeake Bay. "I think it's a healthy future. In some respects, the media hype is good because it's heightened people's awareness of what could happen if we don't wake up and smell the coffee. I think nine out of ten people in general care deeply about the Bay.

"My individual contribution is to be informed and pass on good information about what I know to be beneficial. Where does it start? It starts with composting chickens properly. It starts with removing litter properly, applying it to the fields properly. It starts with Realtors, developers, and homeowners having an attitude of stewardship, placing worth on the *health* of the Bay, as part of property value. It's common sense and caring, even though it doesn't always directly benefit you monetarily. I think that's the attitude we all have to have. You do it because it's the right thing to do."

EDMUND SNODGRASS ∽
LUCIE SNODGRASS ∽

Street, Maryland

Specialty Farmers

ONE NIGHT ABOUT TWENTY-FIVE YEARS AGO, ED SNODGRASS had a dream about a llama. The next day at a cattle auction, there happened to be one for sale and Snodgrass brought it home. At the time, the 365-acre Emory Knoll Farm that the Snodgrass family had farmed for five generations was producing corn and soybeans. Since Snodgrass's father had converted the farm from a dairy operation to grain production, there hadn't been a cow on the property for about ten years, and there certainly had never been a llama. Dating back to the mid-nineteenth century, the farm has produced a variety of goods—milk, corn, Christmas trees. "Every generation has to figure out how they're going to make it work," Snodgrass reveals. "This is not your average farm. We're adapting to modern conditions in new ways. We've broadened the horizons of farming to include more sustainable practices and high-intensity agriculture on less land. For about ten years now, we've been doing llama treks and environmental education focusing on stream ecology. We installed a greenhouse to grow vegetables, rock-garden plants, and container gardens. We also sell about ten species of bamboo for staking and landscaping and consult with each customer on the appropriate use and location of each species. We've installed an off-the-grid solar system to produce our own electricity and fenced the animals away from our streams to reduce the nutrient load on the Bay. We are constantly trying to find ways to promote a more sustainable way of conducting our operations."

In 1972, Snodgrass, in his early twenties, started farming with his father. "We had about four hundred acres of corn and soybeans," he recalls. Today, sandwiched between residential subdivisions, the property has been partitioned into five contiguous farms, including Snodgrass's eighty-nine-acre plot, on which some family members still live. His farmstead has the homey feel of a place invested with decades of use and care—rolling hills arrayed with shade trees, barns, weathered outbuildings, farm machinery, duck-dotted ponds, flowerbeds, a vegetable garden, and a herd of eighteen llamas, including several baby llamas, called *crias*. Snodgrass farmed full-time until 1983. "I got hit hard when commodity prices dropped in the late 1970s and early 80s and the price of corn dropped in half," he says. He worked off the farm until early last year, when he returned to full-time farming. In the interim, he worked as the director of education for the Living Classrooms Foundation, a nonprofit outdoor education program for incarcerated juvenile delinquents.

"That's where I came up with the idea of a land program here. I'd bring the kids hiking and camping for a few days to help them transition back to the real world. Since then, we've had thousands of kids tour the farm. We take them backpacking with the llamas, and study stream ecology. Our small stream feeds into Deer Creek, which flows into the Susquehanna River and then to the Bay. We teach a simple curriculum to help them understand the connection of a watershed. For instance, we pour a gooey organic mess through different mediums to show what it's like when this stuff runs down the city street, the suburban parking lot, or through wetlands. We talk about things like why we're building water treatment plants when nature could do the same thing for us."

About five years ago, Snodgrass married Lucie, a spunky first-generation Swiss-American who affectionately calls her husband *Schatzi* (German for "treasure") and who gave up a high-level public policy career in Washington, D.C., to move to the farm. "Lucie and I have been trying to figure out how to go back to making a living on the farm," Snodgrass explains. "It's become a much more hybrid economy—we still raise some rye, we grow wholesale and retail perennials, we sell llamas, and we take groups on llama treks. Most recently, we've gotten set-aside funding for wildlife habitat from the Maryland Department of Natural Resources, the Federal Agricultural Stabilization and Control Service, and Ducks Unlimited. We put in fifteen hundred trees to reforest farmland into native hardwoods—oak, sycamore, poplar, black gum, and magnolia. There's a similar program where we'll plant about twenty-two acres of warm-season grasses to encourage reintroduction of upland grass birds, like pheasant, quail, and turkey. I do consulting and someday we may sell solar electricity.

"This generation of farming is going to be different," he continues. "It's not going to be the traditional commodity agriculture where we're producing milk or grain. The world economy has changed and commodity agriculture is now a function of the stock market. The price of grain is set in Chicago every day and farmers have no control. It's not the same as a local economy where you can set your price based on what it costs to produce goods, and regional environmental concerns. That's not part of the equation anymore. I don't want to be in that equation," he declares. "I don't want to give away my cost of production as an insignificant factor in an economic formula. On the other hand, *we* set the prices of the perennials in our greenhouse and our wares at local farmers' markets." He goes on to explain that traditional crop farming produces about $400 of revenue per acre. "So with about forty thousand square feet in an acre, that's about a penny a square foot," he calculates. Picking up a twelve-pack of greenhouse plants, he says, "These twelve plants sell for $3 apiece and are roughly a square foot, so that's $36 a square foot. So it's thirty-six hundred times more return! That's something of a wake-up call to us."

"Although we go at it in different ways," Lucie says, "we're both committed to positive change in the world, and giving something back. Ed has a million ideas and I'm good at implementing them. We think more and more about how we can combine my passion for public policy with using the farm as an outdoor classroom. You can really use nature as a learning tool. We experience that clearly when kids visit whose whole life experience centers on a few city blocks. They're such cool kids—there's such brightness and curiosity there."

Ed explains that there aren't many working models of this approach to farming. "One of my ideas for the farm is to make it a viable economic model that is in tune with nature and actually exploits some elements of nature—solar panels, wildlife habitat, wetland education—to create revenue streams. The consulting I'm doing is around sustainable business design. We're redesigning processes and materials so we don't create landfills, unnecessary transportation, or effluents that go into the watershed. Essentially, we want to expand the carrying capacity of the earth. Rather than trying to turn everybody into environmentalists, we design systems where consumers are part of a natural process—let them be the typical American consumers. There's never been a successful movement that recruited everyone into their philosophy. I don't foresee that happening around environmental issues, but I do see designing for economic benefit as a universal objective. For example, our greenhouse can produce year-round gourmet organic lettuces without expending the fuel to transport it from California or Florida. Twenty-five percent of the nitrogen in the Bay watershed comes from car exhaust, so by developing a model that reduces the amount of transportation without reducing the benefits of the end product, we're developing sustainability."

Lucie, too, has promoted localized sustainable agriculture and expanded farmers' markets in her work as Director of Governmental and Community Relations for Harford County. "We've been investigating bringing in a small milk and ice cream processing facility as a tie between local farmers, our high school [agriculture] program, and school cafeterias. I have the opportunity to push the envelope on some of those things. I'm very committed to people and products staying where they live and produce."

"With a local value-added processing plant, farmers get better margins," her husband concurs. "Kids get better product, there's less diesel fuel spewed out, and the local tax base increases. Anything we can do to strengthen links to local farms is important."

Working to construct a new rock garden, Ed explains that he and Lucie grow the attractive plants not only for aesthetics but also to conserve water. "People use drinking water to water lawns, flush toilets, and wash cars. We should be using closed-loop water sources for that, such as recycled 'gray water' from kitchen and bath use. By designing gardens using perennials with low-water needs, we're reducing resource requirements. The analysis comes from an ecological perspective rather than strictly on appearance. I build these as I go along, intuitively."

"And I'm the perpetual garden expansionist," Lucie adds, indicating numerous flower and vegetable plantings in various stages of completion.

"It's her frustrated European colonialism," Ed quips. "I'm analytical. I like to think a problem through to a sensible solution."

"Schatzi sees things in whole pictures," Lucie agrees.

"And," Ed assures, "I have faith that the next rock I find in the field will fit."

HOWARD WOOD ∽

Centreville, Maryland

Farmland Conservationist

Humorist will rogers once said, "land . . . they ain't makin' it anymore." This rustic observation has taken on a crucial significance for people like Howard Wood, after generations of their families have lived off of the land. A small sign posted at the entrance to the Wood family's waterfront farm reads preserved forever. this property has been preserved for the future with a conservation easement.

Maryland's middle Eastern Shore, one of the most productive farming regions on the Eastern Seaboard, is particularly threatened by soaring land values, unplanned growth, and increasing population. Parts of the region are already counted in the metropolitan Baltimore statistical area. Competition abounds for the "highest and best use" of historic farmlands throughout the area. Between 1992 and 1997, development depleted a total of 27,184 acres of farmland in Talbot, Queen Anne's, Caroline, Dorchester, and Kent Counties. On a plat titled Middle Chester River Protected Lands, Howard Wood's influence in local land preservation is evident in the twenty-one parcels, including his own 332 acres of farmland and seventy-two acres of woods, placed under the perpetual protection of conservation easements. Today, at age eighty-three, following decades of gentle, patient persuasion, Wood is known as a founding father of land conservation.

Grizzled and distinguished, Wood is a pillar of integrity in this rural community. Like many families that live on necks and rivers throughout this region, the Woods have strong ties to the soil and conservation. Their holdings comprise two adjacent family farms: Poplar Grove, with its historic manor and dock houses on the Corsica River and Emory

Creek, and Indiantown Farm on the Chester River and White Cove. The Emory family, from whom Wood is descended, acquired these properties in 1660 by a grant from Lord Baltimore. "My grandmother and mother were both born and brought up right here," Wood says. "My mother married a Philadelphian, so I lived in the city but spent several months every year on the farm. I loved sailing and the whole river. I went to college and law school and decided I'd rather be a country lawyer than practice in the big city." In the 1940s, Wood and his wife moved into his parents' farmhouse. A few years later, he bought out his sisters' shares in the property. He practiced law for forty-two years and once made an unsuccessful bid for state senator. "I would push my son around in a baby carriage with 'Wood for Senate' on it," he remembers.

In 1986, Wood, his sisters, and their families met and granted a conservation easement on Indiantown to the Maryland Environmental Trust (MET). In 1997, Wood persuaded his cousin, Lloyd Emory, to place Poplar Grove in conservancy as well. Today, Wood's son James and his wife live at Indiantown, where they raise corn, soybeans, wheat, and barley. Their home-schooled children spend their days learning and frolicking on the same riverside property their grandparents, great-grandparents, and great-great-grandparents knew as children.

Today, Wood says, he is only semiretired. "After so many years, my clients still call me. They're like members of the family." In 1976, a client who owned about five hundred acres south of Kent Narrows on Craballey Bay asked Wood to prepare a Deed of Conservation Easement. "This is how I learned about MET conservation easements," he recalls. "That was the first one I'd ever heard of. I liked the idea of giving conservation easements and getting tax advantages at the same time. This allows families to pass on the farm *intact* instead of having to sell it in parcels."

Maryland was one of the first states in the country to establish land trusts. Now the state is one of the most active in the nation, ranking fifth in conservation acreage. In the 1980s Wood became a MET trustee, and in 1988 the trust developed a Local Land Trust Assistance Program to aid citizen groups in the formation and operation of land trusts. The program works with more than forty private nonprofit land trusts, including the Eastern Shore Land Conservancy (ESLC).

ESLC formed out of concern that sprawling development was causing permanent loss and fragmentation of habitat, productive farmland, traditional small-town settlement patterns, and rural economies. The conservancy believes that preserving farms, forest, and other natural areas for future generations is essential to maintaining the character of the Chesapeake Bay region. It has one of the most successful records in the country and holds over twenty thousand acres of preserved lands and a cumulative total of over 50 percent of the total acres protected by local land trusts in Maryland.

Since the ESLC's founding, Wood has worked alongside the conservancy's director, Rob Etgen (shown here with Wood), convincing landowners along the Chester River and its tributaries to place their land into permanent trusts through conservation easements, farmland preservation, endowments, and other protective mechanisms. Reviewing the Chester River plat, Etgen says, "This is a piece of Howard's handiwork. He's been getting landowners comfortable with putting their land in preservation easements for twenty-five years. At one time, education carried this movement. Government farmland preservation programs are often financially strapped, so it's important for local communities and private landowners to get involved in promoting farmland stewardship and protection. Because Howard's voice is respected in the community," Etgen continues, "all kinds of landowners say to me, 'If Howard Wood endorses the idea, that's good enough for me.'"

The main objective behind a land conservation easement is to restrict future development through a deed agreement between a landowner and the conservancy. The pact permanently limits future development of the property to an agreed level. The conservancy and landowner draft restrictions that protect the environmental and cultural resources of the property while allowing reasonable use for the future. The owner retains the right to sell the property, with the condition that the easement transfers to the new owner. ESLC is affiliated with the Maryland Agricultural Land Preservation Foundation, a state-funded program that preserves productive farmland by purchasing development rights in return for a permanent easement. "The owner can still use the land just the way a farm ought to be used," Wood explains, "instead of growing houses."

Both Wood and Etgen relate that getting families to concur on the terms of the agreement is not always easy. Concerns for the needs of future generations often cause some family members to shy away from the permanence of the decision. "When we had our family conference," Wood recalls, "one of my nieces spoke up and said, 'There's not many times when you get the chance to *do* something like this.' That remark was enough to resolve any doubts." Etgen has witnessed this scenario many times. "Deals are often on the precipice of falling apart because there's no internal agreement in the family," he notes. "The mother will say 'This property's been in our family for ten generations. It doesn't look like it's going to make it. We've got an opportunity to do something, and by golly, we're going to do it!'

"Every agreement is different," he continues, "depending on the people involved. Families that have deep roots in their land have a very personal image of what the property means to them. Today, there are lots of easements in Maryland and there's a *whole* lot of them on the Eastern Shore, thanks to people like Howard who promote the concept to their neighbors."

Over the years, Wood's sway has grown through his everyday life in the community. While waiting to take the bar exam, he worked as a substitute high school teacher. Harry Hughes, the former Maryland governor who initiated the first Chesapeake Bay Agreement, in 1983, was in his class. Wood recalls, "He was my favorite student! When he instigated the Chesapeake Bay Program, I attended the first Bay summit. It was a big meeting of governors and senators, the beginning of the idea of a signatory agreement between the states in the Chesapeake watershed."

Many of the watershed issues that people are addressing today were formulated during that time. "Today we know a lot more about how what we do on the land affects the Bay," Wood says. "Farmland often gets a bad rap, but large housing developments do a lot more damage from runoff, traffic, and too much powerboat activity. People put so doggone much fertilizer on their lawns—they figure if one bag is good, two bags is better. Powerboats create waves that are as damaging to the shoreline as a winter storm. We've had to build jetties and shore up banks because of it. That sort of pollution is worse for the river than farming. Many farmers use best management practices. We use buffers, filter strips, and terracing along the shoreline. The University of Maryland does research here. This farm has a mile of shoreline. We're very conscious of the threat of houses being built.

"The designation of critical areas is a wonderful thing. I worked with the Queen Anne's County Conservation Association to support the Critical Areas law before it was passed." Today the Critical Areas law protects a 1,000-foot strip around the shore of the Bay and its tidal tributaries from development.

Etgen adds that conservation easements are an important augmentation to regulation and zoning. "We've got great plans all over the state that have analyzed zoning issues in great detail—set up development zones with infrastructure for sewage, transportation, and commercial use so people don't have to drive as much. But in every county on the Eastern Shore over 50 percent of growth goes on land that's zoned for conservation, so we're not getting there with the current system. Unlike zoning or regulation, conservation *easements* protect land in perpetuity. They also have environmental restrictions that protect water quality in the Bay."

Wood and Etgen conclude that, beyond the efforts of conservation easements and concentrating growth in towns, there are other considerations. "Even if the water was perfectly cleaned up through scientific and technical means, but the shorelines were all developed, I don't think we would have a Bay that we want," Wood states. "Part of the Bay is beyond the borders of the stream. It includes the land, forested shorelines, the historic landscapes, a sense of heritage and place, and the connection to the people who live on the land and water. Those may be more important than just straight water-quality issues. Certainly here on the Eastern Shore, along these rivers, in these communities, on these family farms, all of those things tug at our hearts."

MYRTHA L. ALLEN ⤳

Baltimore, Maryland

High School Teacher

MYRTHA ALLEN TEACHES SCIENCE TO INNER CITY KIDS AT Patterson High School. Allen's sparsely equipped third-floor classroom overlooks blue-collar Charm City—the Port of Baltimore, Key Bridge, Dundalk Marine Terminal, industrial railroad depots, row homes, strip malls, and strip joints. Day in and day out, like ants in slow motion, a steady stream of teenagers straggle along the sidewalks that lead to Patterson High. Allen has worked here for twenty-five years, teaching environmental science, earth science, biology, and a course she designed herself called Ecosystems of the Chesapeake Bay.

When Allen's parents hear about her many environmental activities, they sometimes ask, "You're a city girl—how come you like the outside?" She says, "I'm a true Baltimorean—born in the city, grew up in the city, went to school in the city, and worked in the city school system all my life." Never married, Allen has been teaching science for twenty-seven years, most of those at Patterson.

Visitors and late arrivals to the school find the front doors locked. A security camera peers down and an intercom demands a pre-entry explanation. Once admitted, entrants must pass muster with the secretary, Mrs. Stanley, a cross between drill sergeant and mother superior. As keeper of attendance records, hall passes, and toilet paper (to prevent vandalism in the locked rest rooms), she stands with arms akimbo, equipped with a walkie-talkie, a lanyard of keys, and the unwavering commands "Come to school prepared!" and "Keep your mouth clean in my hallway!"

Yet behind the confrontational stance of teachers and administrators is an underlying ethic of devotion and affection for the students. "You have to draw a line between teacher responsibility and student responsibility," Allen says. "When students claim I remind them of their mother, I'll say, 'Good! That means we care about you.'"

The school has a high truancy rate and attendance is a major issue. Students still amble in hours after the school day has begun, citing a jumble of endless excuses. They display an "in your face" toughness that is a combination of swaggering coolness, street smarts, and childish rebellion—style counts but neatness does not.

The office is hectic, filled with students, teachers, the principal, a school nurse, and a truancy officer, all vying for one telephone and one copy machine. Between the chaos of the office and a class schedule of ninety-minute periods, Allen, unfazed, squeezes in phone calls to arrange field trips.

Patterson High School's two thousand students are divided into four separate academies. After completing the school's first-year program, called "Ninth Grade Success," students choose between Arts and Humanities, Transportation, Business and Finance, or Sports Studies / Health and Wellness. Each academy is career-oriented and offers internships to prepare students for college or the workforce. Allen explains that there used to be an Environmental Academy, but owing to lack of student interest the academy was dissolved, and the school now offers environmental science courses through a "pathway" in the Sports Studies/Health and Wellness academy, where Allen now teaches.

The staff at Patterson is dedicated to motivating students to want to be successful. "Success is possible," Allen says, "when a classroom offers the type of environment to allow learning to take place. In my classroom, creating a learning environment includes not allowing improper language. If I hear a student speaking in a disrespectful manner, I'll say, 'Wait a minute, you're not out on the street; you don't talk like that in my classroom.' Another key point in creating a successful learning environment is to set and maintain class rules. When students step to my door they know where things stand: no hats, no coats, a book, a pencil, a seat to sit in, turn in your homework in a certain way, follow a grade sheet. With hard work, most of my students are successful."

Surrounded by mismatched furniture, lesson plans, textbooks, a smattering of lab supplies, posters depicting environmental careers, and a tank of fish or Bay grasses, Allen walks the aisles of her classroom clutching papers in her strong hands. She calls her students by their surnames—"Miss Jones" or "Mr. Bates"—celebrates their accomplishments, and fusses with them about throwing away their talents.

When Allen first started teaching, the Chesapeake Bay Foundation (CBF) was establishing an environmental program for teachers at its new field centers. "I had never camped, never been in the woods, never been in a boat, never been in a marsh," Allen recalls. "Then, eighteen years ago, I participated in a CBF trip to Meredith Creek. We slept on army cots in teepees. I had the usual questions: 'Are there bears?' and 'Are there snakes?' The next day while marsh mucking I got stuck in mud up to my hips. After being rescued, I told them, 'I refuse to stay here! I'm going home.' But they convinced me to try again and during the second week

of my 'nature initiation,' I became seasick on the boat going out to Fox Island [another CBF education center on the Virginia side of the Bay]. It was frightening because I didn't know how to swim (I still don't). But as the week progressed, I began to like being outside. The beauty of Fox Island removed all my fears about being out in the environment. Once I returned to the classroom, I even began taking my Biology classes out on school grounds to do activities."

After the episodes at Meredith Creek and Fox Island, Allen continued going on camping and field trips offered by the CBF and the Maryland Association of Science Teachers. "During this time, the CBF guys who now sit in offices were still out in the field working with us. I became so intrigued with 'saving the Bay,' that I would get a group together in the spring to do volunteer work at my favorite place, Fox Island. My love for the Bay and desire to restore it inspired CBF to elect me as a board trustee. It was an honor and a pleasure to serve on the board for nine years. Even though I had to rotate off the board in 1998, I still remain active in CBF and other groups concerned about the Bay. I also write my own activities for my students to do out on the Bay."

Allen maintains a grant-based field trip fund for the students. Her environmental class (pictured on page 158, left to right, Laykeysha Williams, Myrtha Allen, Teresa Fisher, and Christopher Woodrum) recently traveled to North Point Park in southeastern Baltimore County, which includes over six miles of shoreline along the Bay, Back River, and Shallow Creek, and several wetland areas. "I really enjoy taking students to various study sites near the school. Unfortunately, in order to get all students to participate, I sometimes have to say the key word: *mandatory!*

Once we arrive at North Point, I'll ask someone to name the body of water that surrounds the area. Most students won't know it's the Chesapeake Bay. I'll point out the Bay Bridge in the distance. Many, having never seen or crossed it, are getting their first view of the bridge. On my field trips there is work to be done while having fun. I hand out materials and give directions. Students are then free to explore (often for the first time) the forest, the wetland, and the beach, recording data on worksheets. As they explore, I make suggestions on how to obtain data, but offer no answers. I want them to discover the answers as they collect data, problem-solve, and draw their own conclusions. Students soon realize that environmental activities are more than just picking up trash—that they need their skills: math, writing, speaking.

"One of my biggest thrills," Allen remarks, "is to rent a bus and ride around and look at things—smog hanging over the city, the Bethlehem Steel plant, pristine areas like North Point Park. Or we'll visit freshwater areas like Herring Run or Patterson Park. On our first visit, they only see it as a park for recreation. Hopefully, when we leave, they'll see it as an ecological community. I'll direct students to take samples of pond water and observe them under the stereomicroscope. Several of them will say, 'Oh, you don't want to put your hand in that water! It's dirty.' I say, 'Well, who lives here?' Students see the ducks and we discover fish and turtles. We use a big net to pull up some scum and leaves to find leeches. Students begin to see this is a pond community; something lives here. We move from the Bay to the streams to the land, learning about estuaries, watersheds, and groundwater. Every year or so we stencil the storm drains on campus with 'Don't Dump—Chesapeake Bay watershed.' We've been on a skipjack to observe where the Bay meets the Susquehanna River and to Annapolis to complete an environmental scorecard called the Governor's Schoolyard Survey.

"Wherever I travel," she continues, "I'll take slides of the Allegheny Mountains, the coastal plain, the Delmarva Peninsula, and other areas covered in our text book. I use these slides to teach physiographic regions. I have lots of pictures to bring home points like competition, commensalism, mutualism—all those words in the vocabulary section of our textbook. I'll inform students that these concepts exist in the real world; the real test is, Can you apply them? I want to motivate students to take responsibility for helping to protect the environment and taking action. I say, 'It's time to hear from you, because you are the next set of voters.

And you have a right to say, "Why aren't you spending more money on our parks?" Since most of you like to talk and argue, now we need for you to go out and stir things up.'

"Despite everything," Allen says, "I enjoy my job. I like working with students and teaching about the Bay. Especially when they say, 'Yeah, you didn't think I was listening, but I was,' or when I find out that, because of me, one is going into science. One student just sent me a message: 'Tell Miss Allen that because of her I got on the right track. I was hanging with the wrong crowd and she made me stay with her and do activities that got me going in the right direction.' I know I've influenced a lot of students. I've had many students go to college and one even became a doctor. To enhance our field studies, I used grant money to buy a kick seine net, water testing equipment, and identification books for birds, trees, and flowers. One student became very interested in birdwatching and several others really enjoyed identifying flowers. I purchased four binoculars costing $120 each. Some of my colleagues thought that was too much to spend. But I wanted my students to *see* things up close. I thought to myself, 'Maybe if they see it with a good pair of binoculars it might entice them to buy their own,' which it did.

"My most memorable sounds were of students discovering unique forms of life in pond or Bay water. We carry several stereomicroscopes as part of our field trip equipment. As students collected samples and recorded their observations, all I could hear was my name being called: 'Miss Allen, Miss Allen, you've *got* to see this!' That's where we'll turn around the Bay's future and that's why I teach, for that discovery."

GLORIA A. CASALE ⌒

Columbia, Maryland

Preventive Medicine Physician

As a public health physician, Dr. Gloria Casale paid close attention to a 1991 fatal outbreak of cholera. "Suddenly cholera was killing many people in Peru," she recalls. "When there's a huge increase in the number of people dying from a disease that already exists in a population," she explains, "that indicates that a new strain has appeared. Although new strains of old diseases are an inevitable result of human activity, this episode was unusual because it began in three separate port cities over a 1,200-kilometer span of Peruvian coastline, within the same two-week period. It spread very rapidly through South America all the way to Mexico, resulting in more than eight thousand deaths over three years. Authorities found it to be a strain of cholera that originated in Bangladesh, which presumably crossed the Pacific Ocean as a stowaway. We've found this pathogen as far as Mobile Bay, Alabama. Since we weren't seeing sick seamen, we ruled out human carriers. The only other logical consideration was ballast water. Sewer and water systems in many developing nations are unsophisticated; it's very easy for infection to spread. One of my best friends, Hugh Welsh, is Deputy General Counsel for the Port Authority of New York and New Jersey and Legal Counsel for the International Association of Ports and Harbors, a worldwide port organization with United Nations consultative status. I called him right away and said, 'We've got a problem.'"

In the past, different materials have been used as ballast, weight added to increase a ship's balance and efficiency while crossing the ocean. Romans used urns of wine and olive oil, and early seamen used cobblestones. The modern megaships that crisscross the oceans today use tons of ballast water, taken in and discharged at ports around the world. "Therefore," says Casale, "ships putting into North American ports carry not only the cargo intended, but unseen and unwelcome passengers—viable marine organisms and insidious pathogens." She explains that the introduction of nonindigenous species, such as the zebra mussel (*Dreissena polymorpha*), sea lamprey (*Petromyzon marinus*), Eurasian ruffle (*Gymnocephalus cernuns*), and Spiny Water Flea (*Bythotrephes cederstroemi*), into coastal waters is well known and well documented. The resulting economic impact has been the focus of much study, remedial action, and legislative initiatives. It is estimated that preventing zebra mussels (transported to the Great Lakes from Northern European waters) from clogging water supplies will cost billions of dollars over the next decade. The Nonindigenous Aquatic Nuisance Prevention and Control Act (1990) and the National Invasive Species Act (1996) instituted a national invasive species program in U.S. waters. The International Maritime Organization (IMO) has issued voluntary guidelines requesting members to exchange ballast water in open seas. However, Casale points out that "although the goals and intent are essential to reducing the transport of marine organisms, these efforts do not deal with the potential spread of pathogens. While it has been noted that ballast water capable of transporting mussels and fleas can also transport human bacterial pathogens, the public health issues—which have the potential for inflicting far more health and economic damage—have been virtually ignored."

Growing up in a very small, blue-collar New Jersey town populated by the descendants of immigrants, Casale always knew that she wanted to take care of sick people. After high school, she "did the obvious thing for a female in 1957. The choices were being a wife, secretary, teacher, or nurse; so I went to nursing school." While working at a hospital in Kentucky, she remembers, "A lot of the docs were saying to me, 'You know, you really don't think like a nurse—you kinda think like a doctor.' At that point I was thirty-six years old, had been divorced twice, was a single parent of four kids (ages five, six, fourteen, and fifteen), my second husband had taken off for Alaska and left me with huge debts, and my closest family was seven hundred miles away. So I laughed at the suggestion! Finally, one morning when I was working in the operating room the surgeon looked up at me and said, 'You don't have the courage to go to medical school.' The next morning I enrolled.

"First I had to complete two years of undergraduate courses. I took in boarders, traded rent for child-care, worked thirty hours a week, carried twenty credits a semester, and got straight As. It all worked out; the kids and I had a great time doing it. My daughter jokes that it sometimes felt like we were living in the middle of a Sidney Sheldon novel! It wasn't always easy, but it sure was fun." Casale did a residency in anesthesiology and practiced emergency medicine for eleven years. In 1996, she returned to medical school to do a second residency in preventive medicine and environmental health, and she received a Masters of Science in Public Health degree. She served as an assistant professor in the Department of Preventive Medicine and Environmental Health at the University of Kentucky College of Medicine and assistant Medical Director for the Delmarva Health Plan. She says that when she lived on the Eastern Shore of Maryland, she fell in love with the area and the Chesapeake Bay.

Following the Peruvian cholera outbreak, Casale coauthored a paper with Hugh Welsh titled "The International Transport of Pathogens in Ships' Ballast Water." Since its publication in the *Journal of Transportation, Law, Logistics and Policy,* the European Shipping Council and the IMO have formally reviewed the paper. Casale speaks at many meetings and seminars, and she has addressed the executive council of the International Cargo Handling Coordination Association (ICHCA), an international organization with members in more than ninety countries worldwide and consultative status with the United Nations. "We started getting the word out to the ports and international shippers and handlers," she says. The ICHCA accepted Casale and Welsh's recommendations to amend existing legislation to include pathogen transport in ballast water. The group also created an Invasive Species Council to develop a comprehensive plan to deal with the problem and took the issue to the United Nations and the IMO, which is considering an international treaty. President Clinton created a Cabinet-level council to consider the ballast water problem.

"The practice of taking on ballast water in one port and discharging it in another is a game of ecological roulette," Casale warns. She explains that there are about fifty-five thousand vessel entrances into ports in the United States, and ballast water transports about three thousand species of animals and plants around the world every day. One survey identified 367 different kinds of organisms in the ballast water of ships transporting goods from Japan to Coos Bay, Oregon. In addition to marine organisms, bilge and ballast waters contain many bacteria and viruses. "Although some of these are not pathogenic in their native habitat," Casale explains, "they may evolve into pathogens for marine life or humans during their adaptation to a new ecosystem. It is this adaptation, combined with the potential contamination of municipal water systems, that poses the greatest danger."

Cargo ships release an estimated 48 million gallons of ballast water into U.S. waters each day, with 200,000 gallons pouring hourly into the Chesapeake Bay alone by ship traffic destined to Baltimore and Norfolk. The average amount of ballast for container ships in the Port of Baltimore is about 5,228 tons (1,395,000 gallons). Each large tanker can carry 198,000 tons (52,834,000 gallons) of ballast. Colliers (coal ships), frequent visitors to Bay ports, may present the greatest problem of all. Because they come into port with no cargo onboard, they rely entirely on ballast—equal to or more than that of large tankers—to keep trim on the incoming voyage. They discharge this ballast water as loaders fill the ship with coal. Over 80 percent of this water is discharged into the harbors and estuaries when a ship comes in to port.

The National Oceanic and Atmospheric Administration initially thought the answer was to exchange water on the high seas. "As it turns out," Casale reports, "it's not a solution because unbalancing a ship's load in heavy seas can be dangerous to the ship and crew. And often it's more of a 'swish and spit' than an effective flushing. Plus, with the big container ships, to save weight, the hold is so thin that emptying the ballast tank can actually cause that section of the ship to implode from the pressure of the water on the outside. Exchanging ballast at sea discharges the organisms into high-speed currents like the Gulf Stream, which causes an even bigger problem.

"The solution," she concludes, "is shared responsibility. Nobody can afford to do it alone. It looks like the obvious answer is to chlorinate the water after it's taken on in the departure port, let it mix out on the ocean, test it before entering the next port, and add more chlorine if necessary. It's illegal to dump chlorinated water into an estuary, so they'd chemically dechlorinate it before discharging into the next harbor.

"The good thing is that everybody—shipping lines, crews, ports, cargo handlers, governments—is beginning to recognize there's a problem. It's been heartening to see how many people really care. Most developing countries are trying to improve their sewage handling and make their water more potable, but that's expensive. Sustainable development is difficult, and it's going to be a long time before some of them stop dumping 80 percent of their raw sewage into the harbors. This issue is very significant to the Chesapeake Bay region because in addition to the threat to human health, there are problems with oysters (which keep the water clean and filtered), fish, and crabs. There's been discussion about marine organisms losing their immune systems, which usually causes significant infectious disease, resulting in massive fish and marine mammal kills. Keeping invasive organisms out of the watershed will benefit marine economics, improve water quality, and enhance the natural beauty of our estuaries and harbors."

Standing alongside the mammoth vessels at the Port of Baltimore, its loading docks stacked with huge containers, automobiles, and tractors, it's easy to be overwhelmed by the tremendous scale of the problem. Casale, a petite woman, admits that at first she was dismayed by the enormity of the situation. But she smiles when she says, "Little things can have big impacts. Although we've destroyed many of our waterways, they can come back. Everyone hopes to contribute something to improve their world. I think I've found my way!"

RICHARD J. CALLAHAN ∽

Gambrills, Maryland

Eagle Scout

ANYONE WHO THINKS THE ALL-AMERICAN BOY IS A THING OF the past has yet to meet Richard Callahan. At age seventeen, with a 4.5 grade point average, Callahan is class valedictorian, has appeared on *Its Academic,* speaks three languages (English, Spanish, and Chinese), and is enrolled to study chemistry and Chinese at Dartmouth College. He plays the piano and violin, sings and dances in school plays, and is a model son and good friend. Before graduating from Arundel High School, he was vice president of the Earth Club, captain of the chess team, and a board member of the Key Club. He tutors chemistry and math students, volunteers at the local hospital, and is active in his church. "I like to help other people," he acknowledges. He is also a seasoned mountain climber and has earned thirty-six merit badges in the nine years he has participated in the Boy Scouts of America program.

In November 1996, at age fifteen, Callahan began working toward his Eagle Scout badge, a rank that only 4 percent of Boy Scouts achieve. Projects usually entail something like building a storage shed for a church youth group or planting a community garden. But Callahan's project, conceived in simplicity, grew into an entanglement of expansion that tested and refined his leadership abilities. "Because I had grown to really like nature," he recounts, "when I was deciding on an action plan, a Bay watershed project was foremost in my mind. I also wanted to do something that would make a difference and be remembered." The month before, Callahan outlines, the governor's riparian forest buffer panel had submitted their final report outlining the benefits of planting trees along streams; the governor subsequently signed an initiative to plant 2,010 miles of forest buffer in the Chesapeake Bay watershed by the year 2010.

A *riparian forest buffer* is another name for trees planted along a streambed to help clean the water in the stream. The buffer is located between pollution sources, such as pastures, cultivated fields, and lawns, and a body of water. Four hundred years ago, 95 percent of the land that drains into the Chesapeake Bay was forested. Today, less than 60 percent of those forests remain. Trees are important because they protect water quality, provide habitat, and are a food source for fish. In addition, when trees die and fall into a stream, they slow down the water, providing a place for fish to spawn. Every day, thousands of gallons of fertilizers, pesticides, chemicals, and other pollutants wash into the Bay. Trees help reduce this nutrient runoff and prevent soil erosion by trapping sediments and other pollutants with their roots. They also absorb carbon dioxide

from the air and give off oxygen. However, Callahan points out, "with more than 100,000 miles of widely differing streams winding throughout the Bay watershed, there is no 'one size fits all' formula for the forest buffer."

Soon after the governor's initiative was signed, Callahan met with a contact at the Alliance for the Chesapeake Bay (ACB), who suggested that a public awareness project, like posting signs about riparian forest buffers, would be a timely tie-in. "So I wrote up a proposal to design and install ten signs in Anne Arundel County and had it approved by my scoutmaster," he begins. "When it went to the troop committee for approval, they suggested adding an informational pamphlet. All along the way, the project increased in scope and magnitude. At just about every turn, I learned that the road to success is full of detours and roadblocks. Perhaps that's just as well," he shrugs. "If I had known ahead of time exactly what I was getting into, I might have passed up a wonderful opportunity." For more than a year, Callahan marshaled county approvals, raised funds, solicited property owners, and mobilized classmates and fellow scouts.

"First, I needed to come up with some money. We worked it out so I could apply to the Chesapeake Bay Trust [CBT] for a grant (funded through the state income tax and the sale of "Treasure the Chesapeake" commemorative license plates). Here I was, a tenth-grader, and the principle author for a grant request to CBT! I thought, 'Wow, this is starting to sound pretty fun!' I was fifteen and had until eighteen to achieve the Eagle Scout rank, so I decided to do a really good project. I worked up budget figures for cost estimates and 'matching funds' so we could submit a grant proposal. We put in a request for almost $3,000, and they gave us $1,000. Between that and donations of time [465 total hours], transportation [1,500 miles], and materials—lumber, cement, tools, nuts and bolts—we made it work."

However, the grant was awarded "with a little contingency: only when I had the ten sites lined up and a finished copy of the pamphlet could I get the $1,000." For help with the layout of the signs and pamphlet, Callahan put together a "research and development team" of Boy Scouts. "I showed them a few videos on forest buffers and we started designing the signs, which needed to be easy to read, difficult to vandalize, fairly inexpensive, contain good information about streamside forests, and look good." He admits to "minor motivational problems" when trying to get the team to pay attention to the video and develop serious slogans (they liked "May the Forest Be With You"). "We came up with all sorts of incredible ideas using neat pictures and even a talking tree named 'Hobs' (Help Our Bay Survive) that was eventually used on the cover of the pamphlet." In the end, cost considerations forced them to produce the signs in two colors with a simple diagram. They came up with an eye-catching title: "Trees at Work," and added three major points about why forest buffers are important. Lastly, they displayed the logos of the CBT and the ACB, along with the phone number of the Chesapeake Regional Information Service (CRIS) so people could call for more information. "A good friend of mine who is a computer whiz helped produce the pamphlet. It was neat because he wasn't on the original R&D team, but that ended up being a good thing because he was the guy who didn't know anything about forest buffers. He could tell if something was confusing or didn't make sense."

Next Callahan started contacting state parks with forest buffer demonstration sites already in place and private landowners to get permission for installations. "These calls were stressful for me," he confesses, "since I had to sound very professional and not leave them with the impression that I was 'just some teenager.' My worries increased when almost every person I spoke with requested a project proposal. So, I'm thinking, 'Yeah, now I need a whole project proposal!'"

Using the grant approval and completed pamphlet as a project proposal, and working through last minute complications with the sign manufacturer, Callahan finally jumped through all the necessary hoops, and, in October 1997, he was ready to post the signs. "This is a year later," he recollects, "and we're still getting through the *planning* phase. The *execution* phase—when my friends helped me buy the stuff, load it into cars, and put up the signs—that part was easy! When you're a teenager," he reveals, "it's much easier to lead other teenagers than to lead adults!"

Working with Troop 813, the ACB, concerned citizens, park rangers, and the Earth Club, doing installations every weekend, Callahan got the signs, along with two thousand informational pamphlets, installed before the end of the year. As it turned out, only one sign out of the ten was posted in Anne Arundel County, installed at a hard-won site on a heavily traveled, forested stretch of Route 450 near his home. Other signs were erected throughout the state: at Mount Pleasant Farm and Fair Hill Natural Resource Management Area in Cecil County, at Gunpowder

Falls State Park and Boordy Vineyards in Baltimore County, at Rocks State Park, Rockfield Park, and Eden Mill Park in Harford County, and at Fair Hill Natural Resource Management Area in Montgomery County. A site in Carroll County, which was still establishing its demonstration area, was reserved for a future installation.

In early 1998, Callahan submitted his final report in a two-inch thick binder to his scoutmaster. "It was really neat," he exclaims. "One person could not have done this project. It was many people getting together: politicians, scouts, environmentalists, my friends and my family. I was real happy that my dad, who took me on so many great trips, got to be part of it before he passed away last year. I certainly learned a lot. I hope other people of all ages will, too. That's the point."

Callahan's work exemplifies the Boy Scout directive, "Leave the campsite as you found it, if not better, for you are just passing through." In conclusion, he says, while people will read his signs for many years to come, "the real test is to see if we have five hundred miles of forest buffer in Maryland, and 2,010 miles in the Bay watershed by 2010. That's the ultimate goal. People react to problems like *Pfiesteria* by boycotting fish. But that doesn't stop the problem. A primary way to stop the pollution of our waters is to plant trees. Maybe my project will help in some small way."

DANIEL J. FISHER ∽

Queenstown, Maryland

Environmental Biologist

A S AN ENVIRONMENTAL BIOLOGIST SPECIALIZING IN AQUATIC toxicology at the University of Maryland's Wye Research and Education Center (WREC) in Queenstown, Maryland, Dan Fisher studies the effects of pollution on the Chesapeake Bay and its tributaries. He directs a bioassay laboratory that is run by the Maryland Department of the Environment (MDE) and housed in the WREC Environmental Research Laboratory. There, Fisher and his staff conduct effluent toxicity compliance testing on industrial and municipal discharges into state waters. Fisher has managed the bioassay lab under contract since 1987, and he has written more than forty technical reports and publications on a wide variety of environmental issues.

He reports that the three most critical areas of toxic concern in the Chesapeake Bay are the Anacostia and Elizabeth Rivers and the Baltimore Harbor. "One of the major concerns in these areas is contaminants in the bottom sediments and their impact on the environment," he explains. "We do a lot of sediment toxicity work, where we bring samples to the lab and expose clean organisms to them, to see if the sediments can support life. Today, the harbor bottom isn't quite at the 'black mayonnaise' stage, but it's pretty close," he explains with easy-going expertise. ("Black mayonnaise" is a term used to describe foul, toxic sediment covering bay and harbor bottoms that have become anaerobic, that is, devoid of oxygen and thus unable to support life.) Measurements taken in the early 1990s in the Bay's deep channels revealed that 15 percent of the 15-trillion-gallon volume had little or no oxygen. Final results from Fisher's study indicated acute toxicity at approximately 25 percent of the sites sampled in the Baltimore Harbor–Patapsco River system.

Today, Fisher is studying sediment samples as part of a study in conjunction with the University of Maryland and the MDE to establish chemical and biological background information on causes of contamination in the Inner Harbor. The University's Chesapeake Biological Laboratory in Solomons, Maryland, collected sediments from eighty stations and analyzed them for metals and organic pollutants. The laboratory also analyzed the existing benthic community structure at forty-five of these sites. (*Benthic* describes the bottom life zone of a water body, inhabited mostly by decomposers, detritus, suspension-feeders, insect larvae, and fish that eat these organisms, such as catfish, spot, and croakers.)

"In addition," Fisher explains, "twenty-five of those forty-five samples were delivered to my lab for toxicity testing using bioindicators [organisms that, by changing behaviors or dying, may indicate the presence of hazardous pollutants that have escaped other detection methods]. Meaning we put cultured crustaceans called estuarine amphipods in the samples, and observed them to see if they would survive, grow, and reproduce. It's a neat organism because it's a native species that lives naturally in areas from almost no salinity to full-strength seawater. It also lives in sediments that are almost completely sandy to ones that are almost entirely muddy. So it spans the whole range of possible environments that you might want to test in the Chesapeake.

"The theory is, if you put the amphipods in any healthy bottom sample, they will live, flourish, and reproduce. If they die, the sample is considered acutely toxic. But we have an end point of, not only 'will they survive?' but also 'will they *reproduce?*' If their reproductive ability is impaired, the species will not survive, and the sample is considered chronically toxic. But we don't know from the test what ingredient in that sample is toxic. That's why we analyze the chemistry and benthic community structure to determine toxic chemical levels, and if the distribution of species represents a healthy community. This is called the 'Sediment Quality Triad': chemistry, community structure, and toxicity. With all three of those parts we can make a judgment about how healthy the sediment is, and what's causing the toxicity. Some cases result in no chemistry or toxicity problems, but no live amphipods in the field, because the *habitat* has been physically destroyed to the extent that they can't survive."

So even "dead" sediment samples are tested. "We do it all the time, because it helps distinguish between habitat problems and toxics problems. We bring the samples to the lab and aerate the water, so there's no dissolved oxygen problem. In a lot of these areas there's no dissolved oxygen in the bottom, which is part of the reason why there's no life. The Inner Harbor is a dead-end part of the estuary because of the way it's been built up. The natural streams that used to feed into this area have been built over. There's very little flushing, not a lot of water movement or input from other sources, except for runoff from the streets of Baltimore. So not much can live in the sediment. When we pull up a sample it just reeks of sulfur dioxide [the 'rotten egg' smell]. We have to wear gloves when we manipulate those samples. Up in the creeks where there's not much industry, there's good survival, but still a gradient of toxicity. The range of effects in the Harbor is quite large," he says. "Some areas support 100 percent survival, in others all the amphipods tested die; some areas support reproduction similar to control-sample reproduction, and others support no reproduction."

The MDE will use Fisher's findings to help direct future cleanup efforts in the harbor, which often pose a dilemma. "Do we want to spend money on the areas that are so severely contaminated that it's going be expensive to clean them up?" Fisher proposes, "or do we want to concentrate on less polluted, more residential areas?

"Sediment toxicity testing is going to be increasingly important," he advises, "because, as we clean up inputs, there are still huge amounts of contaminants already trapped in the sediment. Although the system reaches equilibrium, the chemicals are slowly released back into the water column. So the sediment is now acting as a *source* for contaminants—either by seeping out of the sediment into the water, or contaminants getting into the food chain. It will probably never cycle out. In most cases, it gets covered up, which is what happened to the Kepone in the southern Bay."

Fisher conducted his masters and Ph.D. research on Kepone, a potent pesticide that, in 1975, manufacturers discharged in large quantities into the James River at Hopewell, Virginia. Concern over possible carcinogenic effects on people eating large quantities of Kepone-contaminated fish led to a ban on commercial fishing in ninety-eight miles of the river, from Richmond to the Hampton Roads Bridge Tunnel. The ban was lifted in 1989. However, while the Kepone has been gradually buried by sediment, making it less accessible to fish and plant life, it is not gone. Because there is still some concern that a severe storm could stir up the sediments, Kepone levels continue to be monitored.

"Because it was too economically and environmentally damaging to get rid of the Kepone by dredging the entire James River," Fisher continues, "the most realistic thing to do was to continue to monitor it as it got covered up. There's no more Kepone being made—but it's still in the river. It doesn't go away, it just sits there. In estuaries there's a fairly rapid sedimentation rate, so now it's buried under new sediments."

Accelerated sedimentation may have applications in the future. "In the Baltimore Harbor," Fisher explains, "one of the techniques they may use at bad sites is to cap them by discharging clean sediments over top of 'hot spots' to bury them. In most areas of the Bay most of the living takes place in the upper couple inches of sediment. Even in a natural system, there's no oxygen transfer between the upper and lower layers, so nothing lives underneath, except species of bacteria that don't need oxygen.

"There is a tremendous amount of sediment removal necessary to keep the channel dredged fifty feet for shipping. From a disposal standpoint, anything from the mouth of the harbor inward is considered toxic. A capping system would eliminate having to relocate toxic dredge material. There are enough problems trying to figure out where to put *clean* sediments. Bringing in unpolluted materials from outside the harbor would kill two birds with one stone by providing disposal sites for clean sediment, and by slowly lowering contaminants by covering them up."

He goes on to say that historically the focus has been on reduction of inputs from factories and wastewater treatment plants into state waters. "All facilities with point sources that discharge waste into state waters operate under a mandatory permit. In accordance with the Clean Water Act, that permit prohibits discharging anything that's toxic to organisms—which kills them or affects growth or reproduction. My bioassay lab does effluent testing, where we introduce organisms to predischarge [prior to dilution by the receiving stream] waste samples. From the permit and the samples we can determine what is in the waste. If we find it's toxic, then it's up to the industry to find out what's causing the toxicity and get rid of it. Depending on the complexity of the problem, it can take from months to years."

Fisher's written report on the effluent-testing program concludes that "a biomonitoring program following accepted test procedures can reduce the toxicity of point-source effluents to receiving waters." He explains that his group is a semi-independent entity that "basically serves as a police-type of regulatory tool, conducting tests to determine if industries are meeting environmental requirements. We use a biomonitoring procedure called 'whole effluent toxicity monitoring,' where we actually let the *organisms* tell us if waste is toxic. Maryland was one of the first states to use it."

Fisher says that most industries don't resist permit regulations. "There are some bad actors, but most companies know it's bad publicity if their waste kills fish. If they can't meet the environmental regulations, then they're out of business. In every case that I know of, there are ways to clean up waste. Whether they can afford to pay for them, or whether it's more cost-effective to shut down, is another story. But that doesn't happen much. Most of the techniques used to clean this stuff up are not super expensive. Once they get it cleaned up, it's fairly easy to keep it that way. We continue to test these facilities to make sure they are meeting their permit requirements."

Another example of science and industry cooperating can be seen in Fisher's work with the MDE and the EPA. Rain and storm water were sampled during deicing "events" (clearing snow and ice during storms) at Baltimore/Washington International Airport (BWI). "For years people thought the deicing agent, ethylene glycol, wasn't a serious environmental problem because it's organic, and certain organisms like to eat it, so it would disappear pretty quickly. The problem is, in the middle of winter it's cold and the bugs don't act that fast. And since they were discharging so much of it, it would overwhelm the system and eventually end up in the Bay. Because it was a point source, the airport was forced by their permit to look at this and, once we found out the severity of the toxicity problem, to design ways to stop discharging that waste."

Studies conducted by Fisher's group in 1993 concluded that deicing discharge is a serious environmental concern when it drains into the Chesapeake watershed. "Our reports led MDE to recommend that a system be implemented to rectify the situation. Deicing agents are a critical component of keeping planes flying in the winter, so they didn't want to say the airport couldn't use them, because there would be a direct impact on safety. BWI complied with MDE recommendations by building a special deicing pad and containment system. Prior to completion, the airport was required to collect fluids with sweeper trucks for offsite treatment, until the new facilities were put into use in 1996.

"This is an excellent example of science and a concerned industrial facility working together for the betterment of the Bay," Fisher says with satisfaction. "Before we did our study, the deicing agent was discharged right off the runway. Now they collect and store it in a 600,000-gallon tank so it doesn't run off. Then they slowly discharge it into the sewer system of a local wastewater treatment plant, which is a controlled environment with microorganisms that break down waste. Ethylene glycol is a good food source for some of the bugs in the treatment plant—they chow down on it. As long as it's metered in very slowly, it gets broken down there."

These approaches, along with the findings of groups like Fisher's, will continue to improve the well-being of the Bay. One of Fisher's recently published papers states that the frequency and severity of toxic effluents "have decreased dramatically since the inception of the [effluent testing] program," resulting in elimination of acute toxicity in over 200 million gallons of effluents per day. "From a standpoint of toxics—stuff that comes out of the pipe—the health of the Bay is getting better," Fisher confirms. "Those are the types of wastes and discharges that we can control because we can test them and identify a problem that industry has to fix or they can't continue to discharge. MDE and most of the states have done a good job in most instances of regulating point-source discharge. Now the big problem that we face is non–point-source pollution—the nitrogen, phosphorous, and toxic chemicals that are running off, not only from farm use, but from urban centers and residential properties. Residential runoff can be a major source of pollution, especially as the population grows. These problems are much harder to monitor. The same thing happens on the Eastern Shore with farming. On one hand, farming is the biggest industry in the state, and the farmers are proud to tell you that. On the other hand, they are the most difficult industry in the state to regulate because they don't have pipes—agricultural runoff discharges from a very wide area.

"It's not a trivial problem," Fisher warns. "What will happen is, we'll get as much as we can out of reducing toxics from point sources, and we'll still be left with the problem of runoff and atmospheric inputs from factories. A lot of pollutants come from burning fossil fuels, including auto emissions that settle down. Scientists are finding chemicals like PAHs [polycyclic aromatic hydrocarbons] in areas of the Bay that aren't located near industry. When you burn petroleum products, you get mercury and PAHs, which are transported through the air to sediments throughout the Bay.

"There are a lot of problems that still need to be solved, a lot of work that has to be done. I've seen us clean up our act. But long-term habitat destruction and low-level pollution persist. We have to wonder, 'How clean can we make the Chesapeake Bay and still maintain a sound economy and have places for people to live?' It's a pipe dream to think we can return to how it was before there was such great human impact. And you can't rush science. It's a slow, tedious process. But it's pretty cool—it's good, fulfilling work. My perspective is to look at the whole ecosystem. Reaching a point of balance is what it's all about."

PATRICK J. FASANO ∽

Oxford, Pennsylvania

Forestry Consultant

A N OLD SAYING GOES, "YOU CAN'T SEE THE FOREST FOR THE trees." The unique part of Pat Fasano's work is that he sees the forest *and* the trees. "Sound forestry management starts with a long-range plan," he says. "Conducting a timber stand analysis prior to harvesting or to determine the best forestry management application is essential. Unlike many lumber mills that take every tree over fourteen inches in diameter—which doesn't take any thought and is a very poor application for long-term management—my work is not a cookie cutter deal; it's a combination of art and science."

Ever since he was a kid, Fasano wanted to be a wildlife biologist. In 1975, he received a Bachelor of Science degree in Wildlife Management from the West Virginia University School of Forestry. He began his career as a procurement forester for a New Jersey lumber mill. When one of the mill's suppliers, a resort in the Poconos, offered him a job supervising fifty-five hundred acres of property for forestry and recreational activities, Fasano says, "I loved the place so much that my wife and I packed up our newborn daughter and moved to Skytop, Pennsylvania." He subsequently served as watershed superintendent and director for the Octoraro Watershed Association, managing three thousand acres of property surrounding the 600-acre Chester Water Authority drinking water reservoir. In 1990, Fasano became affiliated with Forest Management Associates (FMA), an integrated team that has a unique outlook on harvesting timber. In 1998, he branched out and established Comprehensive Land Services, his own land planning and management company. He has managed over eighty-five hundred acres of property, primarily in Pennsylvania but also in other parts of the Chesapeake watershed. He performs forestry consultation, riparian buffer management, watershed planning, and land conservation. He regularly advises the Brandywine Conservancy and Octoraro Watershed Association, as well as many state, nonprofit, and private entities.

"I've been involved in the timber harvesting industry for twenty-five years," he says, "and each woodlot still provides a new challenge. My prevailing thought is to leave the best trees and remove competition from inferior ones. My approach is to conduct a series of light thinnings on an eight- to twelve-year rotation. This gentle augmentation of the entire ecosystem is a new approach to attaining increased productivity and health through minimal impact to Pennsylvania's forests."

Pennsylvania (meaning "Penn's Woods," for founder William Penn) was once 99.8 percent forested. Some of the world's finest hardwoods grow here, and trees are the state's most valuable natural resource. Each year, mills deliver about 1 billion feet of lumber, valued at $4 billion, to domestic and international markets. In the nineteenth century, these timberlands rang with the sounds of axes and saws as a booming industry created lumberjacks and millionaires. Crews bound logs destined to become masts or spars into huge rafts and floated them hundreds of miles down the swift-flowing Susquehanna River to places as faraway as Havre de Grace, Maryland, where they were disassembled and sold to eager buyers from Baltimore and Philadelphia. At one time, in Williamsport, at the Long Reach of the West Branch Susquehanna, a person could walk for miles upriver on a solid bed of tightly packed logs, released into springtime's swollen current and collected in a log boom (a floating toll barrier to catch logs as they come downstream).

By the end of the 1860s, more than a million logs had passed through the boom and the race was on to harvest the centuries-old virgin forests. Susan Stranahan, chronicling the Susquehanna's history, wrote, "Into the West Branch forests marched an army of loggers, and the trees came down like tall grass before a giant scythe." The theory was that, through a natural progression, timber resources could never be depleted. However, this theory failed to take into account the effects of forest fires and what would happen downstream once the hills to the north and west were rapidly denuded of their protective cover. By the end of the nineteenth century, rapacious loggers had all but eradicated Pennsylvania's virgin forests. By the early twentieth century, the lumber industry was well into its long decline.

"Logging throughout the Chesapeake had been like a plague of locusts, moving westward, taking the best, clearing for agriculture, industry, and homes," Fasano says. "Every one of our job sites has been cut at one time and most have a history of disregard for the future. Historically, woodlots have been 'highgraded.' This practice targets all trees of high quality, leaving a residual stand of inferior trees. The reason is twofold—the landowner receives more money and it's the easiest and most productive and profitable method for the logger. Most don't analyze the stand, mark trees, or cull. Cutters swarm the site like bees and the resulting woodlot looks like it's been hit by a bomb! This common 'forestry' practice gives timber harvesting a very bad name. Yet it is the most common practice of timber harvesting in our area. Some landowners scoff at the idea of sustainable forestry because the financial considerations are vastly different compared to highgrade applications. I decline to work for those clients because my ethics, credibility, and referral base would suffer greatly. I tell them I'm the wrong man for the job."

Fasano works closely with Tim Nilan (pictured on right), president and professional forester for FMA. Together they review every tract, conducting a "point sample cruise" and timber stand analysis. They assess many elements, including past logging practices, the number and condition of trees, percent stocking (species composition), volume by board foot (the measurement by which standing timber is bought and sold), timber quality, residual stocking and spacing, mast and coppice regeneration, aesthetics, and objectives of the landowner (e.g., maximum income, long-term productivity, wildlife habitat and game management, hiking and riding trails, preservation of rare or threatened plant communities). "By reviewing a host of factors and computer calculations, all of those elements tell us the right application," Fasano explains. "The selection method of harvesting is the only way to assure that the remaining timber is properly spaced to grow to maturity. Prescribing the same method for cutting, regardless of the stand, can lead to terrible long-term results," he warns.

After determining factors such as thinning method and marketable board footage, Fasano negotiates a contract with the landowner. Then he and FMA's forest technician Frank Rohrer, Jr. (pictured, center) use paint to mark mature "sawlog" trees. Additionally, they mark diseased, poorly formed, and cull trees with an *X*, slating them for removal to improve the species composition and spacing of the stand. Before a job begins, Fasano painstakingly plans the implementation of the actual harvest. This includes surveying property boundaries, devising haul-road access to public routes, laying out skid trails, designing the loading deck area, and submitting a timber harvest plan for approval by various government agencies. He also addresses sediment and erosion control, including buffer zones for riparian areas, construction of water bars (diversion ditches in sloped skid trails to slow storm water runoff), and restoration of the site. "The process is extremely time-consuming and tedious," Fasano admits. "Often it takes two or three months to get approval for something that only requires a half-hour review. The process can be very frustrating, but we *always* play by the rules.

"More often than not," he adds, "loggers will come in with three skidders and six men, and they're gone before anybody knows what happened. It's very challenging because we're competing with others who can often pay more because they're profit-driven. They cut it fast, make their profit based on volume, and move on to the next job. Most of the guys who are in the woods are strictly tree-cutters—if it has paint on it, they cut it. If we marked one hundred trees and they marked one hundred trees, they'd be very different ones. They may be similar in volume, but probably grossly different in value because they would take the cream and we would leave a lot of the cream for the next thinning. It's difficult for some landowners to differentiate and visualize why we're not comparing apples to apples. It isn't always a level playing field. We maintain integrity and know that what we do is the best job. But that doesn't always put food on the table or make the payment on that $170,000 skidder." He goes on to explain that, unlike many loggers who adopt a "pay as we cut" format that gives them an "out" on the contract price, FMA pays a guaranteed balance before cutting. "Often, based solely on my recommendation, Tim will buy a job site-unseen. As the contractor, he's the one doing the cash-flow dance, and I'm the one that better be right about the inventory and quality of those trees.

"It's a unique scenario for us to be in the woods, each having a degree in forestry and the technical understanding that we share," Fasano reveals. "Tim and I are both state-certified in forest stewardship. Our goal is low-impact forestry—to think about den trees, snags, brush piles, and habitat. We're not thinking solely about the value of trees as lumber. We have to find the balance between cutting as thinly as possible and commercial viability. We also bring in issues like watersheds, water quality, and ecological communities. Everything that we do, we try to do it right. Some methods may hurt our profit margin, but they give us great referrals, which are the heartwood of our operation."

Fasano goes on to explain that *heartwood* is a forestry term for the center of a tree. It is, he says, an ironic word because the life stream of a tree lies just inside the bark in the cambium, conduits where water and nutrient uptake flow to the branches and leaves; heartwood is actually deadwood. That is why hollow trees can survive. This is also why girdling into a tree's cambium layer will kill it. "For me, it's the opposite," he imparts. "It's way bigger than skin deep; it's in my heart! That's the paradox of viewing timber as board feet of lumber versus the basis for a productive ecosystem. Holistic land management views market value as only one component. In the fragmented and poorly managed woodlots in our region, I consider many things before I mark a tree. I always think about what trees I should *leave* in the woods for the future. A gentle hand and thoughts for tomorrow guide my judgment. My objective is to leave the best for the future."

LESLIE MATHIESON AND CREW ∽

Arnold, Maryland

Wetland Nursery Workers

Like the intertwining vegetation of the wetlands they help create, Leslie Mathieson and her crew are deeply rooted in their environment. These workers are employed by Providence Center, a community-oriented, private, nonprofit corporation serving Anne Arundel County, which provides professionally managed and individually designed programs for adults with disabilities. Providence Center offers an employment enterprises division, crafts and pottery programs, a woodshop, and an art institute. Mathieson has worked for fifteen years in horticulture. Her current position is production manager for the center's horticulture program, which generates income through the sales of hanging baskets, seasonal crops, and wetland plants. The tidy complex of computerized greenhouses is an anthill of activity performed by a conglomeration of extraordinary workers. Their joyful smiles, ingenuousness, and hard work make up for what they may lack in mental and physical capacity. Mathieson, a devoted cross between line boss and coach, insists on taking a backseat to the accomplishments of her crew members (shown here, left to right, on a Magothy River beach with Mathieson are Carver Jones and William Boyd, and in the greenhouse are Michael Holbrook and Shannon Hunt). "Willie's learning all the time, aren't you, you rascal?!" she teases as William beams.

Since 1981, in a joint effort with Anne Arundel Community College Environmental Center, horticulture crews have raised a wide selection of shoreline grasses, herbaceous perennials, shrubs, and trees used for the creation and restoration of wetlands. These include the quintessential aquatic emergent grasses, smooth cordgrass (*Spartina alterniflora*) and saltmeadow cordgrass (*Spartina patens*), which the program produces by the tens of thousands. The many other flora cultivated here, such as duck potato (*Sagittaria latifolia*), stout bulrush (*Scirpus robustus*), giant smartweed (*Polygonum pennsylvanicum*), rose mallow (*Hibiscus moscheutos*), and sweet gum (*Liquidumbar styraciflua*), are aesthetic and stabilizing, trapping sediment and providing habitat, food, and cover for waterfowl and other aquatic life. In the near future, the crew will add submerged aquatic vegetation and water gardening plants to their wetlands catalog.

Wetland restoration is a new science, developed in the last twenty years or so. In the past a structural approach was taken, using bulkhead retaining walls to "harden" the shoreline. Now, in place of these artificial devices, which have little environmental benefit, bioengineering and natural techniques, like plant replacement, are often used to control erosion by reclaiming and re-creating habitat. It should be noted, however, that we cannot reestablish the amount of wetlands that historically existed; we can only stop the net loss of current wetlands. Also, ecological restoration often falls far short of fully restoring damaged ecosystems. Preventing ecosystem damage in the first place is more effective and much cheaper.

According to the Chesapeake Bay Foundation, the Bay watershed has lost 60 percent of its wetlands, a double-whammy in areas where the harmful effects of growth and development could have been offset by the wetlands developers destroyed. The health of the Bay is inextricably linked to wetlands. Wetlands, often called the kidneys of an ecosystem, help maintain the quality of coastal waters by diluting, filtering, and settling out sediments, excess nutrients, and pollutants through a thick tangle of emergent plants and grassroots like those produced at Providence Center. In addition, wetlands protect lives and property during floods by stabilizing and anchoring shorelines, and they act as a buffer against storm damage and erosion.

Wetlands are transitional zones, regions containing a highly diverse mixture of species in a tightly linked food chain. Estuaries, swamps, and marshes are among the earth's most highly productive ecosystems, comparable to rainforests. It has been estimated that one acre of tidal estuary provides about $75,000 worth of annual "biocapital" in free waste treatment. And, because grasses are vital food sources for fish and other aquatic life that humans eat, that same acre has an annual value of about $83,000 when production of fish and recreational value are included.

Providence Center's horticultural program is beneficial not only to the environment but also to its workers. "This is a wonderful opportunity for them," Mathieson says. She oversees twenty-one workers and three staff members, performing about forty different tasks. Workers are paid on a piece-rate basis. "We break the tasks down according to production needs, then assign the workers various jobs so they will be successful. Quality control is a big issue, especially in wetland production, because there are standards that have to be met.

"It's a unique situation, because to manage this operation requires both a knowledge of retail greenhouse operations and the people skills to work with this clientele—behavioral issues, the need to refocus their attention, physical disabilities. I have a degree in human services, with a strong working knowledge of horticulture. It's my job to keep them motivated, safe, and comfortable."

The atmosphere here is productive yet low-key. Feelings and emotions are free-flowing and refreshing—with open smiles, boisterous greetings, candid musings, pouts, and hugs—as warm and close as the humid glass houses in which the clients work. As one man loads plants for transport to a nearby beach restoration, he good-naturedly tousles the hairy plant tops and, with an impish smile, bids them a fond farewell, "Aww, I'm going to miss you!" In another greenhouse, top-forty radio plays, with Elton John belting out, *How wonderful life is when you're in the world.* There is an obvious mutual affection between supervisors and workers. "Enjoying our work is an important attitude to convey. We want to make it a fun place to be and still have good production," Mathieson confirms.

Plant production begins in a storage shed of sundry jars sloshing with what looks like grass seed stuck to sponges, grimy coffee beans, or slippery pods; this is actually the carefully harvested seed of wetland plants. "Seed collection is a complex procedure," Mathieson explains. "We get our stock from the college. Their students collect wild seeds in the fall. They bring them back to their labs and analyze things like salinity levels, germination rates, and overwinter storage requirements. It's a great partnership because the students are being educated and we get viable seed."

The crew has three heavy production time frames, each spanning about eight weeks, beginning in January and running through May. "Workers take the seed out of the big jars and put them in saucers," Mathieson illustrates. "Then they sow a little pinch in each section of the plant tray. The seeds are all different sizes depending on the type, so the task changes for every crop. Some orders require thousands of plants, so it can be quite a daunting task. Our workers enjoy physical work and the security of repetition."

"I like watering. It's a good job," Michael confirms.

"The interest and willingness of our group is very consistent," Mathieson continues. "Our employees are trained for certain skills, such as filling trays with soil, sowing seed, tip cutting, fertilizing, watering, and grooming dead plant growth. We strive to introduce new tasks and expand training. Just like any other employer, we encourage increased production through learning more, attaining new goals, and picking up the speed."

The center's inventory and customer list are continually growing. "We raise the basic stuff, but we try to add new things all the time," Mathieson says. Landowners and other customers purchase directly from the greenhouses, while community associations, schools, and businesses contract with the center for large jobs. "There aren't many suppliers for these plant materials. We get orders from across the state and all along the East Coast. Sometimes we work from a prepared plan; other times we consult with the customer and make recommendations about what to plant."

Occasionally, workers perform on-site transplanting for projects aimed at erosion control and eradication of phragmites, an invasive perennial weed that outcompetes indigenous grasses and offers little food value to wildlife. Using a string line, a bulb planter, and numerous

SAVING THE BAY

trays of spiky grass plants, the crew sets up a production line, planting in neat rows that look like tufts of hair pulled through a hairdresser's frosting cap. "The first person digs the hole," Mathieson outlines. "The next one dumps in slow-release fertilizer, then, tray in arm, the next one inserts a transplant, and the last person tucks sand around it. We move back a foot at a time until the expanse is covered."

Today's sparse, freshly planted shoreline will, in a few years, be established and spreading to reclaim the river's edge. "It's a good feeling to know that, barring major destruction, these plants will be there for hundreds of years, working in balance with other living things," Mathieson projects. "We enjoy this work so much. It's so valuable to these people, to be involved in the whole process—starting with the seeds, watching them grow, and eventually seeing them planted on the shoreline. Our crews know they're contributing to the environment and helping the future of the Bay. It's a unique and very rewarding contribution to restoration of Bay watersheds."

JUSTIN LAHMAN ⤳

Easton, Maryland

Director of Mapping Services

JUSTIN LAHMAN IS A BRIGHT YOUNG FAMILY MAN WHO WORKS as Northeast Regional Director of Mapping Services at 3Di, LLC (pronounced "three dee eye," short for three-dimensional imaging), a geographic information firm. He has over twelve years of experience in computer science, photogrammetry (the science of making maps directly from photographs), and related mapping sciences. His primary responsibilities are to manage the 3Di Northeast photogrammetry business unit and to evaluate changes in new technology so that his division remains a leader in the industry. The facility has the feel of a scientific frontier: fast-paced, progressive, high-tech. Everything, from the computers to the file systems to the furniture, right down to the pencil sharpeners and message pads, is brand-spanking new.

A pioneer in geographic technologies, operating since 1974, 3Di was one of the country's first privately held photogrammetry companies. In 1993 3Di had a total of three employees; today Lahman works with more than sixty other photogrammetry employees on the leading edge of geographic information and product development. The company is a member of a consortium known as the Chesapeake Region Technical Center of Excellence, which is establishing the NASA Regional Application Center, allowing access to NASA research and technology. The consortium, which also includes research facilities, educational institutions, and state and local governments, focuses primarily on environmental issues, the Chesapeake Bay, and precision farming on the Eastern Shore. The firm is expanding rapidly and expects to employ nine hundred to twelve hundred people in the future, about one-third of whom would be located at the Eastern Shore headquarters.

A total spectrum of technology for the acquisition, analysis, and presentation of geographically oriented information is offered at 3Di. These technologies encompass three distinct yet overlapping areas: photogrammetry, GIS (global information systems), and remote sensing. "Very few other companies actually do all these applications," Lahman says enthusiastically. "It's a technology that's going to explode."

From the tool-making revolution of the Stone Age to the invention of the plow during the agricultural revolution to the coal-fired steam engine of the industrial revolution, technology has played a key role in human impact on the environment. In the early 1960s an environmental awakening in the United States led people to question unbridled progress, eroding their faith in technology. In recent years, the American environmental movement has moved from a general disenchantment with technology to an emphasis on certain technologies that reflect sustainable values. One dimension of this emphasis is the ability of technology to measure the extent of environmental damage and restoration. An important general principle, "standards based on best available technology," has evolved for setting governmental regulations, linking technological development to environmental standards.

Many environmentalists believe that the next significant development, an environmental revolution, will take these principles a step further by using technological innovation to help provide solutions to environmental problems. Photogrammetry is a geographic technology that opens up a new vista for data gathering and evaluation. Lahman (shown on the right) reviews shoreline and wetland maps of Queen Anne's County, Maryland, produced on an analytical stereo plotter by data acquisition group leader Brian Tolley (seated). This equipment uses digital orthochromatic (high-contrast, two-tone) photography to transcribe an aerial photograph, shot with a special stereo-lens camera called a "Wild RC 30," into a direct representation of the actual terrain. This technology minimizes the visual distortion of conventional single-lens aerial photography.

Explaining the advantage of deriving maps from an actual bird's-eye view of the earth, rather than the traditional planimetric and topographic techniques using ink, lines, symbols, and text, Lahman says, "An image is worth a thousand vectors." Not only does this technology offer increased interpretation, but it also allows end-users to see what actually makes up a site. For instance, the composition of a tree line, whether coniferous, hardwood, or wooded wetland, can be distinguished. Besides its ability to show more detail, the technology is more accurate and affordable than conventional mapping.

"We fly the job, get it controlled [surveyed with reference to ground points], and produce the orthoimage. Straightforward. Whereas it would take a survey team many years and many dollars to achieve the same detail and accuracy." In addition to charting such factors as erosion, wetland delineation and restoration, environmental impact and biomass studies, and critical areas, Lahman's department can also easily monitor and assess changes over time by simply updating the mapping data.

Monitoring and evaluation are two primary focuses of today's geographic technologies. GIS, the merging of cartographic mapping and database management, is a technology that, in Lahman's words, "manages data with a picture." For example, a database can be linked to a map, making it possible for erosion control personnel to simply click on a location or touch a computer screen to view a record of sea-level readings. In this way, data can be more easily managed, viewed, analyzed, and understood. These are vital functions for increasing the environmental awareness of those living and working in the Chesapeake Bay watershed.

Other technologies are revolutionizing the farming practices of the region. Use of the Global Positioning System (GPS), owned and operated by the U.S. Department of Defense, was once limited to the military, science, engineering, and big industry. But it has become cheap and accessible enough for individual use, opening up a whole new realm of agricultural technology called precision agriculture. Farmers can optimize pesticide and fertilizer use by custom-calibrating mixtures and application rates rather than applying uniform applications calculated from spot samples. Chemical companies, too, are interested in this data, which allows their customers improved benefits from their products.

Hyperspectral imagery is also instrumental in contemporary agricultural innovations. Using a hyperspectral sensor, one can view a band of information far beyond the spectral range of the human eye. "With the bands comes intelligent information," Lahman notes, such as detection of potential crop stress from pests or soil fungi. "This technology is making it big in the way of precision ag," Lahman explains. "We can fly over a field and tell you what vegetation is there. We can tell where the Canadian thistle is, so that just one square foot can be sprayed rather than the whole field. We can detect crop damage before it becomes visible to the naked eye. This leads to higher yields and better farm management, which means sustainability. The farmer can focus on prevention instead of defense and reaction.

"The technology is emerging mainly on large company farms in Pennsylvania and the Midwest. Nobody's harnessed it in the East where there are small, diverse farms with differing soil types. I've seen farmers that get most of their information from the county office, from outdated soil maps that are, if you'll pardon the expression, old as dirt. More and more the younger farmer has a college degree and is less reluctant about computers and other technologies. It takes time to educate people. We're the precursors of precision ag in the Bay area."

The future of these technologies certainly seems wide open and promising. As for the future of the Chesapeake Bay, Lahman is optimistic and progressive. "Increased integration of data and technology will result in better environmental monitoring capabilities in the future." For example, he explains, buffer zones could be enforced more effectively, and changes to the condition of the watershed as a result of growth and development could be exacted. A digital airborne sensor can provide information about factors such as nutrient runoff, a key issue in the current *Pfiesteria* dilemma.

Regarding *Pfiesteria,* Lahman notes, "It hasn't been validated that agricultural nutrient runoff is the cause. We don't know yet how or even if agriculture is responsible. There are so many other variables. What is the effect of increased urbanization and landfills? Are the commercial harbors involved? What's the effect of thermal pollution, industry dumping hot water into wetlands? Our access to NASA research and technology is being used to try to detect algae blooms by taking images of the Bay and its tributaries. Ideally, accurate data needs to be established before we react. We can lend a hand in that. As technology gets cheaper, accurate data will be increasingly available and reliable. It's only going to get better."

KAREN HARRIS OERTEL ❧

Kent Narrows, Maryland

Owner, Seafood Packinghouse and Restaurant

KAREN HARRIS OERTEL HAS SPENT A LIFETIME WORKING IN HER family's waterfront seafood business at Kent Narrows, where, connected by the Route 50 causeway, Kent Island shakes the hand of Queen Anne's County's mainland. The upper deck of the 450-seat Harris Crab House offers a spectacular view of the Chester River, Prospect and Eastern Bays, and the old Kent Narrows drawbridge. Oyster boats pull up to the adjacent dock to sell their catch to the W. H. Harris Seafood Packinghouse. The Harris family has been in the seafood industry for over fifty years, running one of the last remaining packinghouses in Maryland and shipping products across the United States and Canada. "One of the things that's made Harris a quality operation," Oertel reveals, "is that it's a very 'hands on,' family-operated organization. We enjoy talking to our customers about the Bay and the seafood industry." Although she knows this business like the back of her hand, Oertel is unsettled by the plight of the oyster in the Bay and the resultant inconstancy to her industry.

At one time, there were thirteen seafood-processing houses at Kent Narrows. "My father and brother were watermen," she recounts. "That's where our family heritage comes from. At one point, it was not unusual for us to ship out eight thousand gallons of oysters a week." Today, because of diminished local supply and a reduced labor force (making it necessary to bring in migrant labor during the peak season), the production line operates below capacity.

Oertel goes on to say that for the first time in the history of the industry, there is a machine that not only opens oysters but also kills bacteria and increases yields. "In five years it will revolutionize this industry," she predicts. "If the southern markets, which have been diminished by the threat of an oyster disease called *Vibrio*, can market their oyster as being safe for human consumption, grow their product year-round, get a better yield, and produce it cheaper, we're not going to be able to compete."

Oertel hopes that public awareness will help revive the struggling industry, and several times a month she guides tours through the packinghouse. Here Oertel talks with, left to right, shuckers Penny Ross, Christine "Pee Wee" Atkins, and Helen Wright. At the end of the boardwalk (across which about 300,000 visitors stroll each year as they wait to eat or visit the gift shop and ice cream parlor that flank the packinghouse) stand two large aboveground tanks that serve as a demonstration for Maryland's Oyster Recovery Partnership (ORP).

The ORP grows "certified seed" (disease-free spat, or baby oysters) at state-owned hatcheries at Deal Island in Dorchester County, Piney Point in St. Mary's County, and the University of Maryland Oyster Hatchery at Horn Point in Cambridge, Maryland. The partnership distributes spat to oyster gardeners like Oertel, who raise them for a year before volunteers plant them in Bay waters. In 1999, the program distributed more than 24.5 million oysters in the Severn, Wicomico, and Choptank Rivers and Baltimore Harbor; it plans to plant 40 million more each year in 2000 and 2001. "Our goal," Oertel says, "is to increase oyster population to at least ten times the 1995 numbers by 2005."

Restoring the oyster population is a complex task. It requires more than the hatch-and-release strategy successful with many fish—it also requires full-scale habitat re-creation, mainly reef reconstruction. In the nineteenth century, mounds of oyster reefs were so expansive that they became navigational hazards and were exposed at low tide. From 1870 to 1940, during the heyday of Maryland's oyster industry, watermen harvested up to 4 million bushels of "winter gold" each year. Until the mid-1980s, oystering was the most valuable commercial fishery in the Bay. However, decades of overharvesting, disease, and pollution have taken their toll. "In the 1970s we were still harvesting nearly a million bushels a year," Oertel says. "But in the nineties, we got down as low as forty thousand and saw a large exit of watermen. This season will be about 125,000 bushels.

"The writing was on the wall," she shrugs. "Since 1870, people have known we were overharvesting. Harris's has been sustained by the versatility of dealing with other states so we can continue to supply the product. If we hadn't made those connections, we would have been gone just like the others. Ten years ago, there were over thirty of us in Maryland; now there are only a handful."

By harvesting more efficiently than the earlier hand-tonging, the introduction of dredging and hydraulic tongs kept oystering economically viable. But these methods also chipped away at ancient oyster shell reefs, eventually reducing them to flat layers of shell on the bottom. Two devastating parasites, MSX (*Haplosporidium nelsoni*) and Dermo (*Perkinsus marinus*), exacerbated the situation. These problems continue to impact the industry, as well as water quality, which depends in part on the cleansing effects of filter-feeding organisms.

"Oysters are much too valuable to the ecological balance of the Bay to think of them only as food," Oertel warns. In the past, tall reefs elevated the shellfish into food-rich currents and provided a host of protective nooks and crannies, which also supported complex communities of barnacles, mussels, clams, crabs, worms, and fish. Oysters play an important role in the Bay cleanup effort because they filter plankton, nutrients, and sediment particles out of the water column, then deposit "pseudofeces" for hungry bottom scavengers. "One oyster can filter about fifty gallons of water a day," Oertel says. "We used to have enough oysters to theoretically filter the entire Bay waters in three days," she reports. "Now it takes over a year."

Oertel explains that political factors also contribute to the Chesapeake's oyster predicament. "In the late 1800s, the state designated Maryland waters as a public industry, governed and run by the Department of Natural Resources [DNR]. Subsequently, seafood-processing houses are one of the most regulated industries, and Maryland does not allow for private farming." Unlike those in other oyster-producing states, most of Maryland's oyster beds, by tradition and by law, are public grounds. While approximately 285,000 acres are publicly owned, DNR leases only about ten thousand acres to private individuals. Further, because the bottom is too muddy, most leased grounds are unproductive and have been abandoned. "We don't have a private sector that encourages the entrepreneur to farm oysters," Oertel complains.

"As a processor, we do some farming," she continues. "We've been able to secure a few leases left over from the 1800s. They're minimal in acreage and very controlled by the DNR. We have a seed-growing area, a grow-out area, and holding areas. The concept is no different than farming land. The Japanese have said, 'Give us Chesapeake Bay and we'll feed the world.' They know how to farm. But if a farmer does not cultivate his land and plant seed, what's his harvest going to be? If he walks into a weedy field and throws down a handful of seed, what's his harvest going to be? This is what we're doing in the Bay because we don't encourage the spawning mechanism on a private level—we only allow for the public level, which is minimal."

Oertel attributes this circumstance to over a century of political influence from watermen who fear the loss of their independent lifestyle. "They're afraid the market won't bear the supply if the harvest is too plentiful, which is foolish because there is a huge worldwide demand that we're not able to supply now. Most watermen don't really understand what happens after they sell their catch at the dock. They've never had to risk their labor or money to grow oysters," she points out. "They only take the oyster up. But when we're operating at 1 percent of the catch we saw one hundred years ago, doesn't that tell us we're doing something wrong?" Her voice rises with emotion as she elaborates: "You need to be part of making this happen, guys! What's wrong with three of you getting together and raising five acres of oysters, damn it? You can take it up and have a contract with me and I can buy it from you in the summertime. Makes sense to me!

"But the watermen will dispute that. They'll tell you, 'We've tried oyster growing and it didn't work.' Well, I'm going to dispute *that* because they didn't give it their best shot. When I look at growing oysters, I want to succeed—I want to prove that we can make it happen in Maryland waters. It's very difficult for the public to realize what's on the bottom of the water and what a difference it makes to the Bay. If I had my way, you'd see a mound of oysters built up out of the water so people will ask what it is.

"There are people who would like to see us dry up and go away. Yet I see hope. Some of the younger watermen realize there won't be a future unless we wake up. But they're few and far between. I see a light at the end of the tunnel, but I'm not sure I'll see it happen in my lifetime. Only one of my nephews is involved in the business. My children have all worked here, and I would have loved for them to stay, but I encouraged them to fly. I didn't see a secure future in the seafood industry; I saw a real battle. If I can't grow an oyster, if I can't have them available year-round, I can't control our destiny.

"What most people know about oysters is how they like them prepared. But as goes the oyster, so goes the Bay. When people start to understand what needs to happen and when *those* votes begin to override politics and tradition, we'll start to make a difference. One of the most important things we can do is to look these problems in the eye and figure out how we can turn them around."

ROBERT K. DEAN ⤾

Norfolk, Virginia

Founder, "Clean the Bay Day" and the Elizabeth River Project's Derelict Vessel Removal Subcommittee

ONCE UPON A TIME, ROBERT DEAN SWAM IN THE ELIZABETH River—one of the most polluted bodies of water in the Chesapeake Bay watershed today. Dean also frequently cruised the Bay. "I was disgusted by how much trash was floating in the water," he recalls. "I finally just said, 'Let it begin with me; I'm going to start something.'" In 1988, he called together twelve friends to found the Clean the Bay Day (CTBD) organization, dedicated to preserving the shorelines of the Chesapeake Bay watershed and the adjacent oceanfront and inland waterways through annual volunteer cleanups and campaigns to raise public awareness of problems from marine debris. "I figured we'd start out very small," he says. "But the first year we had two thousand people turn out! We cleaned up fifty-two miles between the North Carolina border and Virginia Beach. This was before I even had a computer and ran everything from my house. Today the event has grown tremendously—into Pennsylvania, Maryland, Delaware, and the District of Columbia. Our ultimate goal is to include every river and tributary in the Chesapeake watershed."

For seventeen years, following his service in the Marine Corps, Dean worked as a retail manager for J. C. Penney. He left his job in 1983 to care for his cousin, who had cancer, which led him to a full-time volunteer career working with mentally and physically disabled persons and addressing environmental issues. He serves in many environmental and civic capacities; he spent several years as chairman of the local Earth Day celebration and was on the Virginia Beach City Council from 1992 to 1996. He says his ten-year-old daughter, Alyson, is his best friend. Big-hearted and hard working, he is an aboveboard, brass-tacks kind of man—not one to toot his own horn.

Since its modest beginning, CTBD has been recognized with national, state, and local awards. Twelve consecutive events—annual one-day, three-hour efforts—have recruited 53,470 volunteers—zone captains, river coordinators, media coordinators, military and civilian scuba divers, small boat captains, and thousands of "mud rats"—who have removed 3,548,216 pounds of debris from 2,408 miles of waterways throughout the watershed. "Considering that over 50 percent of this trash is lightweight plastic," Dean adds, "the volume has been tremendous. The purpose has been not only to enlist the help of citizens to clean up beaches and shorelines, but also to quantify and document the types of litter found. We use the resulting data to help identify and support policies and practices that address the use and disposal of waste, such as plastic."

Following the first cleanup, CTBD had all the collected plastic recycled into plastic lumber, which participating cities assembled into park benches. "In 1990, for the twentieth anniversary of Earth Day," Dean recounts, "we also erected a plastic lumber monolith with the inscription *Earth Day Every Day* in English, French, Spanish, and German at Mount Trashmore." The most-visited park in Norfolk, Mount Trashmore is also the world's first park converted from a landfill.

Dean goes on to say that perhaps the most beneficial impact of CTBD is the education of volunteers and the resulting environmental stewardship. "More and more people are becoming aware of the problem and expressing a genuine desire to help solve it. We've developed a multifaceted awareness program, including public service announcements, research data, a public speaker bureau, and two videos. At the outset, I thought that heightened awareness and stewardship would mean the demise of our organization after a few years," he recalls. "And with the help of the media, we certainly have spread the word about the richness of the Chesapeake Bay and the worth of its bounty, but at the same time, I'm not always sure that the word is getting out to those responsible for the continued degradation."

Each year, tons of refuse, especially plastic, enters the marine environment from ships, recreational boaters, and land-based sources. As it accumulates, the debris is not only unsightly but also life threatening to marine wildlife, especially birds, sea turtles, and fish. "Anything that's dumped in the ocean is either going to sink or float ashore," Dean points out. "This is one of the world's busiest harbors. A lot of ships dump waste overboard as a matter of economics because if they bring it into harbor they have to pay to have it hauled to the landfill. It's local people, too—some guys that work on the river will throw anything over.

"On CTBD I've seen and done it all," he continues. "I've been a zone captain, recorded data, recapped data, and done the final reports. My greatest enjoyment is actually picking up the trash . . . especially in really filthy, hard-to-get-to places, where there are plenty of snakes. It all adds to the excitement! It's an exhilarating feeling to work on a project for several months and then watch it come together in one morning with thousands of people, along hundreds of miles of shoreline, acting in concert to rid the waterways of tons of marine debris. Divers have brought up safes from robberies, stolen motorcycles, decades-old documents, fishing line, anchors, televisions, appliances, huge tandem axles, and tires— lots and lots of tires. They use air bags to bring up heavy items, which they float to a staging area where backhoes pull them out."

CTBD workers also remove many abandoned boats. In 1992, Dean co-founded the Elizabeth River Project, an independent, nonprofit organization formed to build broad community involvement in restoring the health of the Elizabeth River. The project's Derelict Vessel Removal Sub-committee, which consists of twenty-two members from agencies (Army Corps of Engineers, Department of Environmental Quality, and the Coast Guard), shipyard owners, city attorneys, and salvagers, has identified 145 abandoned vessels along the river's shoreline and has removed almost twenty. "We knew all these vessels were out here," Dean reports. "Studies had been made, but nothing was ever *done*. We made tremendous strides in a small period of time because we didn't get tied down in government bureaucracy. We wrote the book on derelict vessel removal; it's a long, slow process.

"Many of these vessels are so aground that we have to wait for high tide. Then we cut them in half with welding torches, hook on big lines to a huge tugboat, and slowly pull them off to a staging area." Shown here, Dean (right) works with Tim Mullane of Rusty Tug and Barge (on left, holding torch). "Once the bottom of a barge begins to rust out," Dean explains, "somebody will buy it for salvage. They'll pour in liquid polyurethane foam, which expands and fills the inside cavity where the rust is—the barge will then float forever. The problem is, when they're abandoned it's very difficult to separate the foam from the metal because it gets into the caverns and structural supports. The easiest way is with a cutting torch. But when you set polyurethane foam on fire it puts off toxic gas, so we have to go in with picks and shovels and do it by hand, which is very labor intensive and expensive. It can cost from $10,000 to $50,000 to remove each vessel. [Renting] the tugs usually runs $1,500 to $2,000 an hour; fortunately, Sandler Materials sometimes donates them. The number one thing we consider is safety. The second thing is the extrinsic value to the community of removing these monstrosities from a grossly polluted river."

Bay writer Tom Horton once remarked, "When you ride up a river and say, 'Jesus, it's starting to go,' it's gone." The Elizabeth River, perhaps more than any other Bay tributary, epitomizes this realization. Encircled by the cities of Norfolk, Chesapeake, and Portsmouth and Craney Island (built of dredge material), the Elizabeth River is often called one of the nation's most polluted waterways—filthy, rat-infested, and opaque, an indescribable color something like stagnant root beer. It consists of a main stem and three major branches generally characterized by a deep central channel fringed by shallows, tidal flats, and developed shorelines. The Elizabeth contains the major deepwater port for the Hampton Roads area, home of the country's largest naval base and a link to the Intracoastal Waterway.

Since the early seventeenth century, this river, named for Queen Elizabeth I, has undergone dramatic changes, particularly in the past century, as a bustling industrial economy attracted an assortment of commercial and military facilities. Dean explains that the constant dredging needed to maintain navigational depth has made the Elizabeth twice as deep as it once was but only two-thirds as wide, so that many areas of wetlands and shallow water have disappeared. Huge, hulking freighters and military vessels line both sides of the main channel, and industry—in the form of fertilizer and pesticide plants, creosote and cement factories, shipyards, dry docks, oil terminals, and coal-loading operations—takes its toll.

Many inactive industrial sites contribute to heavy loads of metals like lead, copper, and mercury, while organic compounds have contaminated bottom sediments and made the river a "toxic hot spot." Because of poor flushing, exacerbated by dredging of the navigational channels, contaminants become trapped in the river. Runoff from highly urbanized

South Hampton Roads and sewage dumped into the river by thousands of recreational boaters also damage water quality. Upland areas are subject to agricultural chemicals, storm-water runoff, aerial drift, and toxic waste dumping.

"You name it, it's been dumped in this river. It's mind boggling!" Dean exclaims. "On the hot spots in the southern branch it's so toxic that the fins on the fish have rotted off and they have cataracts and cancerous lesions. On CTBD, we only put divers in certain areas because if they have any kind of open sore it becomes highly infected. For years, there was no regulation—Atlantic Creosote dumped raw creosote, one of the worst carcinogens. It's still there; it never goes away. And it's still going on. We're not pointing the finger at anybody, but we expect industry to use best management practices as a matter of business ethics. In my eleven years as chairman of CTBD, I haven't received one cent of compensation. That's not why I do it—it's a labor of love and a sense of duty as a citizen. If what I'm doing improves the Bay and its inhabitants, and if it helps my daughter inherit a better natural resource than I received, then it's worth the work. If we continue on the track we're on and the private sector does what they should do, the river will be fishable and possibly swimmable in Alyson's lifetime."

CLIFFORD W. RANDALL ～

Chesapeake Watershed, Various Locations

Environmental and Civil Engineer

WASTEWATER TREATMENT PLANTS DO NOT SEEM LIKE AN AD-
venturesome setting, and Clifford Randall may not look like a
trailblazer, but he has pioneered a process that has consequentially impacted water quality in the Chesapeake Bay watershed. His work is the
sort that boys dream of—ordering up heavy equipment, erecting pipes
and machinery, masterminding chemical reactions, and peering at slime
and squiggly creatures under a microscope—but it is also an example of
applying mechanical and biological engineering toward environmental
and economic gain. Most of us don't give a second thought to what happens after the toilet flushes, the washer empties, or rainstorms flood our
property. However, multiplied millions of times over, these individual
events exert a huge nutrient discharge from wastewater treatment plants,
a primary source of nitrogen and phosphorous pollutants, into Bay waterways. Phosphate detergent bans, along with numerous wastewater
treatment plant upgrades, have played a significant role in reducing nutrient loads in the watershed. Randall is widely recognized as having
done more to reduce nutrient loads in the Bay watershed than any other
single individual. Over his illustrious forty-year career, he helped insti-
gate phosphate bans and developed the process of biological nutrient removal (BNR), which taps internal biological processes, rather than using
or adding chemicals, to remove nitrogen and phosphorus from wastewater. This process is currently used at treatment plants throughout the
Chesapeake region and beyond.

An unpretentious man who grew up in China and Kentucky, one of
seven children of missionary parents, today Randall retains a strong personal faith. For many years, he jogged twenty-five to thirty miles per

week, until eleven heart bypasses forced him to cut his distance in half. His lifework combines ingenious science and relatively simple mechanics. As an undergraduate, he disliked the mathematics of structural engineering, and it wasn't until graduate school, when he took his first microbiology course, that he knew that was what he wanted to do with his life. Today, he is a world-renowned expert on BNR with voluminous curriculum vitae, including positions as Charles P. Lunsford Professor of Environmental Engineering and director of the Occoquan Watershed Monitoring Program at Virginia Polytechnic Institute and State University (Virginia Tech). Randall is a sought-after consultant and lecturer, serves on innumerable committees, and is known as a scientist who is also an effective administrator and educator. He has coauthored two white papers (authoritative reports on a major issue) addressing BNR and nitrogen impacts on the Bay.

Since the mid-1960s, Randall, assisted by graduate students and visiting faculty from around the world, has conducted most of the leading research on reducing the impact of wastewater treatment plants on Bay water quality. It took about fifteen years for Randall's theories about BNR, particularly biological phosphorous removal, to finally prove out. "The technology was in its infancy, but I recognized its potential, even when my colleagues disagreed." In 1984, Randall held a seminar and design workshop in Richmond, Virginia. One attendee was from the Hampton Roads Sanitary District (HRSD), which operated the Lambert's Point wastewater treatment plant in Norfolk, Virginia. At the time, Lambert's Point was performing only primary treatment and discharging large amounts of oxygen-consuming organics, nitrogen, and phosphorus into the Elizabeth River. That plant became the site of the first major experiment with high-rate BNR, in which Randall and others conducted a successful sixteen-month pilot study. Subsequently, Randall helped modify the York River wastewater treatment plant (near Yorktown, Virginia), for BNR operation to obtain data on a full-scale conversion. "Over four years, we ran it in three different configurations and proved we could get nitrogen and phosphorous removal. After that, BNR was pretty much accepted throughout the territory."

During this period, construction began at the Lambert's Point plant, the HRSD's largest facility, designed to treat 40 million gallons per day (mgd). To make the process available in the public domain, rather than reserving it for commercial application, the HRSD patented the high-

rate BNR process under the name of the Virginia Initiative Plant (VIP) Process. The initial plant has been in operation for eight years, and it produces effluent concentrations of 0.4 milligrams per liter (mg/L) total phosphorus and less than 8.0 mg/L total nitrogen. The HRSD currently has two VIP process plants, with a combined treatment capacity of 70 mgd. Using a system of conduits, "mixers," microorganisms, probes, and special equipment such as tall racks of "ring lace" (suspended filaments that keep microorganisms from being prematurely washed through the treatment process), BNR technology provides a cost-effective way to reduce nitrogen and phosphorus discharges.

Over the next decade, Randall worked with the Maryland Department of the Environment, the State of Delaware, the Chesapeake Bay Program, the EPA, and private engineering firms to modify, operate, or evaluate more than eighty plants in Maryland, Virginia, Pennsylvania, Delaware, and New York, as well as Blue Plains in Washington, D.C., a plant that treats over 10 percent of the wastewater in the entire Chesapeake watershed. Among Randall's achievements are the development of the "VT2" process at a plant in Bowie, Maryland, which uses the first oxidation ditch BNR process in the United States, possibly in the world. "It has been an exemplary plant since modification," Randall reports. "Today, that plant has the lowest effluent nutrient concentrations of any in the Chesapeake region." He also developed a retrofit of the Annapolis wastewater treatment plant, with an innovative process called integrated fixed-film activated sludge (IFAS). "Cost estimates for modification of this plant to accomplish year-round, complete nitrification, without any nitrogen removal, using conventional technology were $24 million. That's when they came to me. The cost for modifying the plant to achieve excellent nitrogen removal with IFAS was less than 8 million. We were able to cut both the cost of plant modification and nutrient outputs by about two-thirds which was economically, as well as environmentally, advantageous."

Overseeing bulldozers, budgets, and bacteria may seem like easygoing work (even if it does smell a little funny), but underneath what looks on the surface to be rushing, bubbling water flowing through a series of weirs, pipes, huge concrete vats, and metal chambers are the workings of a basically self-sustaining treatment system that discharges not chemicals but nonpolluting outputs of the process—nitrogen gas and water. Randall explains that in urban areas, most waterborne wastes pass through sewer lines and storm drains, entering a plant where they undergo treatment before being emptied into a natural water body. First, the plant provides primary treatment through the "headworks," "grit chamber," and "primary clarifier," which use physical processes to filter and skim incoming water and minimize odor. Then, in secondary treatment, pumps send the strained, brownish influent to a treatment deck, where successive "activated sludge units" begin a biological process that removes colloidal (suspended and not readily filtered) and soluble organics. "What we're doing here is growing microorganisms," Randall explains. "We feed the sewage to bacteria. Human intestines and fecal matter contain a huge, diverse population of bacteria, all of which constantly cycle through this system. We set up favorable conditions which selectively grow the kind of bacteria we want to work for us at a given stage of treatment."

Randall uses jargon like *BOD* (biochemical oxygen demand), *limiting nutrient*, and *nitrate substitution for oxygen* to explain how the plant exploits bacteria by adjusting conditions such as type and availability of energy (food), dissolved oxygen, and the presence of ring lace traps. For instance, the system can maximize biological phosphorous removal by giving phosphorus-removing bacteria, which are the "fussy eaters" in the crowd, a competitive edge over other types of bacteria. Likewise, bacteria called denitrifiers convert nutrient-rich organic material into ammonia, carbon dioxide, and water. Then nitrifiers take over to convert the ammonia to nitrates and a "mixed liquor" nitrate recycle returns to the denitrifiers for conversion to nitrogen gas. The resultant water then passes through secondary clarifiers, which separate and recycle the bacteria before the treated effluent passes through a disinfection process that uses chlorine, ultraviolet, or ozone, and finally into the receiving waters.

"Before we modified these plants," Randall reports, "the effluent nitrogen concentration would be 20 to 30mg/L. BNR reduces that to a range of 4.0 to 8.0 mg/L. At Bowie, we reduced effluent nitrogen to less than 4.0 mg/L and effluent phosphorus from 7.0 mg/L to 0.2." These are the hard-earned rewards of years of work and dedication. From helping put detergent phosphate bans in place to proving the significance of nitrogen loads in the Bay to developing BNR modifications, Randall's work has steadily reduced nutrient pollution throughout the watershed. Standing at the final discharge pipe, looking out over the Chesapeake Bay, Randall concludes, "We've learned that the Bay and its tributaries are sensitive to nitrogen and phosphorus. While we still have a long way to go, we've made some major, major impacts on the discharge of these nutrients into the watershed. Today, wastewater treatment plants must follow regulatory requirements for these discharges. One good thing about biological phosphorous removal is it doesn't care what our requirements are; it just reacts as much as it can. Maybe that's something else we can learn from."

CARROLL THAMERT ❧

Neavitt, Maryland

Waterman

CARROLL THAMERT HAS BEEN HARVESTING SEAFOOD FROM THE Chesapeake Bay for fifty-three years. Six days a week, at 3:00 A.M., he opens the front door of his small home in the village of Neavitt, on Balls Creek, walks the few paces to his workboat, and heads into the promise of dawn and the Providence of the Chesapeake Bay.

He is the latest, and perhaps last, of four generations of Chesapeake watermen, an independent and resilient breed described by the late Gilbert Byron as "the greatest poets ever," inscribing "Verses of love . . . upon / The bottom of the cove." Thamert's great-great-grandfather was required to sign a citizenship release to the King of Prussia before emigrating to America as a fisherman. His great-grandfather on his mother's side, Grandfather Harrison, was a shipbuilder. Thamert's maternal grandfather supplemented his waterman's income by running a boarding house and taking out fishing parties. And his father before him worked the water while his mother raised the children.

He's seen many changes, from oyster dredging to tonging, diving, and now "motorized" patent tonging. He considers crab pots and peeler pots to be modern methods that have drastically affected the industry. "It's a big difference from when I started." Back then, he says, in his Eastern Shore dialect, there was plenty of everything: oysters, clams, crabs, fish. There were fewer people to take it out. There was more respect for the law. There was a different breed of people—people who thought more about tomorrow and not just about today.

"There's been a decline in everything," he continues. "Twenty-five years ago the grass all left. Now it's coming back. The kill has been here before. This one (*Pfiesteria*) has just lasted longer. I've seen the Bay messed up before. When man puts his hands in it he can mess it up." For instance, he says, if the rockfish moratorium is not properly managed, it could result in overcompensation by bringing back too many and upsetting the balance of nature. "If everyone would have culled according to the law, there'd be no oyster problems today."

Thamert stresses that enforcement is a critical part of environmental protection. Most watermen try their best to follow regulations. "But there's always a bad apple in the barrel. We're required to take either Sunday or Monday off. You're supposed to have it posted on your boat which day you don't work. I've never worked a Sunday in my life, I don't believe in it. But there's some out there who have a sign that says *Sunday* on one side and *Monday* on the other." He's also seen a change in inspection methods. "I'll probably get myself in trouble for saying this, but there's more inspectors today overhauling [enforcing size regulations] from Broncos instead of from boats. There's more officers—colonels and generals—and less inspectors."

Though Thamert has known no other livelihood, he never included his two children in his work. And he is quick to say that he discourages his grandchildren from working the water. Although he has supported his family as sole wage-earner, Thamert realizes that the profits of the men and women who make their living on the Chesapeake Bay are at the mercy of nature and economic markets.

"I take my catch to the dealer in Bosman. I never know what the price will be on a given day." Thamert's seafood passes through the dealer, the city markets, restaurateurs, cargo shippers, and retailers before it gets to the plate. The middleman takes his cut. "You can't count on what you'll make in a year. There's no hospitalization, no insurance. There's no future to it."

Many watermen supplement their incomes with off-water jobs. Thamert's winter-season hobbies of hand-carving wildlife and oil painting have grown to a sideline. "The water and the morning sky is where I get most of the ideas for my pictures," he says. His artwork lines the streets of his community on neighbors' mailboxes and entryways. "The cost of materials has tripled," he says, "but I haven't raised my prices in fifteen years." Tourists attracted to the quaint, natural beauty of the area seek out his wares. "It's all word of mouth; the customers track me down. My work is in every state in America and all over Europe."

Does Thamert foresee the phasing out of the waterman's trade? "There will still be watermen. It's a way of life for some, especially on the islands. It gets in your blood. We don't have meetings. Word gets around. We know the rules and regulations. And, yes, we vote. It's a group that has escaped the rat race, willing to help anybody, especially each other. Like the Amish and barn raising. Watermen are just a fine, hard-working bunch.

"The water tells on you when you get up in years," he continues. "Oyster production is fizzling out, but I can't go oysterin' anyway because my knees are shot from the stress of hauling up the catch." However, when asked about retirement, Thamert replies, "I have no plans to quit crabbing. I'll probably die with my boots on."

As for the future of the Bay, he says, "If it's taken care of, it will last. I think it will come back. Conservation means a lot. We got everything we need right here." With a weathered hand he gestures toward the Choptank River. "We got all the laws we need. Now the lawmen just need to enforce them. I'm law-abiding. That's what I can do to preserve the Bay."

JULIE A. BENINTENDI ∽

Perry Point, Maryland / La Grande, Oregon

AmeriCorps*NCCC Team Leader

At twenty-four, Julie Benintendi is an intelligent, enthuiastic young woman, devoted to her role as an AmeriCorps*NCCC (National Civilian Community Corps) team leader. The organization, which she describes as "a cross between a domestic Peace Corps and Roosevelt's Civilian Conservation Corps," is part of a national service program that began in 1994. Benintendi works in the residential program, in which men and women, ages eighteen through twenty-four, live and work as teams to perform service work for ten months in exchange for an educational award. Teams consisting of eight to fourteen members provide assistance in five categories: education, unmet human needs, public safety, disaster relief, and environmental projects.

"We're based on AmeriCorps*NCCC campuses, which operate under uniform standards," Benintendi explains, "including the best disciplines of civilian and military groups. I applied for the Perry Point campus because I enjoy the atmosphere in this region. Our base is at the northernmost tip of the Chesapeake Bay stem, where it meets the Susquehanna River. It makes an impact when you're helping to clean up something outside your own window."

Benintendi explains that the AmeriCorps*NCCC program "recognizes that as the challenges our nation faces become more diverse, so must the solutions." After an initial training period, members serve on a variety of team-based projects lasting from one day to eight weeks. Benintendi's crew is in the midst of a six-week project sponsored by the Alliance for the Chesapeake Bay and comprising "many completely different assignments that cover the whole Chesapeake watershed."

Benintendi's crew includes, left to right, Valerie Yff (Palas Hills, Illinois), Esther Bain (Philomath, Oregon), Mitch Keiler (sponsor, Alliance for the Chesapeake Bay, Baltimore, Maryland), John O'Farrell (Philadelphia, Pennsylvania), Rose Sherwood (Austin, Texas), Alpacino Carson (Gary, Indiana), Bernard Becker (Martinsville, Virginia), Julie Benintendi (team leader, La Grande, Oregon), and Michelle Maddox (Seattle, Washington). During the first two weeks, the team tackled work assignments involving stream buffer maintenance and shoreline restoration in Lancaster, Pennsylvania, and northern and western Maryland. During the middle two weeks, the crew assisted forest rangers from the Department of Natural Resources in planting and maintaining more than four thousand trees. The project included stabilization of the dredge-material containment facility on Hart-Miller Island, with the help of middle school students and policemen from Baltimore's inner city. The students learned not only how to plant trees but also how those trees relate to the process of relocating sludge dredged from Baltimore's Inner Harbor to uninhabited land.

During the final two weeks, the crew temporarily relocated from their campus to housing at the Wye Island Natural Resource Management Area in Queenstown, on Maryland's Eastern Shore. As one of their assignments on Wye Island, they worked with another group of students from Harper's Crossing Middle School in Columbia, Maryland, who had obtained funds from a state grant to purchase "big flats of shoreline grass like you see at the beach [*Spartina alterniflora*]. The kids learned 'hands-on' how to implement a project from an economic and environmental viewpoint. They learned that grasses are beneficial not only ecologically, but, since the cost of replacement bulkheading is about $1,000 per square foot compared to $70 per square foot for grass, it makes economic sense, too."

Another task Benintendi's crew performed at Wye Island was trimming and removing trees to improve conditions for grass growth. "But it wasn't only a pruning operation," she says. "We piled the cut branches onshore to create wildlife habitat. We spent the first weeks planting trees, and some of the last ones cutting other trees back. They're both important—each has its place in the cycle."

Next, the crew spent two days working in an organic garden at a nearby environmental center, after which they teamed up with the Easton High School Future Farmers of America to work on one of the last

tasks of the six-week stint: a three-day project along eastbound Route 50 in Easton, constructing a "BayScape" at the location labeled Site 5 in the *Maryland Bay Game,* a children's activity booklet handed out by Chesapeake Bay Bridge toll booth tenders.

"They picked the place with the hardest ground possible!" Benintendi exclaims. "That makes it a process! We're hauling one thousand cubic feet each of compost and topsoil, and applying it in layers. Then we rototill, rototill, rototill in-between layers to prepare the ground for planting. People see us laboring here along the highway, and they think because we're wearing black and gray uniforms, that we're juvenile delinquents. It's labor, all right, but the reward is to see these projects completed, and to know we're leaving an educational as well as a visual and environmental mark behind when we move on.

"Also, many crew members are on their own for the first time. I have to be their counselor, liaison, Mom, everything rolled into one, which is probably the hardest part of my job. The best part is getting to work with kids and young adults, and seeing the light in their eyes when they begin to understand a concept or to find their place in the big picture, and to understand, 'Oh, this is what we have to do to save our earth.'"

The function of the crew, though, transcends the "grunt work" of labor. "Service learning is very important," Benintendi explains. "We are required to go beyond the day-labor aspect, and learn from our sponsors about what we're doing and why we're doing it. In turn we teach others. It's kind of cool," she exclaims, "because we find ourselves using skills learned in previous projects on new ones. For instance, we might use an educational skill in an environmental activity, and vice versa."

Educational and communication tools are vital to Benintendi's work. "Getting the job done involves people skills and teamwork as much as muscle management. Transferring understanding involves more than a wheelbarrow. It involves relating to different people on different levels. We're working with young people from all different backgrounds, from all over the country, from cities, suburbs, and rural areas. So maybe what you were raised to believe is different from what someone else was raised to believe, and learning to accept those differences is part of what makes this work. For instance, I worked on a project with a woman who lived her whole life in white, middle-class suburbia. The project was at an inner city middle school, with a predominantly African American and Latino population. It was culture shock. But we all came together to make a cohesive unit. That's the teamwork component: learning to use our own background and personal experience for progress, rather than division."

Benintendi believes unity can also be achieved by realizing the ecological connections to subjects not usually associated with the environment. "I graduated with a degree in architecture and plan to work in urban planning and small commercial and residential design. I was especially enlightened by one of my professors who taught us to think in broader terms beyond concrete, blueprint-type skills—such as the difference in energy conversion between demolishing an old building versus renovating it. Think about the energy that goes into each of those alternatives: knocking down the old building, producing the raw materials for the new one, processing them, shipping them, putting them together—versus recycling some of that original energy into a restoration. That's the kind of thinking we need to understand and consider more often.

"I think perspectives are changing," she continues. "The Bay's future is getting brighter. Humans have exploited the environment ever since we picked up a plow. It's taken a long time for us to realize how much we've destroyed. There's still a lot of work to do, but we're headed in the right direction. Public awareness and publicity about environmental issues have moved to the forefront, even in my lifetime. The younger generations are growing up with better ecological understanding and habits. Education is there from the beginning, and community service is becoming integrated into that. There's been a definite difference in the past ten years. More communities are making efforts to clean up the Bay.

"But there's no set stopping point, it's continual. I've signed up to be a team leader in the Chesapeake region again next year. If one person can influence just five others, it can make a tremendous difference. It's exponential. Like throwing a stone in a still pond—it ripples the water in larger and larger rings, continuously expanding outward."

BARRY L. MONES ❧

Annapolis, Maryland

FBI Special Agent

WHILE THOSE WHO WORK FOR THE GOOD OF THE CHESAPEAKE Bay are armed with a variety of equipment, Barry Mones, special agent for the FBI, is one of a few who legally packs a pistol on the job. Mones acknowledges that most environmental law enforcers are not "blue ribbon tree huggers," but when a criminal violation occurs, he says, "We *are* concerned, and want to do the right thing." The FBI views environmental crime as a serious threat to both public health and natural resources. Since 1982, the FBI and the EPA have joined forces to protect the environment and enforce environmental laws. "Today in the region," says Mones, "our top priority is protecting the Chesapeake Bay, its tributaries, and the associated natural resources."

The FBI hired Mones in 1968 to work as a forensic photographer at their headquarters in Washington, D.C. The next year he applied for agent class. "Ironically, I was initially turned down," he recalls, "because of a now-outdated height requirement. In order to become an agent, I actually had to get Mr. Hoover's personal approval." Mones went on to investigate criminal matters in Knoxville, Tennessee, and Springfield, Illinois, dealing with fugitives, deserters, foreign intelligence, and bank robberies.

In 1972, Mones transferred back to the FBI laboratory in Washington, working to become a certified expert in both document and photographic examinations, handling a myriad of cases, and developing many new scientific techniques. After several promotions, he opted to transfer to the white-collar squad of the FBI's Baltimore Division, where, for three years, he was involved in the first Environmental Crimes Task Force in the Bay region, located in the Silver Spring (Montgomery County) and Calverton (Prince George's County) areas. "The group had a tremendous cohesiveness," he says, "to the point where we were supporting each other even when it wasn't our own primary investigation. It became a very effective partnership." In 1998, Mones transferred to the Annapolis Resident Agency office of the Baltimore Division. The office conducts investigations within the Maryland counties of Anne Arundel, Calvert, St. Mary's, Charles, Queen Anne's, and Kent. "My primary assignment here is in the white-collar crimes program, which encompasses the arena of environmental crimes, computer crimes, and fraud in banking, bankruptcy, telemarketing, and health care. I formulated the idea of a similar task force here closer to the Bay. I put together a plan and was successful in selling it to my supervisor and the U.S. Attorney's office in Baltimore. In December 1998, we kicked off the Chesapeake Bay Environmental Enforcement Coalition (CBEEC)."

Mones explains that the FBI regularly participates in environmental crime task forces with other law enforcement agencies and environmental groups to identify crimes, initiate investigations, and bring violators to justice. The FBI recognizes environmental crimes as more than a regulation problem and has established them as one of its top priorities. As of the 1999–2000 fiscal year, the bureau had obtained $51,000,659 in fines and restitution as a result of 110 convictions (with 412 pending cases) from environmental crime investigations. "Our objective," Mones says, "is to reduce the amount of economic loss and environmental incidents attributable to improper and illegal production, distribution, and disposal of hazardous materials and waste." He explains that an illegal point-source discharge into the navigable waters of the United States is a violation of the Clean Water Act. "It can be the smallest stream," he expounds, "but if that stream feeds another one that flows into a river that goes into the Bay, then we're dealing with a federal violation." To document a crime scene, investigators cordon off the area, take samples, and make notes. They photograph the scene from different perspectives, beginning with a wide angle and moving in for closer shots.

"What most people don't recognize about environmental crimes," he reveals, "is that they are financially driven—people don't want to expend funds to comply with regulations or pay to legally dispose of tires or hazardous materials. Toxic materials are mandated—there's a document trail from what's called 'birth' to 'death.' Wherever it goes, there's got to be a paper trail to prove where and how it's been disposed. There are often falsified documents, other violations, and things that counties don't know. For example, under Maryland law, fines generated by environmental crimes go back to the county. So it's a way for them to recoup some funds."

The purpose of the CBEEC is to improve conservation efforts and environmental compliance in Maryland's Bay area. It consists of a core group of enforcers—the FBI, EPA Criminal Division, U.S. Attorney's Office, and Coast Guard—assisted by various other agencies. "I like the task force–multiagency idea," Mones says. "There's too much work for any one agency to handle. We can work more cases more efficiently by taking this approach. My philosophy is the group needed to have a two-pronged attack. We needed a law enforcement focus and a civilian focus. The civilian focus is to educate citizens about environmental laws and concerns at local, state, and federal levels. We created a hotline for that purpose."

The CBEEC has produced attractive informational posters urging citizens to REPORT ENVIRONMENTAL VIOLATIONS TO THE HOTLINE— 1-800-377-5879—TWENTY-FOUR HOURS A DAY, SEVEN DAYS A WEEK. "The hotline number comes into the U.S. Attorney's office," Mones continues. "While it often helps to be able to follow up with callers, people can certainly leave an anonymous report. We farm out the information to the appropriate agency to take action. We also increase public awareness by sending out releases and invitations to charter boat captains, marina operators, and dozens of citizens groups to attend quarterly meetings that are open to the public."

Complaints have addressed wetlands filling, oil spills, suspicious drum containers, tugboat dumping, and illegal septic and sewage disposal. In one case, Mones initiated an investigation after workers at a local public treatment facility complained of high volumes of incoming volatile substances. "We conducted an investigation and ultimately identified the source as a commercial laundry business. These operations do laundering of what is called 'clean' laundry (such as linens from a restaurant) and 'dirty' laundry (from body and paint shops). The 'dirty' wastewater has to be pretreated to meet county regulations before it can be dumped into a storm drain that leads to the public treatment plant. We investigated extensively to be sure the laundry was the only source. The EPA used monitoring equipment in a manhole to test the water coming out of the facility and to verify its content. Then we established sufficient probable cause and wrote a search warrant for a judge to approve. We put together a search team of about forty people. Again, this is where the task force environment came into play—we had FBI, EPA, National Park Police, fire and health department personnel, and the county 'hazmat' team. We executed a search warrant on the facility, interviewed everybody in the place, searched records, and talked to the plumbers. That search took forty people an entire day to complete. We culled through all the records to find what we were allowed to take. We made a mirror image of computer hard drives on an optical disc. We can also recover information that businesses have erased from their hard drives. We try not to deprive companies of their computers because that's a burden on the business.

"We found that the laundry had illegal wastewater bypasses. It had three 10,000-gallon holding tanks in its pretreatment system, into which the wastewater from the dirty side of the operation flowed. If it couldn't get it clean enough to meet the standards, they were required by law to recirculate and treat it again. But meanwhile, there was more dirty water coming down the line. The holding tanks would get full and sometimes overflow. While the laundry had drains built into the floor to keep recirculating this stuff, employees were on a production salary, so things weren't going to slow down. The pretreatment system operator bypassed the system and dumped contaminated water straight out of the system. That company ended up admitting to complicity and paying a pretty stiff fine."

The CBEEC is working hard to get the word out and educate the public about how to report these types of violations. Meetings, posters, and notices in boat registration renewals and water bills disseminate information. "We hope to get other counties that surround the Bay to do the same thing," Mones says. "One person in a leadership role can motivate an entire organization. For example, the president of the Charter Boat Captains' Association takes a strong interest in our efforts. He comes to all our meetings and carries that message back to his members. The agencies can only do so much. We need the help of educated, concerned citizens. A single individual who reports something suspicious can be invaluable."

ANDREW R. McCOWN ∽

Worton, Maryland

Associate Director, Echo Hill Outdoor School

AFTER MORE THAN TWENTY YEARS OF TEACHING SELF-DESIGNED "Bay Studies" classes at Echo Hill Outdoor School (EHOS), Andy McCown still loves his work. From the deck of a forty-foot workboat, *The Spirit* (built in 1944), dressed in waterproof "oil skins" and surrounded by students from throughout the watershed (many of whom have never been out on the water), McCown is in his element, earnestly imparting the Bay's wonders. "I accept the challenge," he says in a raspy voice, worn from use, "to give every class passion and opportunity."

"So what's the big deal about the Bay?" he posits and then navigates his passengers through their own discovery of the answers. Students (like these youngsters from the Key School in Severna Park, Maryland—left to right, Will Schreitz, Caitlin Ivrey, Kelsey McFadden, Sarah Campbell, and Thomas Braithwaite) explore the Bay, the Sassafras and Chester Rivers, and Still Pond Creek. They dip-net for blue crabs, get splashed with brackish water, spy the Piedmont Plateau (which, according to McCown, means "foot of the mountain" in French), correlate maps with reality, and hold fish ("Uh-oh," one student nervously exclaims. "It looked at me funny!"). EHOS issues each student a "passport" booklet, in which they record sightings (of white perch, skink, mosquito, Great Blue Heron, owl, muskrat, jellyfish, sassafras, grass shrimp), observations (of the Bay, a beach, and a swamp), adventures, and notes about night hikes. They learn the meaning of words like *salinity, turbidity, bioluminescence, peat, compost, habitat destruction, resource depletion,* and *personal responsibility.* "The Bay and our understanding of it are always changing," McCown advises. "So we have to constantly be open to new approaches. There's always something positive you can do; there's always a better way."

McCown grew up sailing, fishing, crabbing, and hunting game on local rivers. "I always loved it," he says. "My family's love of nature is deeply rooted in me. I practiced the sport of falconry at a young age with my father, who also taught me to identify duck species by flight patterns." McCown attended nearby Washington College and has been a Coast Guard–licensed boat captain for more than twenty years. In 1978, he "stumbled into" a job as one of Echo Hill's earliest instructors. The following year he founded the school's "Explore" summer program, which runs five-day educational expeditions in the unspoiled regions of the upper Bay and its tributaries. McCown was also a commercial oysterman from 1988 to 1994, renting a workboat from the school. "I was gradually accepted into the waterman community," he recounts. "It gave me a terrific perspective." In his spare time, he became a member of "Chesapeake Scenes," a well-known acoustic group that performs regional music and folklore. McCown moved into his current position as associate director of EHOS in 1980.

Founded in 1972, the school is located on a 350-acre working waterfront farm in Kent County, Maryland. The campus sits on a high bluff overlooking the Bay, the Piedmont Plateau, and, to the north, the Susquehanna Flats (a large freshwater shoal at the mouth of the Susquehanna River). The school teaches up to five thousand students each year through residential education programs, field trips, and outreach programs lasting from three hours to five days. Students and staff stay in platform tents with bunks during most seasons; winterized facilities are available for use during colder weather. Educational facilities include a mile-long beach, "the Big Marsh" (600 acres of freshwater shrub swamp), an extensive adventure-challenge course, and a fleet of historic Bay workboats. Other teaching sites include a barnyard, a garden, a recycling area, a Native American village, local towns and businesses, and a nearby dairy farm. EHOS offers programs for people of all ages. Participants attend a series of classes with a unique combination of three curriculum areas: science and ecology, history and the human environment, and individual and group development. McCown leads a myriad of activities, such as analyzing water quality, sifting bottom samples, collecting plankton, examining fish, crustaceans, mollusks, and other animals, searching for fossils, identifying birds, exploring swamps, forests, and marshes, using a map and compass, and learning about nighttime.

"We use the Bay as a tool to *show* the existence of things that are removed from most of our lives: landscapes, ecological systems, and organisms. We get out there where we can touch them and encourage the children to apply their book knowledge." McCown says he especially enjoys the summer Explore program, an extension of Bay Studies. "Students return on their own," he explains. "It's an opportunity to expand on what we do during the school year. The idea is to get them out on the Bay having fun doing science—fishing, crabbing, navigating, and exploring the shoreline. For five days, we live on the boats. Because they grew out of the great resource of the Chesapeake, we teach the *value* of our historic boats beyond their monetary worth. When we fuel up, students learn that the faint smell of popcorn comes from soy-based 'biodiesel,' a less-polluting fuel mixture of 20 percent soybean oil and 80 percent diesel fuel. When we catch bait with the seine net, we talk about the food chain. When we go to sleep at night, we talk about the stars. In addition to teaching about the wonders of ecology, we talk about human impact. Rather than focusing strictly on water quality, our role is to encourage a wonder of nature and science and to emphasize human values and relationships with the environment.

"New experiences and the challenge of a residential, outdoor setting result in great personal impact on most students and classes," McCown continues. "I like to think that we provide children with hope, rather than despair. It's easy to teach despair. Outdoor and environmental education walk a fine line between teaching and turning children off by overloading them with discouraging facts. It's important that instructors not push their personal opinions and give students an opportunity to discover their own way. We encourage awareness that this ecosystem exists and that it's really fantastic—we should be in awe of it. Yes, humans create tremendous problems, but we also have the capability to solve them. That's the hope I promote—that people *can* do things to make the Bay better. People have choices—we have minds, science, effort, and will. That's the hope we should be empowering children with.

"Echo Hill is a cog in the wheel. Our little part of education is not making *the* difference, it's helping to make *a* difference. The teacher in Norfolk with a cafeteria compost program, the legislative efforts of the Bay Program, and local land conservancies are all helping to make a difference. Collectively, all those pieces of the pie can make the Bay a better ecological system. Can we do it? We certainly see signs that it's possible. When we have students collect, weigh, and record their 'S.L.O.P.' [Stuff Left on Plate] in the mess hall, we're formulating an understanding of what wasted food can *really* represent. We're trying to show our students that with a little effort and consciousness there can be a huge difference—whether it's food waste or natural resources. One program, one person, one tree alone can't solve the Bay's problems. But, as part of a diverse system, those individual contributions are vitally important."

DARRIN L. LOWERY ∽

Tilghman Island, Maryland

Archaeologist

DARRIN LOWERY LOOKS AT BOTH THE BIG PICTURE AND THE little mysteries of life, from a time when sea levels were 350 feet lower than today and the Chesapeake Bay did not exist. An outgoing fellow, unfazed by the tide of popular opinion, Lowery has lived on Tilghman Island, a finger crook of land between the Chesapeake Bay and Choptank River, for all of his thirty-one years and has studied archaeology for almost as long. Much of his work focuses on Paleoindian investigations, studies of prehistoric human culture in the Western Hemisphere from earliest habitation to around 9,000 B.C. Lowery has performed twenty-two years of archaeological survey work within Talbot, Queen Anne's, Dorchester, Somerset, Kent, and Caroline Counties in Maryland and Accomack and Northampton Counties in Virginia. He has discovered and documented more than twelve hundred archaeological sites, has held research positions with Temple University, the Smithsonian Institution, the Maryland Historic Trust, the University of Delaware Center for Archaeological Research, the Virginia Department of Historic Resources, and various historical groups, and has written and coauthored numerous publications and research reports. Active in several archaeological societies and archaeological conservancy groups and a frequent speaker at lectures and presentations, Lowery is enthusiastically encyclopedic about his work and how it applies to the record of the Chesapeake Bay watershed.

He was only eight years old when, playing on the beach near his home, he stumbled upon an oddly shaped object—a small, triangular stone tool made of jasper, called a Clovis point, used by members of a prehistoric human culture widespread throughout North America from about 11,000 to 10,000 B.C.—that pricked his curiosity about ancient peoples. He found the relic on Paw Paw Cove, which today, protected by its landmark status and an archaeological easement, is an overgrown patch of land, with one edge lapped by the Chesapeake Bay, surrounded by mowed fields. Since that first discovery, Lowery's archaeological finds have included thousands of projectile points (not called arrowheads, since they possibly predate the bow and arrow), numerous prehistoric cultural objects, and even fossilized clam shells from the Miocene epoch (about 18 million years ago) that prehistoric peoples crafted into oyster-shucking knives about three thousand years ago. "Native Americans were using old mollusks to process living mollusks!" Lowery delights. "Isn't that pretty durn cool?" Near a "midden" (huge mound of prehistoric refuse) on Taylors Island in Dorchester County, he has also unearthed large numbers of potsherds, animal bones, and cooking tools.

Lowery applies his findings from the ancient past to help understand modern Bay studies. During the past 3 million years, he outlines, the earth has experienced cycles of ice ages, each lasting about 100,000 years, followed by warmer interglacial periods lasting 10,000-12,500 years. About eighteen thousand years ago, the glaciers began to melt, and the meltwater eventually filled the surrounding lowlands and ultimately created the Chesapeake Bay. Twelve thousand years ago, prehistoric inhabitants of the Bay region lived in a frigid climate and shared a landscape of boreal forest with woolly mammoths, mastodons, and the occasional saber-toothed tiger. The climate made it necessary for humans to walk hundreds of miles to hunt and gather food; in doing so they showed a resourcefulness that Lowery says modern people can learn from. "Humans were much more in tune with the environment than we are now or ever will be again. When they went to a spot and settled, it was because there was something on the landscape—converging streams, a bog, a grove of trees, a hummock—that was essential for their existence. We have lost a lot of that survival connection to our environment."

Lowery maintains that the prehistoric period is poorly understood by Bay-area scientists and environmentalists. "Prehistoric archaeology," he emphasizes, "shows how humans have been impacted by *change*. Scientists talk about change—dying organisms, sea-level rise, wetland destruction, pollution. Guess what? Change has been happening from the human perspective for the past twelve thousand years! We're standing on a beach that twelve thousand years ago was a boreal forest that looked a lot like northern Canada; oysters, crabs, clams, and fish were invasive species, the Bay did not exist, and we might see an occasional mastodon mosey on by—now *that's* change!"

The relatively warm interglacial period (the Holocene) during the past ten thousand years has been a major factor in the changing character of agriculture, human civilizations, and population growth. However, Lowery goes on to say that most environmentalists and ecologists fail to incorporate humans into the picture as anything but a negative force. "They'll study the impact a squirrel has on the distribution of an oak tree, but they view anything humans do as detrimental. Hominids have been on this planet for millions of years. Sure we're impacting the environment; but we're impacting it just like everything else is impacting it."

He attests that hypotheses are often based in part on speculation about unanswered questions from the past. "Sea levels rise and fall in a natural cycle that's been occurring like a heartbeat—up and down and up and down for all of human habitation. Each time it goes down it cuts a deep valley; each time it goes up the valley fills with water and silts in. We don't know for sure what the sea levels were twelve thousand years ago or what caused the warming that led to the interglacial we're in now, but it wasn't us! The preceding interglacial period was 125,000 years ago. Sea levels were twenty meters [sixty-five feet] higher than they are today. Now, who was burning and creating hydrocarbons 130,000 to 140,000 years ago to make that happen?"

Lowery also points out that "the nature of an estuary is to fill itself in" and that factors such as artificially increased siltation, runoff from agriculture, and population pressures that have lowered the aquifer must be considered when studying Bay ecology. "We're on top of the paleochannel of the ancestral Susquehanna River, which is just loaded with cobbles," he continues. "And if you lower the aquifer in a paleochannel that's filled with gravel, you're going to have settling and the landscape will become inundated by the modern Chesapeake Bay. Sea levels are going to fluctuate no matter what. And," he deduces, "our impact as far as hydrocarbons will be insignificant when the next glacial kicks in. When you take into consideration that this has been a natural cycle for millions of years, the current brouhaha over ozone depletion, sea-level rise, and estuarine wetland destruction is severely shortsighted."

Without pause he declares, "I'll let the secret out. If you're a biologist, an environmentalist, an ecologist, a marine coastal guy, how you keep yourself in a job is to scream bloody murder to the public. But archaeology doesn't just look at biology or forestry or marine biology or geology. It looks at it all. Then it incorporates humans into the equation." Lowery explains that an archaeological site, the area where people actually lived, is our best representation of peoples of the past. "It makes them human. The site can tell you that people were not backward and crude because of their stone tools. They were probably much more brilliant than we are today if thrust into the same situation."

However, because most primitive settlements were situated along what is now mutable shoreline, Lowery is concerned about shoreline erosion that destroys archaeological sites. "Obviously," he laments, "there's the danger of losing a significant portion of the archaeological record. This would be a crucial loss, because in the future I see an extermination of the last vestiges of these types of cultural ties to the land. Archaeology can tell you about that because it tells you what humans were taking out of the ecosystem. We have found evidence that people in this region were eating everything from deer, elk, and bear to fifteen-foot sturgeons, sea turtles, and a variety of marine life. On the other hand, I see a definite future trend to aquaculture as a method of subsistence within the Bay area. Watermen are the closest modern counterpart to the people I study. Yet at the Taylors Island site people were doing the same thing that we do today at oyster packinghouses. Rather than packing them in cans for shipping, they were roasting and drying them to use immediately or over the next season. People are predictable. So archaeology gives us hints that things haven't really changed too much. There's a truth and excitement about holding something in your hand that is thousands or even millions of years old, something that a human, not entirely different from us, utilized for subsistence. We can apply that link toward sound decisions for today and tomorrow. The research potential of these sites holds exciting promise for the future."

PATSY KERR ⟋

Langley Air Force Base, Hampton, Virginia

Natural Resource Planner

Pᴀᴛsʏ ᴋᴇʀʀ, ᴀ ғᴏᴄᴜsᴇᴅ, ᴜᴘʙᴇᴀᴛ, ᴀɴᴅ ɢᴏᴏᴅ-ɴᴀᴛᴜʀᴇᴅ ᴡᴏᴍᴀɴ, is the antithesis of what one might expect from a person who lives in a place called the Dismal Swamp. "I'm way down there, almost in Carolina," she says in a southern drawl that smiles even when she does not. Kerr, who has three sons (ages eight, six, and, two months), commutes to her job as natural resource planner at Langley Air Force Base (an hour away) in a pickup truck arrayed with lab equipment, field reports, smashed Cheerios and gum, and a backpack baby carrier for toting her youngest child while she does inspections around the base. Langley is situated at the confluence of the north and south branches of the Back River, a short river close to the Bay. "Working with the Chesapeake Bay Program is not formally in my job description," Kerr says. "But it's something we feel is very important to our conservation efforts."

Born and raised in Lynchburg, Virginia, Kerr says she has always had a special place in her heart for the water. In 1984, she received a Bachelor of Science degree in horticulture and landscape design from Virginia Polytechnic Institute and State University (Virginia Tech). Kerr then spent twelve years with several nurseries, including the landscape division of the Chesapeake Bay Program for the City of Norfolk, where she worked for eight years. In 1996, she began a civilian career in her present position.

"The Air Force had been coordinating the bases within the Chesapeake watershed—Bolling [Washington, D.C.], Andrews [Maryland], and Langley—from regional offices in Atlanta, Georgia. They had somebody out of Atlanta following the Bay program. You can't do that; it has to be someone in the region. I battle that to this day," she adds, "because most of the base population is here short term and then they're gone. I live here—I'm here for the long haul.

"Unless you're dealing with endangered species or noncompliance, there's not a lot of conservation money for DoD [Department of Defense] facilities," she reveals. "Our headquarters does not fund this work—it comes out of our hides and whatever grant monies we can secure. We 'buddied-up' with the Navy, Army, and Marines and wrote a Chesapeake Bay initiative covering several areas: submerged aquatic vegetation (SAV), riparian forest buffers, invasive species (such as phragmites), and shoreline stabilization. As the lead for the Air Force bases in the watershed, I was able to network with the Environmental Protection Agency, the Alliance for the Chesapeake Bay [ACB], the Chesapeake Bay Foundation, and the National Aquarium in Baltimore, which have provided expertise, personnel, and grant funding opportunities. We're trying to be a real proactive base."

Established in 1917, Langley Air Force Base is among the oldest continuously active air bases in the United States. Today, Langley's 1st Fighter Wing flies the F-15 Eagle and provides headquarters for the Air Combat Command, which supplies air combat forces in war-fighting commands and supports intercontinental ballistic missiles; fighter, bomber, reconnaissance and battle-management aircraft; and command, control, communications, and intelligence systems. Home to more than eighty-eight hundred military and approximately twenty-eight hundred civilian employees, the base covers twenty-nine hundred acres.

"Originally they chose this site because it's flat. The whole base has only about eleven feet of relief, so it was easy to close off and fill," Kerr explains. "Basically, the whole base is a filled wetland. It's filled with various soil types, concrete, rebar, and building materials. To reestablish our native wetlands, we go in and excavate to an elevation that will reestablish the ebb and flow of the water, and replant with native marsh grass. It's very expensive—about $100,000 an acre. We're also taking out rubble from the shoreline—it's all asphalt and concrete, there's no filter cloth or anything. When we get a bad northeaster, our shorelines erode and we're knee-deep in water. People's cars get flooded and it's a mess. You can't just take whatever you have and chuck it down there. It's got to be the right composition, and have filter cloth underneath it. Otherwise, when water rushes through the rocks it continually erodes the fines, and we lose land, which defeats the purpose.

"In 1998 we started pulling out concrete and planting trees. Concrete is our business—breaking up and repairing runways—so we have an unbelievable amount of it as fill. It's a commodity that we could recycle for shoreline stabilization. But you've got to crack it to size. In the past they've used *huge* pieces of it, which doesn't do any good. It's got to be sized based on the wave energy of the particular site. Ideally, we'd rather have our shoreline in forest or shrub line, but that doesn't always work with our flying mission requirements. For instance, we have a memorial tract with planes on display. That's our show area and parade grounds, so there's a lot of lawn care and fertilization there. We wanted to install a buffer to filter the runoff before it reaches the river. But that's an area where they don't want any trees, so we replaced the rubble shoreline with a restored tidal marsh. In about a year that's going to be an awesome fringe marsh!"

Recently Langley won the Air Combat Command Natural Resources Award, owing, in part, to Kerr's SAV work. Across the river, her group monitors a successful eelgrass bed, which serves as a control site and from which divers harvest transplants. Every two weeks, she takes water samples to qualify new areas for transplanting. The Langley Fire Department supports the sampling exercises with its rescue boat and personnel. Fire Chief Charlie Bowen and firefighter Walter Costa (pictured above, in boat) sponsor the SAV project as volunteer boatmen. "Walter supports us wholeheartedly. He never blinks an eye at what we need to do for sampling," Kerr acknowledges.

"I drop a 'Secchi' disk over the side," she says, outlining the process. "It's black and white, with measurements marked on the rope. I dip it down and record the clarity based on the footage of the string when I lose visibility. I also filter fixed measurements of water through pads, which we send to the Virginia Institute of Marine Science for water clarity tests of total suspended solids and chlorophyll *a*. We're testing to see how much light is getting through the water column. We provide these samples as part of ACB's citizen monitoring database."

The ACB staff and scuba divers provided by the aquarium and the fire department have tested and planted several acres of SAV. "It's very tedious," Kerr says. "The divers bring up plants from the control site. They hand them to somebody in the water (sometimes that's me), who passes the sprouts up to the boat, where somebody else untangles them. We harvest for a full day, keep the shoots in coolers overnight, then transplant the next day. Divers use bamboo skewers to hairpin the grass to the bottom within a plastic grid so we can track mortality."

SAV species such as wild celery (*Vallisneria americana*), common waterweed (*Elodea canadensis*), sago pondweed (*Potamogeton pectinatus*), and eelgrass (*Zostera marina*) are found in shoal areas of the Bay, from its mouth to the headwaters of its tributaries. SAV plays an important ecological role to the aquatic environment by:

- providing food and habitat for waterfowl, fish, shellfish, and invertebrates
- serving as nursery habitat and hiding places for many species of fish and soft-shell blue crabs
- producing oxygen in the water column through photosynthesis
- filtering and trapping sediment, which can cloud the water and bury bottom-dwelling organisms such as oysters
- protecting shorelines from erosion by slowing down wave action
- removing excess nutrients such as nitrogen and phosphorus, which

can fuel unwanted algae growth (Bay grasses require these nutrients for growth and reproduction)

Historically, growing in up to 600,000 acres along the shoreline, SAV has contributed to the Bay's high productivity. In 1984, at their lowest point, only thirty-seven thousand acres of underwater grasses remained, a figure that fluctuated moderately into the 1990s and rose to about sixty-eight thousand acres in 1999. Because the single most important factor determining SAV growth and survival is the amount of light that reaches the plants, scientists correlate this dramatic Baywide decline of all SAV species with increasing nutrient and sediment inputs from development of the surrounding watershed. The strong link between water quality and SAV makes this type of vegetation a good barometer of Bay health. The 1992 amendments to the 1987 Chesapeake Bay Agreement state that "distribution and abundance of SAV . . . will be used as an initial measure of progress in the restoration of living resources and water quality."

In the past four years, Kerr has overseen the installation of sixty plots of eelgrass, restoration of two acres of riparian forest buffer, planting of two thousand native seedlings along tidal ditches and the banks of the Back River, and stabilization of thirteen hundred feet of shoreline. Her program is also growing oysters in tissue culture and for use on local reefs. "As you can see," she exclaims, "we're on a roll. It is so exciting! We're blessed with people who make the extra effort to work with us."

Sitting on the side of the boat in a dripping wetsuit, Captain and Fire Protection Specialist Nelson Williams, Jr. (pictured, in the water), who has been diving for ten years, says, "I've seen the water quality improve dramatically. It's incumbent upon all of us as citizens to see that it continues to improve."

"We all have a real appreciation for the water," Kerr says of her crew. "My family likes running the rivers. We've fished for years and do a lot of kayaking and whitewater canoe racing. When we moved here ten years ago, we passed a billboard that said *Clean Water and Clean Beaches.* I looked at my husband and said, 'Why do we have to *advertise* that? That should be a given.' It just ruined my day. That billboard is still up there; and I'm still adamant about keeping our rivers clean and leaving things better than we found them."

JOSEPH V. STEWART ❧

Baltimore, Maryland

Marathon Swimmer

T HERE'S SOMETHING ABOUT DEFYING THE ODDS AND THE TIDES of nature's water that beckons humans with a challenge. Not only has Joe Stewart accepted the challenge, but he's also using it to give something back to the waters in which he swims open-water marathons.

Stewart is an attorney who lives in Baltimore City with his housemate, Flash, and dog, Fritz Odaat. He swims at a pace of two miles an hour and is a daily lap swimmer at Meadowbrook Swim Center. When in training, each week he swims laps for about an hour on five days, does an hour and a half on one day, and hits open water for a three-mile swim on the remaining day. He also has a passion for photography and organizes events that call attention to the environment or increase HIV/AIDS awareness. As a volunteer event producer, he estimates that he has raised more than $150,000 for AIDS and environmantal organizations. He has coordinated and participated in many open-water swims:

- Annual 7.5-mile swims across the mouth of the Potomac from Hull Neck, Virginia to Point Lookout State Park, Maryland (1995–present)
- Competitive and noncompetitive courses of 100 yards, 200 yards, 1.1 miles, and 2.1 miles at Gunpowder Falls State Park (1992–1999)
- A 6-mile round trip across the mouth of the Rappahannock River
- A 7.5-mile swim from Cove Creek to Bennett Point across Eastern Bay
- An 8-mile swim around Tilghman Island
- Swims "from Chestertown to the Chesapeake" down the Chester River with courses ranging from 1 to 9 miles (1998–present)
- A 12-mile swim around Wye Island (1999)

- Courses of 1.5 and 3 miles on the Tred Avon River at Bellevue in Talbot County, Maryland (1999).
- Solo and group swims of 8 to 10 miles from the small Talbot County town of Sherwood, around Jefferson, Poplar, and Coaches Islands in the Bay (2000 to present)

"I was born and raised in Anne Arundel County, so I felt a kinship with the Chesapeake's waters early on. But I didn't start lap swimming until I was in my thirties, to relieve stress and get into shape. And it wasn't until I was in my forties, when friends at the Towson YMCA encouraged me to do the [4.4-mile] 1990 Chesapeake Bay Bridge swim, that I fell in love with open-water swimming. But even though I finished in two hours and fifteen minutes, my personal best, I realized that big starts with hordes of swimmers weren't my thing. Something about the backslapping afterwards left me cold. I really didn't like my reasons for doing that swim," he admits. "I wanted to do something with more social relevance."

It was the annual Swim for Life around the harbor just off Cape Cod in Provincetown, Massachusetts, that led to Stewart's enjoyment of open-water swimming events. "The giving spirit of the race made the event meaningful to me. As I swam and spent the day at the festivities I started thinking about the planning that went into it. I guess I was already considering organizing my own event." In May 1993, he decided to do a swim to benefit the environment. "I like the idea of focusing on the environment, particularly with the Potomac swim, since water quality is such a crucial issue. For a swimmer, it seems like a natural thing to think about."

He originally made the three-hour Potomac River crossing alone. Standing on the beach at Point Lookout Park at the completion of his swim, Stewart distributed $1,300 in pledges to organizations working to protect the Potomac River. The Potomac River Swim for the Environment continues to raise donations for five groups working for the river's health: the Interstate Commission of the Potomac River Basin, Point Lookout State Park, the Potomac River Association, Southern Maryland Sierra Club, and the St. Mary's Friends of the Chesapeake.

While it may be fulfilling, distance swimming, especially solo, can also be taxing and tedious. "To keep focused during a swim I chant to myself and the river, and think about the people waiting on shore. After my first crossing I wrote my poem 'On Swimming an Estuary' as part of my process when solo swimming the Potomac in '93." In part, the poem reads

When we've colonized our moon and terraformed the face of Mars,
will we remember the Piscataway and the Potomac?

I stroke and stroke and stroke chanting "for the river's sake"
across the mouth of a cold river churning into a still and abundant bay
sweeping in and out of a mighty sea bearing both unbelievable
and untapped resources and the time bombs of nuclear debris

Merge my spirit, set me free, give me—water—a new identity!

Tired, aching, cold, stroking still, not seeing land ahead,
wondering whether I am making any forward movement at all,
I remember the rock passed from friend to friend, affirming
my ability, reaffirming my determination, warming me with familiar faces
which might be awaiting me on shore and "for the river's sake" I stroke
and chant and kick and breathe and stretch and pull my way across the
    Potomac

Wash away our foolishness and fear
and as the sun burns our planet's face
and we find safety far away on terraformed Mars
remember I swam the Potomac in the former land of the Piscataway
for the river's sake

Stewart's "Splash for Cash" has grown to the Annual Swim for the Environment and includes over a dozen participants. The event benefits efforts to clean up the river and Chesapeake Bay. "I picked the Potomac because it was so challenging. It's something that people have to train for. It's not only the distance, but the wind can be coming from any and all directions. There can be whitecaps. It can be choppy, and rather chilly [the water temperature was sixty degrees for the 1993 swim]. But with long-distance swimming, unlike in the pool, you don't have to keep turning around [the Potomac River Swim is equal to approximately 240 laps]."

The behind-the-scenes organizing is time consuming, and Stewart spends most of the year preparing for the summer events. "For instance," he explains, "scouting out new sites and coordinating a swim with the Coast Guard and Natural Resources Police is a major undertaking." His events are known for being well-organized and incorporating culture

and music into the day's activities. "I take a vigorous grassroots advocacy approach," he says. "But it's not force-fed. My intent is to be creative and absorbing. You'd be surprised by the comments swimmers make about the quality of the event. In other swims, they are usually treated like a number and there is hardly any opportunity for social interaction."

The safety of swimmers is of the utmost importance. A kayaker and support boat, which can dispense food and drink as needed, as well as directions and encouragement, accompany each swimmer. Water-safety officials have the authority to determine when swimmers need to be removed from the water. While the fastest swimmers finish in two to three hours, the maximum length of time anyone is allowed to remain in the water is six hours. Besides the Coast Guard and marine police flotilla, volunteer organizations such as the Chesapeake Bay Boston Whalers Club, the Chesapeake Paddlers Association, and local volunteer fire companies, churches, marinas, and restaurants contribute their services to the events.

While coordinating these crews is a huge job, Stewart contends, "One of the bonuses I've gotten from producing these events is making so many wonderful friends." Individuals from all ages and walks of life are invited to garner a required minimum of charitable pledges and participate. Some come from other states; others have participated in marathon swims such as the Snake River Swim in Idaho and events in Key West, Florida, and Wildwood, New Jersey. Many have become regular participants of open-water swimming on the Chesapeake.

How does Stewart assess the quality of the waters he swims? "Where I've been seems pretty clean. I really like the Patuxent—early on, at least, before the nettles get there. The Bay, on the other hand, can be sort of depressing, on account of oil slicks and trash. And the Potomac, of course—I spend a lot of time in D.C., so I know it's not at its best. People ask me if I have any aspirations do something like the English Channel. Why would I? There are so many wonderful spots on the Bay. I don't have any plans to quit open-water swimming anytime soon. I enjoy finding different courses for events, places where I feel like I'm a part of the small-town community."

When asked about the future of the waters in which he strokes, Stewart replies, "Let's say I'm nervously optimistic. There's certainly good reason to support environmental groups and population control. It's a constant battle that takes constant vigilance. Especially the fragile peninsula of the Southern Maryland groups, which D.C. developers are eager to build up. I'm glad to see that there's still some farmland left. There's always a delicate balance between the welfare of the Chesapeake Bay and profit-making, priorities between poverty and the environment, the economics of the waterman and tourism. We need to investigate ways to rejuvenate the waterman's industry. I say *nervously* optimistic because it's a tricky balance.

"But there seems to be a growing consensus that this is a natural resource that we all share. People need a place to spend time for their soul and for their pleasure. They want to feel like they're making a difference. Public awareness is very important—the environment doesn't vote. I'm happy to do my little part to add to that.

"Organizing events is sort of like having a child," Steward confides. "You watch it grow and see it happen. It's become like a second job, but it's very rewarding. I like to think I'm on the path but off the trail, using my God-given talent to be creative in a way that allows me to follow my dream and honor nature, harmony, and cooperation. I've found that I have an easy job of raising money. When you're doing something you like, the whole universe opens up to you."

Each of the twelve swimmers who participated in the 1998 Chester River Swim received a small ceramic bowl, specially designed by Baltimore artist Sandra Magsaman. Inside the bowl is a painting of a woman and an inscription that reads: *And she understood that her life was like a river. She could wade by its edge or jump in and swim.*

GLOSSARY

airshed — An area within which air pollutants are transported and deposited on land and water surfaces. Boundaries vary with weather conditions, but the Chesapeake Bay airshed may include pollution sources as far away as the Ohio River Valley.

aquaculture — The growing and harvesting of fish and shellfish for human use in freshwater ponds, irrigation ditches, and lakes or in cages or fenced-in areas of coastal lagoons or estuaries.

best management practices (BMP) — A wide variety of agricultural techniques aimed at increasing soil productivity and reducing pollution; examples include plowing along the land's natural contours to reduce erosion from rainfall, planting winter grasses to reduce wind erosion, and storing manure to keep it out of streams.

biofilter — Filter that removes contaminants by allowing fouled water to flow across and through packing materials coated with living microorganisms that eat or detoxify contaminants.

brackish — Somewhat salty water resulting when fresh water from tributaries and land runoff meets salty water from the sea.

carrying capacity — The maximum population of a particular species that a given habitat can support over an indefinite period of time.

Clean Water Act — The Federal Water Pollution Control Act of 1972 (renamed the Clean Water Act when amended in 1977), which, with the 1987 Water Quality Act, forms the basis of U.S. efforts to control pollution of the country's surface waters. The main goals of the Clean Water Act were to make all U.S. surface waters safe for fishing and swimming by 1983 and restore and maintain the chemical, physical, and biological integrity of the nation's waters.

competition — Organisms of the same or different species attempting to use the same scarce resources in the same ecosystem, as in available habitat, space, or food supply.

dissolved oxygen (DO) — The level of oxygen in the water; more than five parts oxygen per million parts of water is considered healthy, while below three is generally stressful (most organisms die without adequate oxygen).

ecology	The study of the structure and functions of nature—namely, the interactions of living organisms with one another and with their nonliving environment of matter and energy.
ecosystem	Interrelated and interdependent parts of a biological system.
erosion	A process or group of processes by which loose or consolidated earth materials are dissolved, loosened, or worn away and removed from one place and deposited in another.
estuary	Partially enclosed coastal area at the mouth of a river or bay where fresh water, carrying fertile silt and runoff from the land, mixes with salty seawater.
eutrophication	Physical, chemical, and biological changes that take place after a waterway has received excessive inputs of land nutrients—mostly nitrates and phosphates—from natural erosion and runoff from the surrounding land basin. In the Bay, this can cause an overabundance of algae growth, which prevents light from penetrating to the lower layers of water. When these algae fall to the bottom, they decompose there and consume life-giving oxygen.
eutrophic	Overenriched or overfertilized.
fishery	The commercial or sport catch of a given fish species.
global positioning system (GPS)	A "constellation" of twenty-four satellites that orbit about 10,500 miles above the earth, spaced so that from any point on earth four satellites are above the horizon; the satellites' computers and atomic clocks determine where the satellite is located at any given time, and their radios broadcast that information to ground receivers. On the ground, a GPS receiver "triangulates" its coordinates and expresses the result as a geographic position.
greenhouse effect	A natural effect that traps heat in the atmosphere's lower layer (troposphere) near the earth's surface. Water vapor, carbon dioxide, ozone, human-made chlorofluorocarbons (CFCs), methane, and nitrous oxide (referred to as greenhouse gases) in the troposphere absorb some of the sun's heat as it flows back toward space from the earth's surface, causing it to radiate back toward the earth's surface.
groundwater	The subsurface collection of rainwater that percolates through the earth rather than running immediately off into waterways; groundwater ranges from a few inches deep to aquifers far below the surface, and represents a significant source of water to the Bay.
non–point source pollution	Pollutants that wash or drain off large or dispersed land areas such as cropfields, streets, and lawns.
Pfiesteria (*Pfiesteria piscicida*)	A potentially toxic organism, one of many algae of the order Dinoflagellata, that has been associated with fish lesions and fish kills in coastal waters from Delaware to North Carolina. A natural part of the marine environment, dinoflagellates are microscopic, free-swimming, single-celled organisms, usually classified with plankton algae. The vast majority of dinoflagellates are not toxic.

Discovered in 1988 by researchers at North Carolina State University, *Pfiesteria* is now known to have a highly complex life cycle with at least twenty-four reported forms, a few of which can produce toxins. Although many dinoflagellates are plantlike and obtain energy by photosynthesis, others, including *Pfiesteria,* are more animal-like and acquire some or all of their energy by eating other organisms.

point source
A single identifiable source that discharges pollutants into the environment, such as the smokestack of a factory, the drainpipe of a meat-packing plant, or the chimney of a house.

runoff
The movement of pollutants from the land into water due to rainfall.

salinity
The amount of salt dissolved in water, expressed in parts per thousand (fresh water has a salinity of zero; the ocean is about 33 parts salt per 1,000 parts of water, a salinity of 33‰).

sediment
Soil particulates—sands, silts, and clays—which can accumulate at the bottom of a water body and be suspended by waves or currents. Sediment from farms, construction sites, or other land that runs into the water during rainstorms can be a significant pollutant.

spawning
The reproductive method of fish, whereby sperm and eggs are deposited directly into the water.

stormwater
Rainwater that runs off the land, paved surfaces, or compacted areas, which can be a significant source of pollution.

submerged aquatic vegetation (SAV)
Vegetation rooted in the bottom of the Bay's shallows (usually no deeper than 10 feet); more than a dozen varieties are found in the Chesapeake, and they are important in controlling water quality and providing food and habitat for wildlife.

watershed
A region bounded at the periphery by physical barriers that cause water to part and ultimately drain to a particular body of water; a drainage basin.

wetlands
Areas of vegetation that are periodically flooded or saturated by water, which have great value for wildlife and water quality; wetlands may range from coastal salt marsh, inundated on every high tide, to nontidal wetlands far inland that are dry most of the time.

REFERENCES

INTRODUCTION

Chesapeake Bay Program. "Chesapeake 2000 Agreement." Annapolis, 28 June 2000.

Horton, Tom. *Bay Country.* Baltimore: Johns Hopkins University Press, 1987.

———. "Chesapeake Bay: Hanging in the Balance." *National Geographic,* June 1993.

———, and William M. Eichbaum. *Turning the Tide.* Washington, D.C.: Island Press, 1991.

Lopez, Barry. *Crow and Weasel.* San Francisco: North Point Press, 1990.

Maclean, Norman. *A River Runs through It.* Chicago: University of Chicago Press, 1976.

Pringle, Laurence. *The Environmental Movement: From Its Roots to the Challenges of a New Century.* New York: HarperCollins, 2000.

Taylor, Marianne. *My River Speaks: The History and Lore of the Magothy River.* Arnold: Bay Media, Inc., 1998.

Womack, Harry. "The Chesapeake Lives!" Salisbury State University Office of Cultural Affairs and Museum Programs, *View* 1, no. 4 (fall 2000).

WILLARD N. HARMAN

Biological Field Station: <www.oneonta.edu/~biofld>

Harman, Willard N., Leonard P. Sohacki, Matthew F. Albright, and Daniel L. Rosen. "The State of Otsego Lake, 1936–96." Occasional Paper 30. Oneonta: State University College at Oneonta, 1997.

MICHAEL J. OGBURN

Virginia Polytechnic Institute and State University Hybrid Electric Vehicle Team: <http://fbox.vt.edu/org/hybridcar>.

WILLIAM ARTHUR EBERHARDT

Alliance for the Chesapeake Bay: <www.acb-online.org>

Eberhardt, W. A., and J. W. Plageman. "Realizing the Total Value from Waste Prevention and Beneficial Use During Manufacturing." Mehoopany, Pa.: The Procter & Gamble Paper Products Company, 1989.

Stranahan, Susan Q. *Susquehanna, River of Dreams.* Baltimore: Johns Hopkins University Press, 1993.

ABBY CHAPPLE

Friends of the Cacapon River: <http://users.sgi.net/~cacapon>.

West Virginia Rivers Coalition: <www.wvrivers.org>.

LLOYD (LOU) WELLS

State Use Industries: <www.dpscs.state.md.us/doc/sui>.

ALAN C. GREGORY

Ballaraon, Paula B., Christopher M. Kocher, and Jerrald R. Hollowell. "Assessment of Conditions Contributing Acid Mine Drainage to the Little Nescopeck Creek Watershed, Luzerne County, Pennsylvania, and an Abatement Plan to Mitigate Impaired Water Quality in the Watershed." Publication no. 204. Harrisburg: Susquehanna River Basin Commission, 1999.

Stranahan, Susan Q. *Susquehanna, River of Dreams.* Baltimore: Johns Hopkins University Press, 1993.

KHALIL HASSAN

Friends of the Rappahannock: <www.crrl.org/community/for>.

ANDREW JOHNSTON

EcoVillage: <www.ecovillages.com>.

ANDREW MCKNIGHT

Falling Mountain Music: <www.fallingmountain.com/mcknight.html>.

McKnight, Andrew. "Letter to Colonel Mosbey" and "Western Skies," *Turning Pages* (CD). Winchester, Va.: Falling Mountain Music, Catalooch Music, BMI, 2001.

Shenandoah Acoustics: <www.shenandoahacoustics.com/andrew>.

RUFUS S. LUSK, III

Lusk, Rufus S., III: <www.revlusk.com> or <www.porttownscenter.com>.

Prince Georges County Department of Environmental Resources: <www.goprincegeorgescounty.com/Government/DER/PPD>.

JOLINE P. FROCK AND JOSEPH R. FROCK

Center for Watershed Protection: <www.cwp.org>.

Montgomery County Recycling Program: <www.mcrecycles.org>.

Alliance for the Chesapeake Bay, U.S. Fish and Wildlife Service, Chesapeake Bay Field
Office. "BayScaping for the Long Term: A Homeowner's Guide." Annapolis, 1984,
and <www.acb-online.org/longterm.htm>

JAMES T. COTTLE

Boyle, Mary. "Something Is Fishy about These Decoys." *Washington Post,* 23 Jan. 1997.

Cottle, James T. *Carving Fish Decoys: A Traditional American Folk Art.* Harrisburg: Stack-
pole Books, 1990.

LORI SANDMAN

Environmental Quality Initiative: <www.eqinitiative.com>.

BENJAMIN K. SYMONS

Interstate Commission on the Potomac River Basin: <www.potomacriver.org>.

Westbrook Elementary School: <www.mcps.k12.md.us/schools/westbrookes>.

ROBERT E. BOONE

Anacostia Watershed Restoration Committee. "American Heritage River Initiative:
Nomination of the Anacostia River." Washington, D.C., 1997.

Anacostia Watershed Society: <www.anacostiaws.org>.

CAROLINE SUZETTE PARK

Georgetown University Law Center: <www.law.georgetown.edu/clinics>.

ELIZABETH S. HARTWELL

Mason Neck State Park: <www.state.va.us/~dcr/parks/masonnec.htm>.

RAY R. WEIL

Brady, Nyle C., and Weil, Ray R. *The Nature and Properties of Soils,* 12th ed. Upper Sad-
dle River, N.J.: Prentice-Hall, 1999.

Clagett Farm: <www.clagettfarm.org>.

"Delmarva Poultry Industry Resource Guide." Georgetown, Del.: Delmarva Poultry Industry, Inc., 1999.

Miller, G. Tyler, Jr. *Living in the Environment.* 10th ed. Belmont, Calif.: Wadsworth Publishing Company, 1998.

Weil, Ray R.: <www.agnr.umd.edu/users/agron/faculty/weil.htm>.

Weil, Ray R. "Defining and Using the Concept of Sustainable Agriculture," *Journal of
Agronomic Education* 19, no. 2 (fall 1990).

ELIZABETH A. GIBBS

Gibbs, Elizabeth Alexander. "Testimony of Elizabeth Alexander Gibbs," Democratic Task Force on the Environment, Committee on Resources, United States House of Representatives, 26 Feb. 1996.

Harper, Scott. "Leave Environmental Laws Alone." *Virginian-Pilot,* 18 Oct. 1995.

MARLENE MERVINE

Delaware Adopt-a-Wetland Program: <www.dnrec.state.de.us/fw/are.htm>.

Lukowsky, Andrea M. "Adopting Wetlands." *Outdoor Delaware,* spring 1994.

Nanticoke Watershed Alliance: <www.nanticokeriver.org>.

BILLY W. MILLS, JR.

Hornsby, Lisa M. "Blazing New Trails in the Water." *Tidewater Review,* 29 Sept. 1999.

———. "Linking Our Waterways to a Network of Trails." *Tidewater Review,* 6 Oct. 1999.

———. "Clearing a Path for the Water Trails." *Tidewater Review,* 13 Oct. 1999.

Latané, Lawrence. "County Hopes Trails Lure Eco-Tourists." *Richmond Times-Dispatch,* 11 Oct. 1999.

Mattaponi and Pamunkey Rivers Association: <www.mpra.org>.

Mills, Sally. "The Middle Peninsula: Virginia's Pearl." *Virginia Wildlife,* Feb. 1998.

———. "Lending a Helping Hand: A 100-year Tradition Focuses on the Recovery of American Shad in Virginia's Coastal Rivers." *Virginia Wildlife,* May 1999.

MARC S. CRUZ

The Accokeek Foundation: <www.accokeek.org>.

LOUISA ROGOFF THOMPSON

Maryland Native Plant Society: <www.mdflora.org>.

Reshetiloff, Kathryn. "Native Plants Help to Save Time, Money, Chesapeake Watershed." *Bay Journal,* March 2000.

Thompson, Louisa. "Control of Invasive Non-Native Plants: A Guide for Gardeners and Homeowners in the Mid-Atlantic Region." Silver Spring, Md.: Maryland Native Plant Society, March 1999.

Voris, Sally. "Woman Comes to Rescue of Native Plants." *Baltimore Sun,* 23 Aug. 1999.

RANDOLPH L. ESTY

Hardin, Garrett. "The Tragedy of the Commons." *Science* 162 (1968): 1243–48.

Keep America Beautiful campaign: <www.kab.org>.

BILLY FRANK LUCAS

Galeone, Daniel G., and Edward H. Koerkle. "Study Design and Preliminary Data Analysis for a Streambank Fencing Project in the Mill Creek Basin, Pennsylvania." U.S. Department of the Interior, U.S. Geological Survey Fact Sheet 193–96. Washington, D.C.: Government Printing Office, 1996.

Pennsylvania State University, College of Agricultural Sciences, Cooperative Extension. "Peaquea-Mill Creek Information and Leaflet Series." Smoketown, Pa.: 1994–95.

Spotts, David E., Lance J. McDowell, and C. Mark Hersh. "Aquatic Assessment Report, Muddy Run Stream Bank Fencing Study, Peaquea-Mill Creek Hydrologic Unit Area Project." Pennsylvania Fish and Boat Commission, Division of Environmental Services, and U.S. Fish and Wildlife Service, Pennsylvania Field Office. Elm, Pa.: August 1997.

Upper Thames River Conservation Authority, Rural Clean Water Quality Program: <www.thamesriver.org/Projects/nutrient_management.htm>.

CATHERINE CLUGSTON

Clugston, Catherine: <www.FarmFinder2000.com>.

"Delmarva Poultry Industry Resource Guide." Georgetown, Del.: Delmarva Poultry Industry, Inc., 1999.

EDMUND SNODGRASS AND AND LUCIE SNODGRASS

Emory Knoll Farms: <www.emoryknollfarms.com>.

HOWARD WOOD

Eastern Shore Land Conservancy: <www.eslc.org>.

GLORIA A. CASALE

Casale, Gloria A., and Hugh H. Welsh. "The International Transport of Pathogens in Ships' Ballast Water." *Journal of Transportation, Law, Logistics and Policy* 65, no. 1 (1997): 79–87.

Miller, G. Tyler, Jr. *Living in the Environment.* 10th ed. Belmont, Calif.: Wadsworth Publishing Company, 1998.

RICHARD J. CALLAHAN

Callahan, Richard J. "Trees at Work" brochure. Annapolis: Chesapeake Bay Trust, 1998.

DANIEL J. FISHER

Fisher, D. J., M. H. Knott, B. S. Turley, L. T. Yonkos, and G. P. Ziegler. "Acute and Chronic

Toxicity of Industrial and Municipal Effluents in Maryland." *U.S. Water Environment Research:* 70, no. 1 (1998): 101–7.

Wye Research and Education Center: <www.agnr.umd.edu/maes/wrec>.

PATRICK J. FASANO

Pennsylvania Department of Environmental Protection: <www.dep.state.pa.us>.

Stranahan, Susan Q. *Susquehanna, River of Dreams.* Baltimore: Johns Hopkins University Press, 1993.

LESLIE MATHIESON AND CREW

Chesapeake Bay Foundation: <www.savethebay.cbf.org/statebay/habitat.html>.

Environmental Concern Inc.: <www.wetland.org>.

Miller, G. Tyler, Jr. *Living in the Environment,* 10th ed. Belmont, Calif.: Wadsworth Publishing Company, 1998.

JUSTIN LAHMAN

3Di LLC: <www.3dillc.com>.

Allen, John L., ed. *Environment,* Annual Editions Series. Guilford, Conn.: Dushkin Publishing Group and McGraw-Hill Publishers, 1997.

Miller, G. Tyler, Jr. *Living in the Environment.* 10th ed. Belmont, Calif.: Wadsworth Publishing Company, 1998.

Pringle, Laurence. *The Environmental Movement: From Its Roots to the Challenges of a New Century.* New York: HarperCollins, 2000.

KAREN HARRIS OERTEL

Harris Crabhouse: <www.harriscrabhouse.com>.

W.H. Harris Seafood, Inc.: <www.harriscrabhouse.com/seafood.htm>.

ROBERT K. DEAN

Clean the Bay Day: <www.cbf.org/calendar/ctbd.htm>.

Elizabeth River Project: <http://mh106.infi.net/~erp>.

Horton, Tom. *Bay Country.* Baltimore: Johns Hopkins University Press, 1987.

CLIFFORD W. RANDALL

Randall, Clifford W., James L. Barnard, and H. David Stensel, eds. *Design and Retrofit of Wastewater Treatment Plants for Biological Nutrient Removal.* Vol. 5 of the Water Quality Management Library. Lancaster: Technomic Publishing Co., Inc., 1992.

CARROLL THAMERT

Byron, Gilbert. "Chesapeake Calendar." From Gilbert Byron, *Selected Poems.* Chester-
      town, Md.: Washington College Literary House Press, 1953.

JULIE A. BENINTENDI

Alliance for the Chesapeake Bay: <www.acb-online.org>.
AmeriCorps*NCCC: <www.americorps.org>.

BARRY L. MONES

Federal Bureau of Investigation: <www.fbi.gov/contact/fo/balt/envircrm.htm>.

ANDREW R. MCCOWN

Echo Hill Outdoor School: <www.ehos.org>.

DARRIN L. LOWERY

Gosier, Chris. "Bay May Claim Prehistoric Bits on Tilghman." *Capital News Service,*
      reprinted, *Star Democrat,* 18 May 1998.
Lowery, Darrin L.: <www.intercom.net/~xenndar>.

PATSY KERR

Amendments to the 1987 Chesapeake Bay Agreement. Annapolis: Chesapeake Bay Pro-
      gram, 1992
Alliance for the Chesapeake Bay: <www.acb-online.org>.
Virginia Institute of Marine Science: <www.vims.edu/bio/sav>.
Hurley, Linda M. *Field Guide to the Submerged Aquatic Vegetation of Chesapeake Bay.*
      Annapolis: U.S. Fish and Wildlife Service Chesapeake Bay Estuary Program,
      1990.

JOSEPH V. STEWART

Swinehart, Becki. "Joe Stewart—Parting the Waters for a Cause: Life and the Environ-
      ment." *Sports Focus Magazine,* April 1996.

FURTHER READING
AND RESEARCH

Alliance for Community Education. "This Place Called Home" (CD-ROM). Stony Creek, Conn.: New Society Publishers, 1998.

Baliles, Gerald L., John Morton Barber, and John Hurt Whitehead. *Preserving the Chesapeake Bay: Lessons in the Political Reality of Natural Resource Stewardship.* Charlottesville: Howell Press, Inc: 1996.

Bell, David O. *Awesome Chesapeake: A Kid's Guilde to the Bay.* Centreville, Md.: Tidewater Publishers, 1994.

Brait, Susan. *Chesapeake Gold: Man and Oyster on the Bay.* Lexington: University Press of Kentucky, 1990.

Center for Watershed Protection: <www.cwp.org>.

Chesapeake Basin-wide Information On-line Service Project (BIOS): <www.gmu.edu/bios/project>.

Chesapeake Bay Foundation. *Nanticoke River Watershed Natural and Cultural Resources Atlas.* Annapolis: Chesapeake Bay Foundation, 1996.

Chesapeake Bay Information Network: <www.chesapeake.org>.

Chesapeake Bay Program: <www.chesapeakebay.net>.

Chesapeake Bay Program. "Local Government Pollution Prevention Toolkit: Tools and Models to Help Local Governments Implement Pollution Prevention (P2) and Protect the Chesapeake Bay, Its Rivers and Streams." Annapolis: Chesapeake Bay Program's Toxic Subcommittee and Local Government Advisory Committee and Redman / Johnston Associates, Ltd., 1998.

———. "A Comprehensive List of Chesapeake Bay Basin Species." Annapolis: Chesapeake Bay Program, 1998.

———. "Better Backyard: A Citizen's Resource Guide to Beneficial Landscaping and Habitat Restoration in the Chesapeake Bay Watershed." Annapolis: Chesapeake Bay Program, 1999.

———. "Chesapeake Bay Watershed: Its Land and People." Annapolis: Chesapeake Bay Program, 1999.

Chesapeake Bay Trust: <www.chesapeakebaytrust.org>.

"Chesapeake Restoration and Protection Plan." Publication #5500002495. Washington, D.C.: Government Printing Office, 1985.

Collings, F. d'A. *The Discovery of the Chesapeake Bay: An Account of the Explorations of Captain John Smith in the Year 1608.* St. Michaels, Md.: Chesapeake Bay Maritime Museum, 1988.

Cowing, Sheila. *Our Wild Wetlands.* New York: Julian Messner, 1980.

Curtin, Philip D., Grace S. Brush, and George W. Fisher, eds., *Discovering the Chesapeake: The History of an Ecosystem.* Baltimore: Johns Hopkins University Press, 2001.

Davidson, Steven G., Jay G. Merwin, Jr., John Capper, Garrett Power, and Frank R. Shivers, Jr. *Chesapeake Waters: Four Centuries of Controversy, Concern and Legislation,* 2d ed. Centreville, Md.: Tidewater Publishers, 1997.

Duke, Maurice. *Chesapeake Bay Voices: Narrative from Four Centuries.* Richmond, Va.: Dietz Press, 1993.

Delaware Department of Natural Resources and Environmental Control: <www.dnrec.state.de.us/DNREC2000>.

Delmarva Poultry Industry: <www.dpichicken.org>.

Easterbrook, Gregg. *A Moment on the Earth: The Coming of Age of Environmental Optimism.* New York: Viking, 1995.

Environmental Organization Web Directory: <www.webdirectory.com>.

Glendening, Parris N. "Blue Ribbon Citizens Pfiesteria Commission Report." Annapolis: State of Maryland, 1997.

Goodall, Jane. *Reason for Hope: a Spiritual Journey.* New York: Warner Books, 1999.

Hard Bargain Farm Environmental Center / Alice Ferguson Foundation: <www.hardbargainfarm.org>.

Henry, Kristina. *Sam: The Tale of a Chesapeake Bay Rockfish.* Centreville, Md.: Tidewater Publishers, 1998.

Horton, Tom. *Water's Way: Life along the Chesapeake.* Washington, D.C.: Elliot & Clark Publishing, 1992.

——. *An Island Out of Time.* New York: W.W. Norton & Co., Inc., 1996.

Kline, Benjamin. *First along the River: A Brief History of the U.S. Environmental Movement.* San Francisco: Acada Books, 2000.

Leatherman, Stephen P., Ruth Chalfont, Edward C. Pendleton, Tamara L. McCandless, and Steve Funderburk. *Vanishing Lands: Sea Level, Society and Chesapeake Bay* (includes videotape). College Park: University of Maryland Laboratory for Coastal Resaearch, 1995.

Leggett, Vincent O. "Blacks of the Chesapeake: An Integral Part of Maritime History." Annapolis: Leggett Group and Stoneground Studio Publishing and Distribution Company, 1997.

——. "Blacks of the Chesapeake: The Chesapeake Bay Through Ebony Eyes." Arnold, Md.: Bay Media, Inc., 1999.

Lippson, Alice Jane, and Robert J. Lippson. *Life in the Chesapeake Bay: An Illustrated Guide to the Fishes, Invertebrates, Plants, Birds, and Other Animals of Bays and Inlets from Cape Cod to Cape Hatteras,* 2d ed. Baltimore: Johns Hopkins University Press, 1997.

Managing Planet Earth: Readings from Scientific American. New York: W. H. Freeman, 1990.

Maryland Clean Marina Initiative: <www.dnr.state.md.us/boating/cleanmarina>.

Maryland Conservation Council: <www.us.net/mcc>.

Maryland Department of the Environment: <www.mde.state.md.us>.

Maryland Department of Natural Resources: <www.dnr.state.md.us>.

Maryland Sea Grant College: <www.mdsg.umd.edu>.

Maryland's *Smart Growth* and Neighborhood Conservation Program: <www.mdp.state.md.us/smartgrowth>.

Maryland Watermen's Association: <www.marylandwatermen.com>.

Maurer, George. "A Better Way to Grow: For More Livable Communities and a Healthier Chesapeake Bay." Annapolis: Chesapeake Bay Foundation, 1998.

Meyer, Eugene L. *Maryland Lost and Found: People and Places from Chesapeake to Appalachia.* Baltimore: Johns Hopkins University Press, 1989.

———. *Chesapeake Country.* New York: Abbeville Press, Inc., 1990.

Middleton, A. Pierce, and Gregory A. Stiverson. *Tobacco Coast: A Maritime History of Chesapeake Bay in the Colonial Era.* Baltimore: Johns Hopkins University Press, 1994.

Montgomery County Public Schools, Chesapeake Bay Watershed Project Resources: <www.mcps.k12.md.us/curriculum/chesapeake/resources.html>.

Multinational Exchange for Sustainable Agriculture (MESA): <www.wenet.net/~mesa>.

Murdy, Edward O., Ray S. Birdsong, and John A. Musick. *Fishes of the Chesapeake Bay.* Washington, D.C.: Smithsonian Institution Press, 1997.

New York Department of Environmental Conservation: <www.dec.state.ny.us>.

The Oxford University Press Video Encyclopedia of Science, Nature and Ecology. Las Vegas, Nev.: LDA Video, 1997.

Pennsylvania Association for Sustainable Agriculture: <www.pasafarming.org>.

Pennsylvania Department of Environmental Protection: <www.dep.state.pa.us>.

Race to Save the Planet. Video series. WGBH Science Unit, Chedd-Angier Production Company, Film Australia, and University Grants Commission of India / EMRC / Gujarat University. South Burlington, Vt.: Annenberg / CPB Project, 1997.

Rodale Institute: <www.rodaleinstitute.org>.

Save Our Streams Program of the Izaak Walton League of America: <www.iwla.org/SOS>.

Save Our Streams (Maryland): <www.saveourstreams.org>.

Save Our Streams (New York): <www.esf.edu/esp/prjh2osh/pws5.htm>.

Save Our Streams (Pennsylvania): <www.dep.state.pa.us>.

Save Our Streams (Virginia): <www.sosva.com>.

Save Our Streams (West Virginia): <www.blue-heron.org/sosmonitor.html>.

Schubel, Jerry R. *The Living Chesapeake.* Baltimore: Johns Hopkins University Press, 1981.

———. *Life and Death of the Chesapeake Bay.* College Park: Maryland Sea Grant, University of Maryland, 1993.

Sharpley, Andrew, ed. *Agricultural and Phosphorus Management: The Chesapeake Bay.* Boca Raton: CRC Press, Lewis Publishers, 1999.

Simpson, Ralph David, and Norman L. Christensen, Jr., eds. *Ecosystem Function and Human Activities: Reconciling Economics and Ecology.* Baltimore: Chapman and Hall, 1996.

Stream ReLeaf Program, Maryland Department of Natural Resources: <www.dnr.state.md.us/forests/streamreleaf.html>.

Taylor, John. *Chesapeake Spring.* Baltimore: Johns Hopkins University Press, 1998.

Tilp, Frederick. *This Was Potomac River,* 2d ed. Alexandria, Va.: privately published, 1978.

Trefil, James. *101 Things Everyone Should Know about Science.* New York: Doubleday, 1992.

University of Maryland Center for Environmental and Estuarine Studies: <www.co.cees.edu>.

U.S. Environmental Protection Agency. *Chesapeake Bay: Introduction to an Ecosystem.* Washington, D.C.: U.S. Environmental Protection Agency, 1989.

U.S. Environmental Protection Agency Chesapeake Bay Program Office: <www.epa.gov/r3chespk/>.

U.S. Environmental Protection Agency Great Waters Program: <www.epa.gov/oar/oaqps/gr8water/brochure/chesapea.html>.

U.S. Fish and Wildlife Service: <www.fws.gov/r5cbfo/Ecoteam/cbsr.htm>.

Virginia Department of Environmental Quality: <www.deq.state.va.us>.

Virginia Department of Conservation and Recreation: <www.state.va.us/~dcr>.

Virginia Institute of Marine Science Sea Grant Marine Advisory Program: <www.vims.edu/adv/ed/teach.html>.

Warner, William W. *Beautiful Swimmers: Watermen, Crabs and the Chesapeake Bay.* Boston: Little Brown & Co., 1994.

Warren, Marion E., and Mame Warren. *Bringing Back the Bay: The Chesapeake in the Photographs of Marion E. Warren and the Voices of Its People.* Baltimore: Johns Hopkins University Press, 1994.

Website Maryland, Chesapeake Bay Bookstore: <www.pwl.com/maryland/bookstore/mdches.htm>.

West Virginia Division of Natural Resources: <www.dnr.state.wv.us>.

White, Christopher B. *Chesapeake Bay: Nature of the Estuary, a Field Guide.* Centreville, Md.: Tidewater Publishers, 1989.

White, Dan. *Crosscurrents in Quiet Water: Portraits of the Chesapeake.* Dallas: Mountain Lion, Inc., 1987.

Williams, John Page, Jr. *Chesapeake Almanac: Following the Bay through the Seasons.* Centreville, Md.: Tidewater Publishers, 1993.

Wolf, E. C. *Course Guide for Race to Save the Planet.* Belmont, Calif.: Wadsworth, 1997.